Sex: Lessons from History

Also by Fern Riddell

The Victorian Guide to Sex:
Desire and Deviance in the 19th Century

Death in Ten Minutes: The Forgotten Life of Radical
Suffragette Kitty Marion

Dr Fern Riddell is a historian specialising in sex, suffrage and culture in the Victorian and Edwardian eras. She appears regularly on TV and radio, hosts the well-known history podcast Not What You Thought You Knew, and continues to explore how history has made us who we are today.

FERN RIDDELL

Sex: Lessons from History

HODDER

First published in Great Britain in 2021 by Hodder & Stoughton
An Hachette UK company

This paperback edition published in 2022

1

Copyright © Fern Riddell 2021

The right of Fern Riddell to be identified as the
Author of the Work has been asserted by her in accordance
with the Copyright, Designs and Patents Act 1988.

A CIP catalogue record for this title is available from the British Library

Paperback ISBN 9781473666290

Typeset in Plantin Light by
Palimpsest Book Production Ltd, Falkirk, Stirlingshire

Printed and bound in Great Britain by Clays Ltd, Elcograf S.p.A.

Hodder & Stoughton policy is to use papers that are natural, renewable
and recyclable products and made from wood grown in sustainable forests.
The logging and manufacturing processes are expected to conform
to the environmental regulations of the country of origin.

Hodder & Stoughton Ltd
Carmelite House
50 Victoria Embankment
London EC4Y 0DZ

www.hodder.co.uk

Contents

Contents

Introduction

These are the facts: throughout history human beings have had sex. Sexual culture did not, as Philip Larkin wrote, begin 'in 1963'. It has always been a celebrated, needed, wanted and desired part of what it means to be human. Our ancestors have worried about sex, and attempted to regulate sex, since the dawn of time. So much of our popular understanding of the role sex has played in our historic lives has been drawn from the records of those who have seen sex as a universal experience that must be controlled. Like it or not, we all exist within a sexual culture. It is both individual and shared, unique to ourselves and intrinsically influenced by our experiences with others. We are fed cultural messages surrounding sex first in the home, then school, from our friends and wider society. In the past, our disconnected communities attempted to self-regulate their cultural messages surrounding sex. As those communities expanded, the governance of sexual behaviour became as important to control as taxes, and so our legal and religious systems have always reflected our innate need to define, understand and regulate sex.

The study of our historic sexual culture has long been

the dominion of scientists, sociologists and anthropologists, whose work requires order, statistics, boundaries and clinical analysis. When the founding father of sexology, Heinrich Kaan, published *Psychopathia Sexualis* in 1844, it was the first attempt by any scholar to study what might be considered normal or abnormal in human sexual behaviour. Kaan set out not only to produce a semblance of order to the wild and untamable landscape that is our sexuality, but to prove that sex occurs not only in the physicality of our bodies, but also in our minds. He argued that sexual identities are formed not only by our physical state, but also from our imagination. He was the first person to attempt to unpick that stunningly human aspect of sexual behaviour and identity – free will. To understand that who we love and how we desire is not biologically determined or binary. Since the late 1890s, scholarship on the subject has continued to be driven by the ideas and attitudes of the study of the mind. From Richard von Krafft-Ebing's declaration that 'woman... has but little sensual desire' in 1886 to Freud's examination of sexuality, the world of psychiatry and psychoanalysis has taken over our understanding of human sexual interaction. The emergence of the field of sexology – slowly from the mid-nineteenth century, to its explosive twentieth-century statisticians such as Marie Stopes, Alfred Kinsey, William Masters and Virginia Johnson – has given us a unique window into many aspects of human sexuality, but it has also pathologised us, and demanded we fit our sexuality into prescribed boxes, to be monitored and understood in the name of science and medicine.

So what have we learned about sex from the sexologists? Masturbation has always gained a great deal of attention, with self-pleasure having been a target for both religious and secular authorities alike, long before the sexologists showed up. From the eighteenth-century horror of the sin of 'onanism' to the invention of Kellogg's Cornflakes in the early twentieth century, many early sexologists attempted to expose the supposed dangers of this sexual act, legitimising their studies by conforming to long-held sociological beliefs. But, if we step outside of the worlds of science and medicine, and look at the reality of ordinary people's sexual culture, we find a very different world to the one scientists and sexologists, church or state, identified. This clash between private attitudes to sex, and public medical or governmental disapproval, has been a constant battleground for the sexologists who have tried to reconcile the realities of private experience to the traditional doctrine of public morality.

For many of those who attempted these early studies of sex, their own sexual lives guided and informed their studies. Fresh from the annulment of her marriage in 1914 – due to her husband's inability to consummate their union – Marie Stopes kept a detailed table of her own feelings of sexual arousal when alone, which she titled 'Tabulation of Symptoms of Sexual Excitement in Solitude'. Ranging from a low libido when she is 'fearfully tired and overworked', to peaks in orgasmic activity during 'tenderness in kissing' or 'a desire to be held tightly around the waist', this simple document gives us a unique example of female sexual desire, at a time when our cultural history has traditionally believed sex was not something women actively engaged with. Our understanding of sexual relationships since the 1930s has been guided by these giants, yet as W.H. Auden wrote in his 'In Memory of Sigmund Freud', these voices have become 'a whole climate of opinion, under whom we conduct our different lives'.[1] Our cultural understanding of the sex act since the early twentieth century has been heavily reliant on the constructs of the late nineteenth century with its pathologising and fixation on deviance, and yet often devoid of the history of ordinary people. Historians compile data in much the same way as scientists and sexologists, but our conclusions leave room for one thing – the reality of humanity. It is wild and uncontrolled, it defies expectations. 'Everyone was writing up their sexual experiences,' recorded Anaïs Nin in 1941. '… Invented, overheard, researched from Krafft-Ebing and medical books. We had comical conversations. We told a story and the rest of us had to decide whether it was true or false. Or plausible… The homosexuals wrote as if they were women. The timid ones wrote about orgies. The frigid ones about frenzied fulfilment. The most poetic ones indulged in pure beastiality [*sic*] and the purest ones in perversions.'[2]

This book is an attempt to showcase a different view of our history. Because when you strip away the moral, religious and scientific approaches to sex, you are left with one thing: culture. And the history of our sexual culture

---

1 W.H. Auden, 'In Memory of Sigmund Freud', 1939.
2 Anaïs Nin, *Delta of Venus*, February to December 1941.

tells a very different story to the one you might be expecting. Sex, as an experience, is indefinable, and as you will see, there is nothing new or modern about the sexual culture we live in today. People have always loved the opposite sex. People have loved their own sex. They have loved both their own sex *and* the opposite sex, *and* those without a binary sexual definition. We have always recorded the existences of citizens who have felt their physical body – their genitals, their bodily organs – has forced them to appear as the wrong sex; and some people have felt they are more masculine or feminine, in contrast to what they are told should be their experience as a man or a woman, without the belief or feelings that their body is wrong, but simply that their nature is different. Today, this is something we define as 'gender non-conforming'.

Sexual culture, to me, means anything that encompasses a sexual act, idea, definition or portrayal. It is in the pamphlet wars between the seventeenth-century 'She-Quacks' of London, fighting for their right to sell cures for sexually transmitted diseases in the pages of the Old Bailey Proceedings; it is in the coded diaries of Anne Lister, lesbian and writer, in the early nineteenth century; it is in the dramatic love affair of Heloise and Abelard, and the protests of sex workers in the 1970s for recognition. This book is built on the public and private records of those who have lived and loved before us. It is an attempt to reset the narrative, to change the cultural memory that portrays sex as something our ancestors were ashamed of, to show that in reality, sex has always been at the forefront of our lives.

Writing in the 1880s, the man previously identified as the father of sexology (given that he showed no imagination and borrowed Kaan's title of *Psychopathia Sexualis*) Richard von Krafft-Ebing, declared, 'Love must always have a sensual element, i.e. the desire to possess the beloved object, to be united with it and fulfil the laws of nature. But when merely the body of the person of the opposite sex is the object of love, when satisfaction of sensual pleasure is the sole object, without desire to possess the soul and enjoy mutual communion, love is not genuine.'[3]

Our history of our sexual culture has not been genuine. It has lacked the understanding that our ancestors gloried in sexual connection, and fought to celebrate sex against the doctrines of church and state. And while this book is by no means a complete history of our sexual culture – that would be impossible – what it *is*, is an attempt to change your mind; to remove misconceptions and beliefs about the past that damage our understanding of sexual culture today. Understanding the lives of our ancestors, their passions and their desires, is a fundamental necessity to understanding the problems in our own sexual culture, and, perhaps, even finding a way to resolve them.

---

3 p. 19, Krafft-Ebing, https://archive.org/details/psychopathiasexualis00kraf/page/n37

I

The First Fuck

'It's nice to be able to write the words
"I want to fuck you" in a letter.'[1]
—Kingsley Amís, 1944

Did you know the first reference to the term 'fuck' wasn't sexual? One of the earliest examples of 'fuck' in the English language is the adventurously named Simon Fukkebotere, who lived in thirteenth-century Ipswich, c.1290. Contrary to the modern sexual connotation, the 'Fukke' (or fuck) in his name means 'to hit' or 'to strike' butter, and identifies Simon by his trade, that of a butter churner. In terms of sexual slang fuck is a relatively new swearword to the English language. Although the words fukke, fock, fuk, fuck and fucke all appear during the medieval period, they are most commonly found in either surnames or placenames, devoid of any direct sexual

---

1 Zachary Leader (ed.), *The Letters of Kingsley Amís* (London, 2000), 25 November 1944, letter to Philip Larkin.

connotations and meaning 'to strike'. 'Fuck' as we understand it, is virtually unknown before 1300. But just because what we might view as 'taboo' language wasn't recorded, doesn't mean it didn't exist, it's just that the act of recording it – written, printed or published – comes with technological advances and widening literacy. What gives us a clear picture of our historical sexual culture comes as soon as different people begin to write it down.

So this chapter is on the origin of words. Specifically, those words we have used throughout history to talk about sex. We use language to flirt, to seduce, to love and to shame. It is a key part of our sexual culture, and the words we use to define sex have also allowed us to define ourselves. To be gay or straight, to be trans, have all emerged out of our need to identify who we are and how we want to have sex. The history of the words we use, and their historical ancestors, might surprise you. They show us, merely by their existence, that our ancestors did not live in a barren one-dimensional sexual landscape, but in a world full of exploration, surrender and desire. Our sexual culture today owes everything to the words of the past; without their record we would have no way of knowing ourselves. What it also shows us is that our historic sexual culture is utterly understandable. Our relationship to sex, among ourselves and in our communities, has little changed over the course of millennia. Try as our secular and religious institutions might, sex and the pursuit of sex will always be an uncontrollable form of human expression. It has always been the most important connection one human being can have with another, and how we have expressed that desire and what it gives us in return is as present in the past as it is today.

The recorded word is the most vital source we have to understand the sexual landscape of our past. The poetry, literature, memoirs, songs and stories created across history give us the eroticism of sex, free of the clinical, medicalised language of religious and scientific authorities. Language is one of the most important parts of our cultural sex history; from slang to rules for sexual overtures and the issue of consent, without language our understanding of sex simply would not happen. We've even invented entire secret languages for different sexual identities, from the BDSM (Bondage, Discipline, Sadism and Masochism) community to the nineteenth-century origins of Polari spoken by homosexual men who wanted to avoid discovery. Sexual slang is overt *and* covert. It is a secret, a code, shared and sacred. Slang shows us that every aspect of sex and the human body has been spoken about, discussed, parodied and explored in our culture, throughout time. And no lexicographer has done more for our understanding of the language surrounding sex than Jonathon Green and his *Green's Dictionary of Slang*. Compiled from almost every slang word known in the English language, from the medieval period to today, Green has created a record that is absolutely unparalleled. Because of his work, we can see the cultural landscape of the past, as it was, in the language of any era.

Throughout history we have used words – spoken, recorded and in print – to share and to suppress sexual knowledge, allowing our definition of sex and its extremes to be something entirely individual – what is one person's erotica is another's pornography, while one person's sexual celebration is another's sexual shame. So, if we want to understand the history of sex in our culture, we need to uncover how we have talked about it. Understanding the words we have used in our culture – not the sanitised, respectable language of censorship and State control, but the everyday common language used by those around us – gives us a very clear, and very new, sense of the status sex has had in our culture over the centuries. And it may be one that surprises you.

One hundred years after Simon Fukkebotere, the butter churner, 'fuck' still had yet to appear in sexual slang. For those living in the thirteenth and fourteenth centuries, Middle English used 'swive' or 'swyve' as an everyday term for sex. One of the most important archives that we have for the language of this period is recorded in Geoffrey Chaucer's *The Canterbury Tales*, a collection of poetical and allegorical stories as told by a fictional group of pilgrims on their way to visit the shrine of Thomas Becket, at Canterbury Cathedral. Written in the final decades of the fourteenth century, *The Canterbury Tales* allows us to see the complex attitudes towards sex, gender, relationships and power that could be held by Chaucer and his contemporaries. Here, sex is an overt and central part of the interactions between men and women. And far from being taboo, to 'swyve' was a common part of everyday speech.

In 'The Merchant's Tale', Chaucer depicted the marriage of the old and grotesque January to the young and nubile

May. Not an uncommon theme in poetry and oral stories of the period, this tale focuses on May's attempts to have sex with her lover, and then convince her husband she has not done so, even though, as January insists:

2378 *He swyved thee; I saugh it with myne yen*
[He fucked thee; I saw it with my eyes][2]

To be 'swyved' also appears in the tales of the Miller, the Cook and, most graphically, in 'The Reeve's Tale'. Here, two students attempt to get their revenge on a thieving miller by seducing both his wife and his daughter in a sexual comedy of errors that would not be out of place in a *Carry On* film. Using the cover of darkness, and sharing three beds in the same room, one student, Aleyn, seduces the willing daughter, while the other, John, through sleight of hand and a clever bit of furniture rearrangement, seduces the wife without her knowledge:

4225 *And nyste wher she was, for it was derk;*
[And did not know where she was, for it was dark;]

4226 *But faire and wel she creep in to the clerk,*
[But gently she crept in to the clerk,]

4227 *And lith ful stille, and wolde han caught a sleep.*
[And lies full still, and would have gone to sleep.]

---

2 Geoffrey Chaucer, 'The Merchant's Tale', line 2378.

4228 *Withinne a while this John the clerk up leep,*
[Within a moment John the clerk leaped up,]

4229 *And on this goode wyf he leith on soore.*
[And on this good wife he lays it on vigorously.]

4230 *So myrie a fit ne hadde she nat ful yoore;*
[So merry a time she had not had in years;]

4231 *He priketh harde and depe as he were mad.*
[He stabs hard and deep as if he were mad.]

Eager to escape the miller, their revenge now fulfilled, Aleyn sneaks back to the bed he had supposedly shared with John, and whispers in his ear:

4265 *As I have thries in this shorte nyght*
[I have three times in this short night]

4266 *Swyved the milleres doghter bolt upright,*
[Fucked the miller's daughter flat on her back,]

Even today, we define this need to immediately brag about a sexual conquest as being typically male. Chaucer does not give us the daughter's reaction to her night of sexual abandonment. Only, of course, it is not John to whom Aleyn whispers, but the miller, and the tale ends with the students' dash for freedom, and laughter all around. Chaucer's use of 'swyve', as well as the sexually graphic innuendo of '*he priketh hard and deep*', depicted sex in no uncertain terms. From the eighteenth century onwards, Chaucer's works only grew in popularity, and his audience would've been drawn from every part of British society – men, women and children alike. For those living during the time of Chaucer, and the centuries that followed, the tales gave room for discussion and comparison to their own sexual lives. Modern readers may feel the sexual game played here portrays women without agency, and the thought of being tricked into sleeping with someone you believed to be your husband, only to find out it is in fact a stranger, would most likely result in a rape charge.

Our modern reaction to the sex culture found in *The Canterbury Tales* is perhaps coloured by the fact that Chaucer himself is the acknowledged perpetrator in a possible rape case. In 1380, Cecily Chaumpaigne submitted a legal document releasing Chaucer from any financial responsibility towards her in the aftermath of *de raptu meo* – her rape. The historical record for what happened between them is incredibly sparse, only Cecily's entry into the Close Roll (the records of the royal chancery) contains the reference to rape, and scholars have long argued that the interpretation of this phrase in medieval documents covers everything from the act of rape to the abduction of a minor. (Chaucer's father, John, had been a victim of such a *raptu* – in his case an abduction and attempt at forced marriage by his aunt at the age of 12.)[3] But what *is* clear is that the author of the greatest source of English

3 https://www.oxforddnb.com/view/10.1093/ref:odnb/9780198614128. 001.0001/odnb-9780198614128-e-5191/version/0

language before Shakespeare operated in a sexual land-scape very similar to our own. Sexual relationships were seen as the most important interaction two (or more) people can share, and they can be incredibly complicated.

One of the best records for the words we've used to discuss sex is found in our earliest dictionaries. Not only did they record respectable language, but also the common, everyday language in use around Britain. This is cosmo-politan, drawn from across Europe, and reflects the diverse nature of our historic societies. From the 1470s, after William Caxton imported the printing press and movable type to England from Europe, print culture began to emerge out of the presses of London. It is unsurprising, perhaps, that Caxton chose Chaucer's *The Canterbury Tales* as one of his first major publications, first in 1477, and then again in 1483. Throughout the following century, printing presses and their publishers established a lively and growing culture for the printed word that was cele-brated across Tudor England. And as the printed word became increasingly important, so did standardisation of spelling and meaning, and from here, our earliest diction-aries began to emerge, building on the lists, glossaries and personal bilingual records kept by elites in the previous centuries. From here on, the record of words and what they meant became increasingly universal.

Giovanni Florio's *Queen Anna's New World of Words*, published in London in 1611, presented a dictionary in both English and Italian, which he dedicated to Anne of Denmark. Queen Consort to James I, the Scottish king who had inherited the English throne at the death of

Elizabeth I, Anne was a cosmopolitan monarch, for a new, sophisticated, Stuart England. Published less than a decade after James inherited the English throne, Florio's *New World of Words* showcased this coming together of different languages and peoples under the new British Crown.

Giovanni (or John, as he was also known) Florio was closely connected to the English court. The son of an Italian immigrant, Florio's father had arrived during Edward VI's reign, becoming a member of William Cecil's household, and a tutor to the unfortunate Lady Jane Grey. Part of the Protestant Reformation in England, the Florio family were forced to flee during the Catholic reign of Mary I. But with the ascension of Elizabeth I, Florio returned to England during the 1570s, and quickly became a prolific author of English and Italian texts, recording proverbs and sayings that were in common usage in Tudor England. By the time of his dedication to Queen 'Anna', in the publication of the latest edition of his dictionary, he was tutor to her eldest son, Prince Henry, then heir to the throne before his tragic death at the age of eighteen.

Translations and multilingual texts were a huge part of the emerging book trade in England. And, thanks to their record and preservation, we know sex was not something their authors shied away from. Nestled in among Florio's descriptions of food and greetings lies a large amount of sexual slang. Florio informed his readers that if they wanted to know the Italian word for pit or ditch – **Fóssa** – it was also used to describe '*a woman's pleasure-pit, nony-nony or pallace of pleasure*'. Still in common use, the

Chaucerian 'swyve' (now 'swive') was now found alongside 'fuck'. **Fottaríe:** fuckings, swivings; **Fottènte**: fucking, swiving and **Fottúto**: fucked, swived. The lilting **Fottistèrio** (a bawdy or occupying-house) also ame with the intriguing side point that it hinted at 'the mistery [*sic*] of fucking'. An earlier edition of Florio's dictionary, printed in 1598 as *Worlde of Wordes*, has the honour of being the first instance of 'fuck'.[4] A few pages after *Fóssa*, the entries under 'P' connected food, sex and women with crystalline clarity.

Póto: *any kind of drinke.*

Pótta: *a woman's cunt or quaint.*

Pottácchia: *a filthy great cunt.*

Pótta marína: *a fish in Latin Vrtíca.*

Potteggiáre: *to use, touch or play with cunts.*

Pótto: *any kind of drinking pot.*

Pottúta: *cunted, having a cunt.*

This connection between women's genitals and the aquatic was not unique to the Italians. Sixteenth- and seventeenth-century terms for the vagina included 'watergate' and 'water-pot', while Shakespeare's 1603 play, *Measure for Measure*, referred to a man's infidelity with another woman

---

4 Ruth Wajnryb, *Expletive Deleted: A Good Look at Bad Language* (Free Press, 2005), p. 59.

as 'groping for trout in a peculiar river', while in *Hamlet*, a promiscuous man was identified as a 'fishmonger'.[5] But it's not only bawdy cultural entertainment that made these connections; we also find them in the medical literature of the nineteenth century. Writing in 1844, the founding father of the field of sexology, Heinrich Kaan, in his description of female genitalia, referred to the cervix as '*os tincae*', meaning fish mouth.[6] Kaan was far from alone in using this definition; it occurs in medical books and journals across the nineteenth century, and even earlier. When the Scottish writer, Thomas Urquhart (1611–1660), published his translation of *The Works of Rabelais* (Books I and II in 1653, and Book III in 1693, after his death) the bawdy and viscerally graphic novels of the monk written in the previous century continued that sex and sea connection. 'My Wife will suck and sup me up, as People use to gulp and swallow Oysters out of the Shell', translated Urquhart, depicting fellatio between a married couple in no uncertain terms.[7] These images that we use for sex, our innuendo and slang, are repeated across history. Women are 'wet', vaginas are

---

5 Watergate see: *The Schole house of Women*, Edward More, London 1640; water-pot see; *The London Jilt, or, the Politick Whore...shewing all the artifices and stratagems which the ladies of pleasure make use of for the intreaguing and decoying of men interwoven with several pleasant stories of the misses ingenious performances*, London 1683.

6 Benjamin Kahan (ed.) and Melissa Haynes (trans.) *Heinrich Kaan's 'Psychopathia Sexualis' (1844): A Classic Text in the History of Sexuality (Cornell Studies in the History of Psychiatry)* (Cornell University Press, 2016).

7 *The works of Rabelais, faithfully translated from the French with variorum notes, and numerous illustrations by Gustave Doré*, 1871, p. 280.

rivers or oceans, seas of pleasure in which a person can drown. 'Salt-cunted' was a favoured word of the anonymous Victorian author of *My Secret Life*, a pornographic memoir from 1888; while the twentieth-century eroticist, Anaïs Nin, brought all of these ideas together in the beautifully descriptive *Little Birds*: 'The odour of her sex – pungent shell and sea odours, as if woman came out of the sea as Venus did'. We can see, through these continual and repeating identifications, that language has always been at the heart of our sexual culture. It helps us to seduce another, to identify shared desires, and to fantasise about sex, even when we should not, or cannot, have it. It is also the clearest example of the indisputable fact that sexual desire for the same sex, or all sexes, is not new.

Florio's *Worlde of Wordes*, from 1589, also listed and defined words for gay sex: ***Cinédo*** (a bardarsh buggering boy, a wanton boy) and ***Cinedulare*** (to bugger, to bardarsh). By the 1611 edition the definitions are made even clearer: '***Cinéduláre***, *to play the Sodomite*; ***Cinédulo***, *a bardash, a sodomite*'.[8] There were, of course, multiple entries under 'S' for words describing '*the unnaturalle sinne of Sodomie*' and those who practised it. What this important documentation shows us is that to be gay was not a secret. In fact, if it was so common that someone had to write down its definition in the dictionary, and translate that into other languages, then our historical definition of gay sex, defined by Oscar Wilde as 'the love that dare not speak its name', *must* be re-examined. How

---

8 https://archive.org/details/b30334925/page/102

those who read or created these records felt about the morality of such sexual acts is currently unknown, but what the record shows us is that they were both acknowledged and existed.

Language has also given us a cultural heritage for the origins of individual sexual acts. Take anal sex; English slang for this act emerges in the 1640s, as 'Italian tricks' or the 'Italian sin', and by the 1720s 'swive', that Middle English word for sex, had come to mean anal as well. Contained in the memoir of highwayman James Dalton, and advertised in the Old Bailey Proceedings, 1 May 1728, was a song supposedly sung in the gay clubs (or Molly houses) of the era: 'Let the Fops of the Town upbraid / Us, for an unnatural Trade, /We value not Man nor Maid, / *But among our own selves we'll be free* [...] We'll kiss and we'll Sw--e, / *Behind* we will drive'.[9] Printed and sold by J. Roberts, at the Oxford Arms in Warwick Lane and priced at one shilling, 'A GENUINE NARRATIVE of all the STREET-ROBBERIES committed by James Dalton and his Accomplices' was a rip-roaring tale of criminal life in eighteenth-century England. Dalton was the captain of a gang of thieves who regularly found themselves in the dock at the Old Bailey. He had first appeared in 1720, convicted and sentenced to transportation for stealing aprons.[10] A decade later, after numerous convictions and thwarted transportations for robbery, street robberies (and a Royal Pardon for giving evidence against a number of

---

9 Old Bailey Proceedings, 1 May 1728.
10 James Dalton, John Pindar; *Theft: grand larceny*. 3 March 1720.

his brothers-in-crime), Dalton 'yielded up his breath at Tyburn, the 13th of May, 1730, being then somewhat above thirty years of age.'[11] His 'Grand Narrative', published two years earlier, not only contained his many robbery exploits, but also presented an intriguing view of the sexual landscape of London, from the sex industry to gay culture. This information was not hidden away by blanked-out letters, or coded in canting or secret language, but clearly advertised. 'Some merry Stories of Dalton's biting[12] the Women of the Town, his detecting and exposing the Mollies, and a Song which is sung at the Molly-Clubs: With other very pleasant and remarkable Adventures. To which is added, A KEY to the Canting Language, occasionally made Use of in this Narrative', read the final part of the memoir's Old Bailey advertisement. What this tells us is that for the readers of Dalton's memoir and the Old Bailey Proceedings, gay culture was already known. It wasn't something that eighteenth-century society was unaware of; there was clearly a market for it and an interest in not only the lives, but in the languages of those who were not solely heterosexuals.

Sexual slang was not the sole property of gay men and the Molly houses of the eighteenth century. The understanding that women, too, could desire their own sex was rife in our print culture from the late seventeenth century

---

11 Arthur L. Hayward (ed.), *Lives of the Most Remarkable Criminals who have been Condemned and Executed for Murder, the Highway, Housebreaking, Street Robberies, Coining or Other Offences*, first published 1735, 1927.
12 'Biting' here means pickpocketing.

onwards. Charles Cotton, in his erotic writings on the female body – 'Merryland', as he termed it – identified lesbians as 'she-centaurs', young women who explored their sexual desires by 'first riding one another'.[13] For much of the seventeenth and eighteenth centuries, to be a woman who was sexually attracted to other women was to be deemed as 'classical', to identify with the mythical world of the Greek poetess Sappho, and the island of Lesbos, from which the word 'lesbian' originates. We find it in the diaries of Anne Lister, the famous Yorkshire land-owner, who recorded her many lesbian romances that took place during the first half of the nineteenth century. But to be a lesbian was not a singular identity. As the nine-teenth century moved on, there came an increasing awareness of identities within identities. To be a 'Dyke' or a 'BullDyke' appears to have originated from America, specifically Harlem in New York and the red light district of Philadelphia, at the end of the nineteenth century.[14] It signified women who went to great lengths to dress as men, not merely in everyday workwear, but fashionable, well-cut masculine attire. The *Newcastle Courant* identified 'dike' as an Americanism to mean 'a person in full dress' in 1892, and by 1906, J. Richardson Parke's *Human Sexuality* recorded that 'female inverts, or lesbian lovers, are known euphemistically as "bulldykers"' among the gay scene that could be found along America's East Coast.[15]

---

13 1684 [UK], C. Cotton, *Erotopolis*, p. 148.
14 J. Richardson Parke, *Human Sexuality* (1906), p. 309n.
15 Ibid.

The Jamaican writer, Claude McKay (1890–1948), in his visceral 1928 exploration of the black community in New York, *Home to Harlem*, reflected how quickly the language and visibility of gay culture could be found in post-war America: 'there is two things in Harlem I don't understand/ It is a bulldycking woman and a faggotty man.'[16] Just as Paris had ruled Europe as the capital of sexual exploration in the nineteenth century, as the twentieth century matured, Harlem became 'the Paris of the Western Hemisphere – a museum of occult sex, a sensual oasis in the sterile desert of white civilisation, where conventional people can indulge in unconventional excess…Harlem is the pool of sex, where all colours are blended, all bloods mingled.'[17] Here, gay culture established its modern language and culture, and exported it all over the world. And once again, the dictionaries recorded the unique shifts and heritage of these words. By the 1930s, two years after Radclyffe Hall published *The Well of Loneliness* – banned in Britain and yet published in America – 'bulldyking' was the established term to describe a butch or masculine lesbian.[18] Instead of viewing these words as taboo, we must acknowledge that, simply by being recorded in our print culture, there was a clear, common understanding of the many forms sex, sexual attraction and sexual desire can take. In contrast, 'fuck', which had appeared regularly in dictionaries from Florio's *Worlde of*

---

16 1928 [US], C. McKay; *Home to Harlem* 36.

17 Mae West, *The Constant Sinner*, 1930, p. 158.

18 1931 [US], N. Van Patten, 'Vocab. of the Amer. Negro' in AS VII:1 27.

Wordes in 1598 to John Ash's *A New and Complete Dictionary* in 1775, was quickly relegated to the dictionaries of slang and vulgar terms a decade later, and did not reappear in mainstream dictionaries until the late twentieth century.[19]

So where did our inherited knowledge of sex go? As books and the printed word, the post and public speech were to become targets for government censorship, was there anywhere that the language of sexual knowledge could survive? Innuendo, which had been prolific in the elite worlds of medieval manuscripts, emerged as a shared common language at roughly the same time as the explosion of movable type and the printing press. Although understood to have originated from documents surrounding medieval libel cases, by the sixteenth century innuendo had moved out of the legal world and into popular culture to become what we understand today – something naughty, secretive but shared; normally sexual, the corruption of an innocent idea with lascivious double talk. It can be alienating; it can highlight a listener's innocence and it can make them a figure of fun; but it can also be presented as a common language. And it's in 'innuendo' that our inherited sexual culture survived amidst the growing censorship of the printed word in the centuries that followed. From the oral tradition of Chaucer's *Canterbury Tales*, sex found a home not only in our spoken culture, but also in what is sung.

Songs – the landscapes they create and the knowledge they can transmit – have long been a refuge for illicit or

---

19 Ruth Wajnryb, p. 61.

rebellious language. It is much harder to police the words of songs, and much harder to recreate their history, as the words that have been sung and the music that accompanies them can change with each singer, and each performance. While it is true that some of the song culture of the sixteenth and seventeenth centuries has been conserved, as the eighteenth century began there emerged a desire to create and conserve the secretive, social world and culture of the songs of the streets. These were not the hymns and celebrations of church or state, but the bawdy, licentious, human songs of folk music – the music of the people – that had moved slowly from the villages and hamlets of rural Britain, to the towns and cities of the Industrial Revolution. The growth of technology and urban expansion that dominated much of the late eighteenth century and early nineteenth century brought with it an ancient culture of community, built on the song lines of families, knowledge and culture that had always existed outside of the confines of the elite record. As the traditions of campfires and the rural pastoral life became modernised, our song culture began a long, slow progression indoors, to the firesides of pubs, and the 'Song and Supper' rooms of the early half of the nineteenth century.[20] Of these Song and Supper rooms, Evans', in Covent Garden, was the most famous – a venue that provided sustenance and libation to its patrons, and found both Charles Dickens

---

20 *Morning Post*, 12 October 1895; Stuart and Park, *The Variety Stage*; Baker, *British Music Hall: An Illustrated History*.

and William Makepeace Thackeray in its audience.[21] These public spaces catered solely to a male clientele, where 'the epidemic of vocal music has more particularly spread its contagious and devastating influence among the youth of the Metropolis, the London apprentice boys'.[22] This devastation came in the form of risqué or obscene songs, printed in collections during the 1830s and 1840s such as *The Randy Songster, A Regular Out-and-Out Collection of the most Moving, Licentious, Pathetic, Flash, and Amatory Chaunts, Ticklish Staves, and Lecherous Tit Bits, Ever Before Printed*, and *Fanny Hill's New Friskey Chanter, and Amorous Toast Master, containing a Slashing Lot of Randy, Friskey, Licentious and Slap-Up Flash Songs*. Known as 'chapbooks', these fascinating song collections were, until 2011, thought lost to history, as few had survived beyond their initial publications. But a collection edited by Paul Watt and Patrick Spedding, *Bawdy Songbooks of the Romantic Period*, has recently brought over 1,000 unknown songs to light.[23] This bawdy song culture of the Georgian and early Victorian eras is absolutely riddled with sexual connotations and innuendo, making clear that sexual knowledge will always find a way to be shared, and to be saved. The importance of records like this is that they show us that there is an innate human desire to keep our inherited and shared sexual culture alive and free, almost as if it is, itself,

---

21 *Morning Post*, 12 October 1895; Baker, *British Music Hall*, 3.

22 *The Town*, 3 June 1837.

23 P. Watt and P. Spedding, *Bawdy Songbooks of the Romantic Period* (London, 2011).

a living thing. Carried first by the oral traditions of song
and spoken word, to the printed literature and thrill that
comes with reading and sharing knowledge, sex, and the
celebration of sex, has been central to our language for a
very long time.

The authors who recorded and transmitted sexual
knowledge in this new urban landscape soon had a
powerful form of culture at their fingertips, the music
halls. Although the Song and Supper rooms had been only
for men, the music halls – often simple rooms attached
to pubs, with a raised platform for performers – catered
to everyone. Here, sexual knowledge was spoken and sung
by men and women, to men and women. There was no
restriction placed on who had the right to understand the
language used and the meaning behind it. Taken from a
'cache of songbooks' George Speaight had unearthed in
the British Museum, *Bawdy Songs of Early Music Hall*
(1975) is one of the few surviving records we have for
the sexually explicit and yet universal song culture of the
early Victorian era.[24] Sung between the 1830s and the
1850s, Speaight's collection identified the ribald and cele-
bratory nature of music hall song and its depictions of
sex. With titles such as 'He Did It Before My Face' – whose
opening verse begins: 'One day, as I was walking out/And
crossing o'er the plain/I suddenly beheld, O dear/A very
handsome swain;/ And while I looked at him about/and
viewed his manly grace/A certain member he pulled out/
He did, before my face' – or 'The Flea Shooter' with its

---

24 G. Speaight, *Bawdy Songs of the Early Music Hall*, (Canada, 1975).

descriptions of female masturbation, which are then echoed in 'The Ladies and the Candle', the overt sexual language of these songs is clear.[25] These are not Victorians for whom sex is a prudish, secret thing, and the music halls became a space where sexual knowledge, or sexual knowingness, could be exposed and explored. But the physical locality of the music halls was not solely responsible for the transfer of sexual knowledge by song; it could be found everywhere, and by both men and women.

In 1864, Emma Devine, 'a good-looking girl, only 13 years of age', was accused of stealing from the St John's Wood home of Mr James Tipping, where she had been engaged as a nursemaid.[26] On her arrest, the girl was found to have 'a song of the most infamous character' among her belongings.[27] When asked how she had obtained such a song, the girl replied that she had been given it by another young girl in Lisson Grove.[28] A gentleman had given it to her and it was done up in an envelope. 'That's how girls get them, sir,' Emma informed the judge.[29] Now part of the City of Westminster, Lisson Grove had a dubious reputation in the nineteenth and early twentieth centuries. In 1885, a Lisson Grove side street was revealed to be the home of Eliza Armstrong, the 13-year-old girl procured by newspaperman W.T. Stead to prove the existence of

---

25 G. Speaight, *Bawdy Songs of the Early Music Hall*, (Canada, 1975). p. 27, 45, 56.

26 London Police – *Cork Examiner*, 4 February 1864.

27 Ibid.

28 Ibid.

29 Ibid.

child prostitution in the capital; and it was the birthplace of the fictional Eliza Doolittle in George Bernard Shaw's 1913 play *Pygmalion*, where the cockney flower girl is given a lady's education and introduced to the upper classes (immortalised by Audrey Hepburn in *My Fair Lady*). For over sixty years, the young working-class women of Lisson Grove were found to possess an independence and sexual awareness that many would assume was not acceptable to their wider society, and yet, what this tells us is that women, particularly young women, were just as keen on and interested in understanding sex as any adolescent and they sought that knowledge from the recorded language in the world around them. By the 1890s, as Marie Lloyd sang of winking 'the other eye' and Marie Collins issued her declaration that '*Life was made for pleasure, so enjoy it without measure*', sex in nineteenth-century society is still clearly and openly discussed on the music hall stage.[30] The *Illustrated Police News* ran weekly advertisements for 'French and American Letters', 'Rubber Preventive Devices' and 'Malthusian Appliances' alongside 'Saucy Songs' and general news.[31] The music hall's cultural role as a dramatic entertainment, one with a mass appeal that far outstretched its brothers and sisters – the theatre or 'legitimate stage', the opera, and the races – gives us a unique evolution of social sexual views and attitudes that previously have been

---

30 Marie Collins, 'Take it On, Boys!' (1893); Marie Lloyd, 'Wink The Other Eye' (1890).

31 *Illustrated Police News*, weekly from 15 January 1898, to 17 November 1900.

identified solely through dramatic or literary works – the poetry of John Donne, the plays of Shakespeare, the Earl of Rochester, or the books of the Marquis de Sade. They also show us that if you look further than the works of 'great men', you discover sex was something women were just as interested in and just as aware of. We know that by the 1890s the combined audience figures of thirty-five of London's most well-known music halls reached approximately 14 million each year, to say nothing of the audiences in halls across the country.[32] This was the largest form of cultural entertainment of the nineteenth century, and the language it used to express sex and sexual culture connects our modern-day forms of sexual expression all the way back to Chaucer.

But innuendo, slang and even sexually explicit song culture also show how our sexual language became restricted, relegated by censorship during the twentieth century. It's here, in the changing language of popular culture, the erasing and banning of books, songs and plays that presented the reality of our sexual lives, that we will find a loss of understanding about sex itself. And, surprisingly, we will begin with a return to Simon Fukkebotere, the thirteenth-century butter churner. By 1952, Simon's trade *had* become synonymous with sex; immortalised in the risqué lyrics of the song 'Keep On Churnin' (Till The Butter Comes)' by one of the founding fathers of rock 'n' roll, Wynonie Harris. Harris's name

---

32 Brad Beaven, *Leisure, Citizenship and Working-Class Men in Britain*, p. 51; Susan Pennybacker, *A Vision for London*, p. 211.

may have slipped from popular memory, overshadowed by the likes of Elvis Presley and Buddy Holly, but between 1945 and 1952 he scored sixteen top-ten hits in the American rhythm and blues *Billboard* charts. He was known as a 'blues shouter', often recording and singing on the Decca record label. Harris, the son of an African-American mother and Native American father, became emblematic of a new style of blues. His music was 'slick and urban' and celebrated 'the joys of life in the big city'.[33] His lyrics are full of sex and alcohol, his life was outrageous, and he typified a growing belief in post-war Black America that you could, and should, be 'successful and black and proud'.[34] 'Keep On Churnin' (Till The Butter Comes)', one of his later records from 1952, is undeniably erotic, sexual without any overt sex language: 'First comes the milk, then comes the cream, it takes good butter to make your Daddy scream, Keep on churnin' till the butter comes.'[35]

Just as with Chaucer's *The Canterbury Tales*, sex is depicted as accepted and central to the popular culture of the twentieth century. But across the Western world, during the nineteenth and twentieth centuries, censorship began to take hold. Britain outlawed the distribution of sex guides, erotic literature and educational pamphlets,

---

33 Tony Collins, *Rock Mr. Blues: The Life and Music of Wynonie Harris* (Big Nickel Publications, 1995), p. 10.

34 Ibid.

35 'Keep on Churnin' (Till the Butter Comes)' (Henry Glover), Wynonie Harris, 1952.

under the Obscene Publications Act of 1857. The 'Comstock Laws' in America were passed within a few decades, in 1873, one of the most graphic and reductive pieces of legislation ever created, outlawing the distribution of sexual knowledge and sex education through America's postal service:

Every obscene, lewd, or lascivious, and every filthy book, pamphlet, picture, paper, letter, writing, print, or other publication of an indecent character, and every article or thing designed, adapted, or intended for preventing conception or producing abortion, or for any indecent or immoral use; and every article, instrument, substance, drug, medicine, or thing which is advertised or described in a manner calculated to lead another to use or apply it for preventing conception or producing abortion, or for any indecent or immoral purpose and every written or printed card, letter, circular, book, pamphlet advertisement, or notice of any kind giving information directly or indirectly, where, or how, or of whom, or by what means any of the hereinbefore-mentioned matters, articles or things may be obtained or made, or where or by whom any act or operation of any kind for the procuring or producing of abortion will be done or performed or how or by what means conception may be prevented or abortion may be produced, whether sealed or unsealed; and every letter, packet, or package, or other mail matter containing any filthy, vile, or indecent thing, device or substance and every paper, writing, advertisement or representation that any article, instrument, substance, drug, medicine, or thing

may, or can be, used or applied, for preventing conception
or producing abortion, or for any indecent or immoral
purpose; and every description calculated to induce or
incite a person to so use or apply any such article, instrument, substance, drug, medicine, or thing, is hereby
declared to be a non-mailable matter and shall not be
conveyed in the mails or delivered from any post office
or by any letter carrier. Whoever shall knowingly deposit
or cause to be deposited for mailing or delivery, anything
declared by this section to be non-mailable, or shall knowingly take, or cause the same to be taken, from the mails
for the purpose of circulating or disposing thereof, or of
aiding in the circulation or disposition thereof, shall be
fined not more than five thousand dollars, or imprisoned
not more than five years, or both. (Section 211 (enacted
1873) of the Federal Criminal Code)

By the 1930s, both America and England had set up
organisations to instruct and police their cultural institutions. The BBC had its Dance Music Policy Committee,
which scoured song lyrics for any lewd immorality, and
banned them from the airwaves; while the Motion Picture
Production Code in Hollywood took over the film studios
after a rash of sex scandals, to create a new, clean image
of moving pictures. The institutions that created culture
were scared of sex; just as the dictionaries had sanitised
language, the authorities of popular culture were running
scared. But sex is not something that we have ever successfully restrained with laws or punishments.

The language we use to understand sexual identities

today is entirely modern. In the 1920s and 1930s, to be 'gay' in the homosexual sense emerged in popular culture across the Western world in the work of both novelists and newspapers, from Australia to America.[36] Before that, to be a 'Queen', a 'Miss' or a 'Molly', 'Betty' or 'Nan' was often used either to identify homosexuals by those outside their community, or by gay men within it who portrayed a 'feminised' gay identity, alongside the words 'catamite' or 'sodomite' for gay men whose queerness was performed within predominately tough, masculine boundaries. Turning back to our historical dictionaries, we find that many different words were used to describe someone who was gay, as well as the sexual acts associated with it. For over 300 years, from *Worlde of Wordes* to the eighteenth century, 'bardash' was a popular everyday word (and insult) to identify a gay man, or someone who engaged in homosexual acts.[37] There was little fear of using these words in public, and clear understanding of what they referred to. In 1850, Edward Kenealy, the Irish barrister at the heart of the notorious 'Tichborne Claimant' case – the longest court case in British legal history, resulting in his disbarment – included the line 'Gulligut, boor, filthard, bardash!' in his epic poem, *Goethe: A New Pantomime*. Our record of sexual slang, in dictionaries and popular speech, makes clear that to be gay was an acknowledged part of our sexual culture – however much critics may have wished otherwise. *A new dictionary of the terms*

36 https://greensdictofslang.com/entry/pgc2e4q
37 John Florio, *A Worlde of Wordes*, 1598; R. Nares Gloss. 1822 (1888).

*ancient and modern of the canting crew, in its several tribes,
of Gypsies, beggers, thieves, cheats, &c., with an addition of
some proverbs, phrases, figurative speeches, &c.* from 1698,
contained the simple definition of 'duncarring' for
buggering, and almost thirty years later, the *Weekly Journal,
or The British Gazetteer* recorded that, on 1 October 1726,
'one Thomas Doulton stood upon the pillory at Charing-
Cross, pursuant to his sentence at the last Sessions at the
Old Bailey, for endeavouring (according to the canting
term) to discover the Windward Passage upon one Joseph
Yates, a seafaring person'.[38] When 'cant' or common
speech, slang and innuendo, has made its way into the
official court record, it makes clear that these words and
what they meant were known *everywhere*.

But while our language has always had words to describe
the differing aspects of our sexual identities, the boundaries
our new, modern definitions have placed on our freedom
to express sexual desire and identity have been incredibly
limiting. We have pathologised sex to such an extreme that
we have lost the understanding that it is something ever-
changing. We have created specific communities – which
have been necessary to pull together activists and fight for
the rights of the majority of those within them. But these
communities have also created rigid boundaries, defining
who has the right to belong and who does not. Today,
discussion surrounding gender or sexual fluidity is regarded
as a unique moment in our sexual culture, when in reality

---

38 https://archive.org/details/newdictionaryoftoobegeuoft/page/n3; 1726,
Weekly Journal, or The British Gazetteer, 1 Oct.

it is closer to a return to the understanding of sex shared by our ancestors, albeit with modern protections in law to stop discrimination. But although we have made huge strides in protecting our right to sexual self-expression, our understanding of the words we use to talk about sex and identity can still limit our ability to empathise, and accept those who express these attributes differently to us.

Today, one of the remaining battlegrounds surrounding words, sex and human sexuality revolves around the transgender community. The word 'transvestite' and 'transsexual' arrived in English after 1949, popularised by the work of the American sexologist, David Oliver Cauldwell (1897–1959). His interpretation of the term, already understood by the wider European medical community, shows us just how dangerous words can be in our sexual culture. It is difficult reading, but unless we confront the attitudes and arguments that have formed the worst parts of our sexual culture, we have little ability to confront and defeat them.

One of the most unusual sexual deviations is PSYCHOPATHIA TRANSEXUALIS – a pathologic-morbid desire to be a full member of the opposite sex. This desire is so powerful that the individual insists on – often impossible – elaborate surgery that would turn him into a complete woman, or her into a biologically perfect male ... The condition, incidentally, is not at all rare. Thousands of cases exist. Among both sexes are individuals who wish to be members of the sex to which they do not properly belong. Their condition usually arises from a poor hereditary background and a highly unfavourable child-hood environment. Proportionately there are more individuals in this category among the well-to-do than among the poor. Poverty and its attendant necessities serve, to an extent, as deterrents. When an individual fails to mature according to his (or her) proper biological and sexological status, such an individual is psychologically (mentally) deficient. The psychological condition is in reality the disease. When an individual who is unfavorably affected psychologically determines to live and appear as a member of the sex to which he or she does not belong, such an individual is what may be called a psychopathic transexual. This means, simply, that one is mentally unhealthy and because of this the person desires to live as a member of the opposite sex. That which pertains to the psychopathic transexual may be called psychopathia tran-sexualis. There are varying degrees of psychopathic transexuality.[39]

Cauldwell's presentation – to the English-speaking medical establishment – of trans identities as a mental illness has defined Western sexual culture's interaction with the trans community. They have suffered, and continue to do so, horrific abuse thanks to this attitude – no different from the pathologising of homosexuality or female sexual desire as a mental illness that occurred at the end of the nine-teenth century. What is so deeply disappointing about this

---

39 Dr D.O. Cauldwell, *Psychopathia Transexualis* (originally published in *Sexology*, vol. 16, 1949, pp. 274–80. Copyright 1949, by *Sexology* magazine).

part of our historic sexual culture is that the words '*trans-vestit*' (1910) and '*transsexualismus*' (1923) were both coined by the first doctor to identify and perform the trans surgeries, Dr Magnus Hirschfeld (1868–1935). They were words of acceptance and understanding in German, whose meaning became corrupted in English.

So, can we stop words from defining our sexual lives? Can we undo the power words have to barricade us into entrenched positions, or do we need to accept this is a side effect of the power they also give us for self-expression? Just as 'fuck' has changed its meaning over the centuries, many of our words surrounding sex, love and gender have constantly shifted their definitions. But one thing has always remained absolute: throughout history there has never been only one simple way to have sex, one binary form of gender, or one rule about love that everyone must obey. Language, in its myriad forms, from spoken to written to sung and to censored, has given us one of the most important tools we need for sexual self-expression and communication. Looking at the history of sex and language can surprise us with how long (or how short) words and their meanings have been expressing our sexual desires. The heritage of words like 'salt-cunted' gives us a time when sex was not about using toothpaste to tighten your vagina, but rather a celebration of the earthy, animal human nature of sex. Our history of sex, seen not as an extreme or restricted act, but simply as a universal need felt by many, may go some way to undoing the damage of the language we use today, to demean those whose sexual desires and identities are different to our own. Since the twentieth century, who we say we are and how we love has become a defining part of our identity. The boundaries we now have for our understanding of sexuality and gender have made our sexual culture almost unique in history, as it now goes hand in hand with protections for many of those identities in law. But just because we call ourselves by a modern name, does not mean what or who we are is a modern creation. To be gay, lesbian, bi, trans, pan or even asexual (for starters) has always been part of human sexual expression. For many, gender and sexuality are different things, but in this book, and this exploration of history, they form individual and yet inextricably connected parts of the same idea – identity.

In recent years, the search to find our sex selves in the historical past has become a war zone, as differing identities pursue their search for historical legitimacy. This has often come with a belief that the modern-day definitions we use now existed in the past, or have the same shared meaning. This is not often the case. Searching the past for ourselves will not lead to the happy discovery you might be seeking, but instead to complex, multi-identifiable histories and characters. In our modern world language is how we identify ourselves, it is our own form of self-ID, demanding boundaries and conformity. But as we shall see next, the words we use today are simply expressions of identities and desires that have a far more ancient heritage.

2

Women Loving Women

'I had a feeling that Pandora's box contained the
mysteries of woman's sensuality, so different from a
man's and for which man's language was so inadequate.
The language of sex had yet to be invented. The
language of the senses was yet to be explored.'
—Anaïs Nin, *Delta of Venus*, 1977

It is not difficult to find the voices of lesbians, or women
who have had relationships with other women, in our
history. They are all there, recorded by time in published
memoirs, poetry, diaries and personal histories. It is a
myth to believe lesbians have been somehow absent from
our cultural history, strengthened by the long-held popular
rumour that Queen Victoria did not believe they existed.
Our modern belief that lesbian history is mired in secrecy
and ignorance comes from the 1950s, and the work of the
historian Derrick Sherwin Bailey. In his early study of
anti-gay legislation, Bailey declared lesbian acts were
'ignored by both medieval and modern law', a theory many

seem to have accepted unchallenged until the work of Louis Crompton in the 1980s. Since then, a fascinating portrait of lesbian existence has emerged out of the archives, and shows us that not only were lesbians widely acknowledged by state and religious authorities, but, perhaps surprisingly, they were viewed to be just as dangerous to the fabric of society as male homosexuals. Not only were lesbian women prosecuted across Europe, but they suffered state-sanctioned executions.

We can trace state-led lesbian fear back to the ending of the Classical world. The existence of lesbian desires among women became an obsession for the early Church as it pushed aside the religions of the ancient world and made its move to dominance across the globe. During the Roman Empire, the conversion of Constantine the Great to Christianity stopped the persecutions of many of those in the early Christian faith, and created the perfect atmosphere for the pursuit of a unified and shared Christian doctrine that would govern much of the religious, secular and sexual lives of Europeans for nearly two millennia. In AD 325, Constantine convened the Council of Nicaea, the first meeting to bring together the different branches and ideas of the early Church. In the decades that followed, different scholars and theologians discussed, wrote and argued about the many ways to interpret the words of God and his disciples, at that point only a few centuries old. One of the most important voices to emerge in the fourth century was that of Aurelius Ambrosius, a Roman governor in northern Italy, who became Bishop of Milan in AD 374. We know him as St Ambrose, one of the founding fathers of what is now the Catholic Church. Among his many writings, one text often attributed to St Ambrose is a commentary on the word of St Paul. In it, discussing the history of God, his relationship with, and punishment of humanity, Ambrose had this to say: 'God being angry with the human race because of their idolatry, it came about that a woman would desire a woman for the use of foul lusts.'[1] Establishing lesbianism as God's punishment for men's pursuit of false idols did not stop the Church's desire to punish lesbian women too. Written at the end of the seventh century, the penitential of Theodore – a guidebook to instruct religious confessors in what punishments to mete out to their flock – recorded that 'if a woman practices vice with a woman, she shall do penance for three years.'[2] Knowledge of female sexuality continued to be discussed by Church leaders throughout the medieval period. St Anselm, the Archbishop of Canterbury (1093–1109), declared lesbian women to be 'against nature, because women themselves committed shameful deeds with women'.[3] While his contemporary, the French theological, Peter Abelard (1079–1142) – famously castrated after his sexual relationship with Héloïse d'Argenteuil – went further, arguing 'against nature, that is, against the order of nature, which created

---

1 St Ambrose, *Omnia opera*, 5 vols, in *3: Commentarii in omnes Pauli epistolas* (Basel, 1567), 5:178.

2 McNeill and Gamer, 'The Penitential of Theodore', in Handbooks, p. 185.

3 St Anslem, *In omnes santissimi Pauli apostoli enarrationes* (1547), p. 8v.

women's genitals for the use of men, and conversely, and not so women could cohabit with other women.'[4] For all these early Church philosophers, the sexual desire of women for other women was in direct violation of women's creation as Man's Companion. The idea that Eve might have preferred Lilith to Adam in the Garden of Eden could lead only to the destruction of all concerned. Fears abounded among the clerical community of early medieval Europe that the enclosure of nuns in convent life would lead to carnal lust, lesbian acts and the use of sex toys for penetration. The discovery of passionate poetry, written by a twelfth-century Bavarian nun in Tegernsee to another of her sisters, suggests their fears were not unfounded:

> *It is you alone I have chosen for my heart …*
> *I love you above all else,*
> *You alone are my love and desire …*
> *When I recall the kisses you gave me,*
> *And how with tender words you caressed my little breasts,*
> *I want to die,*
> *Because I cannot see you.*[5]

Five hundred years later, the scandalous life of Sister Benedetta Carlini, Abbess of the Convent of the Mother

---

4 Peter Abelard, *Commentarium super S. Pauli epistolam ad Romanos libri quinque* in *Patrologia latina* ed. J.P. Migne (1844–66), 178:806.

5 E. Ann Matter, 'My Sister, My Spouse: Woman-Identified Women in Medieval Christianity' in *The Boswell Thesis: Essays on Christianity, Social Tolerance and Homosexuality* (2006), pp. 153–4; Sapphistries: *A Global History of Love Between Women* by Leila J. Rupp, p. 42.

of God, in Tuscany, reaffirmed what many Church leaders feared. Born into a wealthy middle-class Italian family, Benedetta entered the convent in 1599, when she was nine years old. Fourteen years later, at the age of 23, she began to have visions. Although they began beautifully, by 1617, Benedetta's visions had become ugly, traumatic things. She was 'pursued at night by handsome young men who wanted to kill her and who beat her all over with iron chains, swords, sticks and other weapons.'[6] These demonic attacks lasted for hours, leaving her screaming in agony. For the convent, the appearance of a mystic – a member of their community so committed to God, they were visited both by angels and demons – was something to be celebrated. It meant the convent itself was in divine favour, increasing their power not only among the local townspeople, but also within the Church itself. To keep an eye on Benedetta, and to be with her in her hours of need, the convent superiors decided to grant her a young female companion, another nun named Bartolomea Crivelli, who was to share her cell and keep watch on her during the night. Not long after Bartolomea joined her, Benedetta experienced the stigmata, all of which was witnessed and confirmed by Bartolomea. 'To receive the stigmata was no ordinary event,' writes Benedetta's biographer, Judith C. Brown, 'it was one thing to have visions ... but to receive the holy wounds of Christ was a miracle of a different order'.[7] The result of this miraculous event

---

6 Judith C. Brown, *Immodest Acts* (Oxford University Press, 1986), p. 54.
7 Ibid., p. 58.

was Benedetta's election to Abbess of the Convent at the age of 29, in 1619.

Benedetta's visions grew more extreme. She was to marry Jesus Christ, and while the convent began to prepare for their wedding, Benedetta was often visited by an angel named 'Splenditello', 'a beautiful boy ... dressed in a white robe with gold embroidered sleeves and wore a gold chain around his neck. His handsome face was framed by long, curly hair crowned by a wreath of flowers'.[8] Her power outside of the convent also grew; stories of the powerful mystic of the Convent of the Mother of God reached the ears of those who feared for their own secular power, if tested by a powerful female religious figure. It did not help that other female mystics had been revealed as frauds, or that Benedetta's visions had begun to be filled with excessive praise for Benedetta herself, as well as threats of damnation against anyone who doubted her. And so almost as soon as she had been made Abbess, Benedetta was removed and investigated. A year later, she was reinstated, having convinced secular authorities of the reality of her still bleeding stigmata, her marriage to Jesus, and the power of her vision over fourteen different visits. Much of her testimony had been shored up by the words of Sister Bartolomea. Perhaps Benedetta believed this would be enough to secure her position, but she had reckoned without the fear of the Catholic Church, who in 1623 sent their own investigators to test the divine mystic. What was revealed horrified

---

8 Judith C. Brown, *Immodest Acts* (Oxford University Press, 1986), p. 64.

them – Benedetta's visions were not divine, they concluded, they were demonic.

Perhaps unwilling to divulge what had been happening at the convent to secular investigators, to those from the Church the nuns gave frightening new testimonies that destroyed Benedetta's miracles. One sister claimed to have seen Benedetta 'smear her own blood on a statue of Christ' only to then profess it had begun to bleed by itself; when she attempted to confront Benedetta publicly, the Abbess had forced her into an act of self-flagellation, whipping her own back until it bled.[9] Another nun told of how Benedetta had revealed to the sisters that Christ had descended from heaven and kissed her on the forehead, leaving a gold star in place. Many of the nuns had seen this star, but, watching through a hole in the door of Benedetta's study, *this* nun had seen the Abbess make it herself out of gold foil, and fix it in place on her forehead with red wax.[10] Most damning of all, a number of the nuns had spied Benedetta inflicting the supposed wounds of her stigmata on herself using a needle.[11] Finally, Bartolomea gave her testimony.

> This Sister Benedetta, then, for two continuous years, at least three times a week, in the evening after disrobing and going to bed would wait for her companion to disrobe, and pretending to need her, would call. When Bartolomea

---

9 Judith C. Brown, *Immodest Acts* (Oxford University Press, 1986), p. 111.
10 Ibid., p. 112.
11 Ibid.

would come over, Benedetta would grab her by the arm and throw her by force on the bed. Embracing her, she would put her under herself and kissing her as a man, she would speak words of love to her. And she would stir on top of her so much that both of them would corrupt themselves ... sometimes one, sometimes two, sometimes three hours ... she [Benedetta] would have her put her finger into her genitals, and holding it there she stirred herself so much that she corrupted herself ... and also by force she would put her own hand under her companion and her finger into her genitals and corrupted her ... to entice her and deceive her further, Benedetta would tell her that neither she nor Benedetta were sinning because it was the Angel Splenditello and not she who did these things.[12]

Benedetta had lived a life of seclusion in an all-female environment since she was a child. And yet her sexual desires had not been restricted by the regime and religion of convent life. Bartolomea clearly viewed their sexual interactions as forced, yet they also show us that, even in a shut-up and confined community where sexual knowledge was supposed to have been rejected by piety, the need and desire for sexual interaction remained. After such stark testimonies, Benedetta's time as mystic and Abbess was over. Faced with the revelations of the sisters, when it came to her own attestation, the investigators found she had undergone a remarkable change. She knew

---

12 Judith C. Brown, *Immodest Acts* (Oxford University Press, 1986), pp. 117–120.

now, she claimed, that her visions had been demonic and she no longer suffered the nightly embraces of Splenditello that had plagued her for years. She was penitent, even humble. No more records of her survive until the diary entry of one of the convent's nuns on 7 August 1661: 'Benedetta Carlini died at age 71 of fever and colic pains, after eighteen days of illness. She died in penitence, having spent thirty-five years in prison.'[13]

So what are we to think of Benedetta? She was undoubtedly a con artist and deeply manipulative, forcing another young woman into satisfying her own sexual urges. She gaslit both Bartolomea and the entire convent into accepting her behaviour in the name of God and their holy duty. But what records like this show us is that lesbian women and the lives they led were not unknown. So how have we created the cultural myth that lesbians flew under our historical radar? Why have we believed their existence was not acknowledged?

I believe this comes from our modern understanding of the term 'sodomy'. Today, our popular understanding of this term is normally applied to anal sex, but before the twentieth century it defined any sexual act that was outside of the missionary position. Most often, it was used to describe homosexuality, not only between men, but also between women. This terminology and understanding of what 'sodomy' meant emerged in the thirteenth century, with the teachings of St Thomas Aquinas (1225–1274), who wrote: 'copulation with an undue sex, male with male,

---

13 ASPi, Corp. Relig., 924, ins. 1.

or female with female ... this is called the vice of sodomy.'[14]
When we understand the terminology of the past, we can
start to unpick the history of those it applies to. Lesbians
were not only a concern of the Church, they were also
prosecuted under secular law. Uncovered by Louis
Crompton, the earliest secular law to set out punishment
for lesbian acts dates to 1270, in a French legal code called
Li Livres di jostice et de plet.[15] The punishment clearly
follows the same lines as St Thomas Aquinas, targeting
homosexual behaviour in all forms, and seeing no difference between men or women who participated in these
acts:

> He who has been proved to be a sodomite must lose his
> testicle. And if he does it a second time, he must lose
> his member. And if he does it a third time, he must be
> burned. A woman who does this shall lose her member
> each time, and on the third must be burned.[16]

There is some confusion among translators as to what
was meant by 'member' in these codes. Theories range
from the loss of a hand or foot, to genital disfigurement
of either the penis or vagina. But what it shows us is that
homosexuality was not viewed as a solely male identity,

---

14 St Thomas Aquinas, *Summa Theologica*, trans. Fathers of the English
Dominican Province, 3 vols (1947–48), p. 1825.

15 Louis Crompton, 'The Myth of Lesbian Impunity, Capital Laws
From 1270 to 1791' (1981), Faculty Publications – Department of
English, 59, p. 13.

16 Pierre Rapetti ed. *Li Livres di jostice et de plet* (Paris, 1850), pp. 279–80.

but with an acknowledged awareness that women could
be queer too. And this acknowledgement, the awareness
of lesbian women's existence, continued to be discussed
throughout Europe across the centuries. Both the church
and the state shared a need to control and demonise those
women who acted 'against nature'. They used a heritage
of religious and secular beliefs to build legal structures
that punished any woman who did not conform. Writing
in 1314, Cino da Pistoia, 'poet and friend of Dante',
published his thoughts – his *Commentary* – on the laws
of the period.[17] Drawing on a Roman imperial edict from
the third century, Pistoia created a heritage for secular
capital punishment of lesbian women that ran from the
ancient world to the fourteenth century.

This law can be understood two ways: first, when a
woman suffers defilement by surrendering to a male; the
other way is when a woman suffers defilement in surrendering to another woman. 'For there are certain women,
inclined to foul wickedness, who exercise their lust on
other women and pursue them like men.'[18]

What this shows us is that by the fourteenth century
lesbian women had been long been acknowledged by both
church and state, and identified as a something that needed
to be eradicated. As Crompton argues, 'throughout the
continent, lawyers ... were encouraged to write provisions
for the killing of lesbians into the civic, regional, and
imperial codes they drafted during the late Middle Ages

---

17 Louis Crompton, p. 15.
18 Cino de Pistoia, *In Codicem commentaria*, 2 vols (1578), 2:546A.

and the Renaissance'.[19] Executions soon followed. In 1477,
a young lesbian girl was drowned in the German town of
Speier; in 1533, Francoise de l'Etage and Catherine de la
Manière were tortured in Bordeaux, while in the same
century, two Spanish nuns were reportedly burned alive.[20]
French records report a woman burned alive in 1535, and
another hanged for sodomy in 1580.[21] The only country
in Europe that appears not to have taken an interest in
the capital punishment of lesbians is England, where such
motivations for the executions of women have yet to be
identified. Yet although England's lesbian heritage seems
to have been, in many ways, immune from continental
fears and state-sanctioned murder of lesbian women, the
English-speaking world was not. Attempts to enshrine
punishments for lesbians in law appear across the emerging
colonies of America. 'Un-natural filthiness to be punished
with death,' wrote Massachusetts' Reverend John Cotton,
in 1636, '...which is carnal fellowship of man with man,
or woman with woman'.[22] There seems, however, to have
been little stomach for such extreme punishments.

---

19 Louis Crompton, p. 16.

20 Rudolf His, *Das Strafrecht das deutschen Mittelalters*, 2 vols. (Weimar:
Hermann Bohlaus Nachf., 1935), 2: 168;Theodor Hartster, *Das Strafrecht
der freien Reichsstadt Speier* (Breslau: Marcus, 1900), pp. 184–85; Antonio
Gomez, *Variae resolutiones, juris civilis, communis et regii* (Venice: Typo-
graphia Remondiniana, 1758), p. 328; Jean Papon, *Recueil d'arrests
notables des cours souveraines de France* (Paris: Jean de la Fontaine, 1608),
pp. 1257–58.

21 Judith C. Brown, p. 134.

22 Louis Crompton, 'Homosexuals and the Death Penalty in Colonial
America', *Journal of Homosexuality* (1967), p. 279.

Brought before the court of New Plymouth on 6 March 1648 was Sara Norman. Little is known of her life outside of the trial; born Sarah White, she had married Hugh Norman in 1639, giving birth to a daughter, Elizabeth, three years later. They had lived in Yarmouth, and it's believed that it was here that Elizabeth drowned in a well in 1648.[23] Within months, Sara found herself abandoned by her husband and accused of a dangerous immorality. She had been found in bed with 15-year-old Mary Vincent, who had been married just that year to an Englishman, Benjamin Hammon. Both women were brought before the Governor, William Bradford, Captain Miles Standish and four other men, to be punished 'for leude behaviour each with the other vpon a bed'.[24] Mary Hammon was quickly cleared; her youth (although old enough to be married) was enough for the court to dismiss any idea that she might have been actively seeking a sexual relationship with another woman. Sara appears to have been left to await punishment. A year later, she successfully beat another accusation of 'sodomy, and other unclean practices', but in 1650 she was finally sentenced by the court. Not only for her lewd behaviour with Mary Hammon, but also for giving 'diverse lascivious speeches', for which she was ordered to 'make a publik

23 Kenneth Borris (ed.), *Same-Sex Desire in the English Renaissance: A Sourcebook of Texts*, 1470–1650 (Routledge, 2015), p. 107.
24 *Records of the colony of New Plymouth in New England : printed by order of the legislature of the Commonwealth of Massachusetts* (1855–1861), p. 137.

acknowledgement ... of her vnchast behaviour'.[25] This public shaming was a far lesser punishment than the death penalty set out by earlier colonialists.

So what of England, our supposed sanctuary for lesbians in the past? In the last few years, our popular culture has begun to acknowledge the lives led by lesbian English women; in 2018 the eighteenth-century-set film, *The Favourite*, became an award-winning hit for its portrayal of the rumoured love affairs of Queen Anne (1665–1717) with Sarah Churchill, the Duchess of Marlborough, and Sarah's cousin, Abigail Masham. A year later, airing to great critical acclaim, the Sally Wainwright-helmed BBC drama, *Gentleman Jack*, presented the life of nineteenth-century Yorkshire woman, Anne Lister. Lister is one of England's most important lesbian figures, keeping, as she did, a coded diary of all of her relationships and female conquests. She was unashamedly queer, in a time before queerness had been defined. But our records of lesbian life in England are not held solely by the upper classes. At the beginning of the eighteenth century, in Taxal, Cheshire, two curious marriage entries for the parish of Prestbury exist: Hannah Wright and Anne Gaskill, 4 September 1707; Ane Norton and Alice Pickford, 3 June 1708. Uncovering these unusual entries, the historian, Mary Turner, remarked, 'these four names are feminine ... why go to

---

25 *Records of the colony of New Plymouth in New England: printed by order of the legislature of the Commonwealth of Massachusetts* (1855–1861), p. 163.

Taxal? Was the incumbent there more lenient? There does not appear to be any attempt to cover up'.[26] It's hard to imagine eighteenth-century Britain as a radical haven for lesbian life among the ravages of her European counterparts, but although no other record of these women has currently been identified, we do know many other lesbian women who lived and loved in Britain at this time.

Anne Lister (1791–1840) is remarkable. Difficult, Machiavellian, if she had been a man we would undoubtedly refer to her as a womaniser. Her self-knowledge led her to pursue lesbian affairs while she was a schoolgirl. At the Manor House School in York, Anne fell in love with Eliza Raine while they were both in their early teens. Eliza had been born in Madras, the daughter of a British surgeon and an unknown Indian woman.[27] After her father's death in 1797, Eliza had been sent to York for her education, and was expected to inherit £4,000 when she reached her maturity at the age of 21.[28] And yet, for some reason, Eliza and Anne did not fit in with the other girls of the school, and they soon found themselves relegated to a lonely attic they shared, rather than the lively dormitories most girls would expect. They rapidly became inseparable, exchanging rings and promising to live together when Eliza came into her inheritance.[29] But they were soon separated, as Anne

---

26 Mary Turner, 'Two entries from the marriage register of Taxal, Cheshire', *Local Population Studies*, no. 21 (Autumn 1978), p. 64.

27 *Gentleman Jack*, p. 7.

28 Ibid., p. 7.

29 Ibid.

was to be educated at home. Here, in 1807, she began an education that would shape her understanding of the world and her place in it. Her classical education allowed her to discover eroticism and sensuality that was devoid of 'Christian moralising'.[30] She read Greek and Latin poetry – Horace, Juvenal and Martial – and from here created lists of sexual words she then defined: clitoris, dildo, eunuch, hermaphrodite, tribade.[31] In the poetry of Martial she found some of her earliest references to lesbianism:

> When she's done with all this, she sates her lust, she doesn't suck cock – that's not macho enough for her – instead she absolutely gobbles up girls' middles.[32]

Desperate for Eliza to share her understanding, Anne often wrote to her to instruct her in classic literature. When the girls were seventeen, Eliza came to stay with Anne in Halifax, and if they had not before, they consummated their love many times over.[33] But the love affair did not last long. For the rest of her life Anne cut a swathe through the women of Halifax, England and Paris. In Paris, 1824, in the company of the 38-year-old Mrs Maria Barlow, Anne attempted to discover if the woman beside her might be willing to become her lover. Using the same commentaries on St Paul that were used by St Ambrose and

---

30 *Gentleman Jack*, p. 11.

31 Ibid.

32 Martial 2013, 503 (Liber VII, 67).

33 *Gentleman Jack*, p. 14.

St Anselm to identify lesbian acts, Anne pointedly asked what they might mean, while taking care to always play the innocent:

> [Anne] pointed to that verse about women forgetting the natural use, etc, 'But,' I said, 'I do not believe it.' 'Oh,' said she, 'it might be taken in another way, with men ... as men do with men'. Thought I to myself, she is a deep one ... I said I had often wondered what was the crime of Ham. Said she, 'Was it sodomy?'[34]

The clever way in which Anne, an educated woman, used what were originally warnings about lesbian women to *identify* someone who shared her sexuality should not be thought of as unique. What her diary entries show us is that many women had access to, and understood, female sexuality in a way that was a far cry from the heterosexual binary dynamic we have always believed in. But one of the dangers of the past is that we require our new cultural heroines to embody the perfect image of queer identity. That is not possible with Anne. She was as much a product of her society and her privilege as any aristocratic male. She supported the Tory party, and, even though her life witnessed the erasure of female voting rights with the Great Reform Act of 1832 – enshrining in law for the first time the right to vote for 'male persons' only – her status as a land-owning woman allowed her a role in politics ordinary women were denied. Although she did not have

---

34 *Gentleman Jack*, p. 121.

the vote herself, she could instruct her male tenants how to vote, and to vote for the candidates she supported. In the first vote that followed after the 1832 Act, Anne supported James Stuart-Wortley, the 28-year-old, Oxford-educated barrister son of Baron Wharncliffe, and nephew of Lady Louisa Stuart. Keen to be seen to support Lady Stuart's nephew, and further enhance her friendship with this formidable and talented writer, Anne used her influence to campaign for, or in many cases, clearly instruct, her male tenants to vote for Wortley. 'Had James Bottomley,' she recorded in her diary, 'having sent for him to tell him to vote for Wortley tomorrow – had 1/4 hour's talk – he promised to vote for him ... seeming to care nothing about it but that he thought he ought to oblige me.'[35] Although Anne's campaigning for Wortley was initially unsuccessful, he became the Tory MP for Halifax a few years later, in 1835.

Anne's views were Tory blue – conservative, through and through. She believed in the integral rights of the land-owning aristocracy. Her dislike of the 'mobocracy' of the Chartists saw her happily billet local dragoons in the hotel she owned in Halifax, to make sure the peace was kept. When she discovered that a number of Halifax's poor were taking their water from a stream on the grounds of her lover, Ann Walker, Anne's lawyer advised them to place a barrel of tar in the stream, poisoning it for months to come. The residents of Caddy Fields, as the poor area was known, were livid and 'burnt A— & me in effigy',

---

35 *Gentleman Jack*, p. 208.

recorded Anne.[36] Perhaps the hardest of her views to acknowledge comes from her visit to Coldbath Fields Prison in 1824. The prison sat in Clerkenwell, and had existed since the seventeenth century. By the time of Anne's visit the prison housed roughly 472 men, women and children, day to day, sentenced for a myriad of offences from 'vending blasphemous publications' and embezzlement, often on short sentences. The prison's population saw a fast turnover; in 1824 alone it held 3,831 inmates.[37] Four years earlier it had housed the 'Cato Street Conspiracy', a group of men arrested for High Treason and sentenced to death for a plot to murder the Tory Prime Minster, Lord Liverpool, and his cabinet. Perhaps this was what drew Anne to Coldbath Fields Prison, a tourist seeking celebrity. She presented her application to view the workings of the prison, believing that 'in a metropolitan prison there is nothing indelicate or offensive – nothing, I presume, which a female might not, with the strictest regard to propriety or decorum, inspect'.[38] Once inside, Anne took great interest in those prisoners sentenced to hard labour, which in Coldbath Fields took the form of a treadmill.

The treadmill was a relatively new punishment in British prisons, initially invented by a Mr Cubbit of Ipswich in

---

36 *Gentleman Jack*, p. 237.
37 https://www.prisonhistory.org/wp-content/uploads/2018/06/Guide-to-the-Criminal-Prisons-of-Nineteenth-Century-England-R1.pdf
38 *Gentleman Jack*, p. 117.

1817, and first installed in Brixton Prison.[39] Writing in 1845, in his *Prisons and Prisoners*, Joseph Adshead reported a graphic description of the Coldbath Fields treadmill: 'In passing through its various yards, many of its inmates, both males and females, may be seen on the exposed tread-wheels, almost fainting under heat and exhaustion in summer, and, in winter, almost petrified with cold.'[40] Anne, with her Tory spirit, had seen things rather differently: 'I got upon it for two or three minutes, and have nothing to say against it – cannot imagine how it can do any harm.'[41] Perhaps her view would have been altered had she tried it for the hours, weeks and months those in Coldbath Fields were forced to endure. Her dismissal of the treadmill is surprising on many levels, especially as it was a form of punishment often faced by those sentenced for acts of 'indecency and immorality' that Anne herself indulged in. Perhaps this shows us that while we can find many examples of our ancestors living sexually diverse lives, unless they were actively engaged in a community that acknowledged those desires, one's experience of your sexuality could be entirely insular. Equally, just like today, simply because one person belonged to the widespread queer community does not mean their personal sympathies would extend to others' experiences.

Throughout the eighteenth and nineteenth centuries

---

39 Henry Mayhew, *The Criminal Prisons of London* (Cambridge University Press, 2011), p. 174.

40 Joseph Adshead, *Prison and Prisoners*, 1845, p. 178.

41 *Gentleman Jack*, p. 117.

lesbians appeared often in pornographic songs and etch-
ings. While the emphasis on women who cross-dressed
and lived as men became a romanticised female aspiration.
But their reality often ended in brutal public exposure.
Carried in the *Derby Mercury* on 7 November 1746, the
notorious story of Mary Hamilton was reported from
Bath:

> We hear from Taunton, that at a General Quarter-Sessions
> of the Peace for Somersetshire, Mary Hamilton, otherwise
> George, otherwise Charles Hamilton, was tried for a very
> singular and notorious Offence: Mr. Gold, Council for the
> King, open'd to the Court, That the said Mary, &c.
> pretending herself a Man, had married fourteen Wives.[42]

The most recent of Mary's conquests was one Mary Price,
'who appear'd in Courts and depos'd, that she was married
to the Prisoner some little time since at the parish Church
of St. Cuthbert in Wells, and that they were bedded as
Man and Wife.'[43] For the last three months, Mary and her
'husband' had lived in what appeared to be matrimonial
harmony, until Mary had made a discovery; her husband
was not, in fact, a man. It's clear from the newspaper
report that the courts – and the reading public – were
fascinated by how Mary Hamilton could have carried out
a successful fraud on her wife, including fulfilling the acts
of a marital bed. Hamilton's lack of discovery had been

---

42 *Derby Mercury*, Friday, 7 November 1746.
43 Ibid.

due to 'the Prisoner's using certain vile and deceitful Practices, not fit to be mentioned.'[44] These 'deceitful practices' were most likely the use of sex toys and dildos to mimic the act of penetration, and were presented in the fictionalised account of Hamilton's life written by Henry Fielding in the same year. This is something that frequently occurs in the history of women who have loved women. Stories like that of Mary Price, of women discovering the bodies of their husbands were actually female, and they had (often) been unsuspectingly penetrated by a dildo or strap-on, are not uncommon. And this causes problems for the modern historian. Given our own binary definitions of lesbian, gay and transgender, where do women like Mary Hamilton sit? Some people would argue she belongs to lesbian history, others that these are clearly trans histories. For eighteenth-century audiences attempting to define and judge Mary Hamilton, the confusion was clear:

There was a great Debate for some time in Court about the Nature of her Crime, and what to call it but at last it was agreed, that she was an uncommon notorious Cheat; and as such, was sentenced to be publickly whipp'd in the four following Towns, Taunton, Glastonbury, Wells, and Shipton-Mallet, to be imprisoned six Months, and to find [sic] Sureties for her good Behaviour for as long Time as the Justices at the next Quarter Sessions shall think fit.[45]

---

44 *Derby Mercury*, Friday, 7 November 1746.
45 ibid.

Five years after Mary's case seized the English imagination, the *Historical and Physical Dissertation of the Case of Catherine Vizzani* was translated and published in London. The original Italian story had first appeared in print in 1744, authored by the anatomist Giovanni Bianchi, and gave his detailed description of the life and autopsy of Vizzani, 'a young woman, born at Rome, who for eight years passed in the habit of a man, [and] was killed for an Amour with a young lady'.[46] In his swashbuckling and graphic account of her life and death, Bianchi revealed that Catherine used a 'rag-stuffed cylinder' to fulfil the masculine parts of her identity that her physical body could not.[47]

Throughout history lesbian identities have existed, many of whom clearly expressed their love of women and their own womanhood. There are also many women who cross-dressed as men and married women – some revealed their female bodies to their wives, others attempted to keep them hidden, and used devices in place of a male penis. We have no right to decide whose community they belong to; perhaps it is, in fact, both or all. What matters is their existence. They lived, they loved, and we must not deny them the right to be remembered.

---

46 Hal Gladfelder, *Fanny Hill in Bombay: The Making and Unmaking of John Cleland* (John Hopkins University Press, 2012), p. 157.
47 Chris Mounsey (ed.), *Developments in the Histories of Sexualities: In Search of the Normal, 1600–1800* (Rowman and Littlefield, 2015), p. 252.

3
Men Loving Men

'Love him and let him love you. Do you think
anything else under heaven really matters?'
—James Baldwin, *Giovanni's Room*, 1956

Just as lesbian women faced the death penalty for their
love, gay men have always suffered at the hands of both
church and state. Nailing their *Twelve Conclusions* to the
doors of Westminster Abbey and St Paul's Cathedral in
1395, the Lollards declared 'The English people bewail the
crime of Sodom'.[1] As an early Catholic reform group, the
Lollards feared that the celibacy enforced by the Catholic
Church would only lead to immorality and 'unclean acts'
among the religious communities of monks and nuns. Less
than 138 years later, in 1533, Henry VIII passed 'An Acte
for the punishment of the vice of Buggerie', the first time
English law took the act of sodomy out of the ecclesiastical

---

1 Carolyn Dinshaw, *Getting Medieval: Sexualities and Communities, Pre-
and Postmodern* (Duke University Press, 1999), p. 55.

courts of the Church, and made it a crime of the state. Henry quickly made use of the new law to seize power and assets from England's many monasteries, sending investigators to uncover any illicit acts. Known as the 'Royal Visitation', their reports were compiled in the *Compendium Compertorum* of 1535. It caused widespread condemnation of the clergy; in 175 entries of different monasteries, 180 monks had admitted to either being a sodomite, or sodomitical practices.[2] Henry's motivation for publicly revealing the homosexuality of priests and monks was entirely self-serving; he wanted the land and money he would gain from their public prosecutions and executions. The punishment for sodomy or buggery was hanging, although members of the aristocracy, such as Mervyn Tuchet, 2nd Earl of Castlehaven (1593–1631), were given the cleaner death of beheading. We don't know exactly how many men died in sodomy executions prior to the 1670s – records are sparse – yet the publication of the proceedings of the Old Bailey from 1674 to 1913 gives us a unique database of convictions and punishments that we can use to better understand how gay men were treated, lived and loved in our historical past.

Within the proceedings there are three main offence categories to search through, on the hunt for those men who may have been living gay lives: 'Sodomy' (regardless of gender or species), 'Assault with Sodomitic Intent' and 'Sexual Offences: Other'. The first two recorded

---

2 Louis Crompton, *Homosexuality and Civilization* (Harvard University Press, 2006), p. 362.

prosecutions for 'Sodomy' in the Old Bailey appear in 1677, and show us that the old definition of sodomy, that of any unnatural practice that is not simply the missionary position, was still very much in play. Both of the first prosecutions refer to bestiality. The first is a woman with a dog (she was found guilty and sentenced to death), the second is a man with a horse (he was found not guilty). It's not until 1694 that the 'most Unnatural and Horrid Sin of Buggery, which is so detestable, and not fit to be named among Christians' is brought to court against a Turkish man, Mustapha Pochowachett.

Most likely part of London's thriving Merchant community, Pochowachett was accused of rape by his 14-year-old Dutch serving boy, Anthony Bassa. As was common across this period, master and servant shared a bed, and on the 11th of May, after they had retired for the night, Bassa alleged that 'the Prisoner assaulted him, and forced his Yard into his Body; upon which the Boy cried out, to prevent which he stopt his Mouth with the Pillow, and used him in a very unnatural manner.' This act of rape could be proved by the fact that Bassa had been examined by a court-appointed surgeon, who gave testimony that he had been infected with a venereal disease after the attack, 'he being order'd to search the Boy, found two great Ulcers on both sides his Fundament, and that he was in a dangerous condition'. Throughout the trial, giving his defence through an interpreter, Pochowachett swore that he had done nothing wrong, and offered to be examined by the surgeon to prove that he could not have infected the boy, who claimed 'the Turk's Members were shanker'd, and much bloody, and a great hole upon the fleshly part of his Yard.' But the jury believed Bassa and chose not to examine his master, instead finding him 'Guilty of Buggery', which carried with it a sentence of death.

Although some historians have presented sodomy cases as evidence of consensual homosexual relationships, criminalised simply because they were sex acts between two gay men, the cases found under 'Sodomy' or 'Assault with Sodomitic Intent' only ever describe vicious assaults and attacks. These *are* criminal sexual assaults, whether or not one or both of the men involved were gay. Take, for example, George Duffus in 1722. Charged with 'Assault with Sodomitic Intent' on a man named Nicholas Leader, Duffus was found guilty of '(being in bed with him) seiz'd [Leader] by the Throat, forcibly turn'd him on his face, and endeavour'd to commit the said crime upon him. The fact being plainly prov'd the Jury found him guilty.' This attempted rape resulted in a heavy fine of 20 marks, one month's imprisonment, and for Duffus to be pilloried near Old Gravel Lane. The pillory was not a mild punishment; locked into stocks displayed in public squares, prisoners were often surrounded by a baying, angry mob, who beat them, threw things, and hurled any form of abuse they could think of. In 1756, the conman Eagan was stoned to death while pilloried, while others were pelted with oyster shells, or beaten within an inch of their lives.[3] This was mob justice, public judgement on the

---

3 Frank McLynn, *Crime and Punishment in Eighteenth-century England* (Routledge, 2013), p. 283.

crimes of those imprisoned after the law had made its decree.

Looking through the assault and sodomy cases held within the Old Bailey Proceedings, we continually find evidence of violent and aggressive attacks that today we would still prosecute. The abuse of a minor, as in the case of Edward Caley in 1730, drew harsh punishment. Caley was only 10 years old when he was assaulted by his teacher, Isaac Broderick, a paedophile who stood accused of numerous assaults on the young boys in his care. Alongside another boy named William Ham, Caley bravely gave a detailed account of the attacks he had suffered, and Broderick was sentenced to 'stand twice in the Pillory, once at Ratcliff, at the nearest convenient Place to where the Facts were committed, and once at Charing-Cross; to suffer 3 Months Imprisonment, and pay a Fine of 20 Nobles'. Ordering Broderick to be pilloried in the heart of the community where he had committed his crimes made sure that mob justice could be carried out – perhaps, as a way for those who had been attacked to obtain some small form of recompense themselves.

Our understanding of the history of gay men in the UK is one often seen only through the horrific anti-gay legislation of the twentieth century. Understandably, this has led to many of us holding onto a strong belief that throughout history gay men have never been treated as human beings. It is, perhaps, a historian's duty to correct and change this broad belief, to show its nuances and alter our misunderstandings of the past. Gay men deserve a historical lineage that does not portray them solely as demonised and shamed, but the reality of the lives many gay men had in their communities.

What the law tells us about gay men in our historic past, and what that means for the reality of sexual culture, seem to be two very different things. Although to be gay was viewed as a criminal act, many gay men have lived and loved across history. In the 1720s, the exposure of 'Molly clubs' and 'Molly houses' in periodicals and the emerging newspapers created a widespread awareness of gay culture in London, and across England. James Dalton, the infamous highwayman, described the Molly culture in his *Grand Narrative*:

> Walking out one night, he met with one – , alias Susannah Haws, a man who was what they called a Bug to the Mollies, and sometimes acting in that Capacity with those that were not established in Clubs, picking 'em up, as if to commit that damnable Crime of Sodomy; and when they had got a Handle, or any Foundation to proceed upon, they extort Money from them.[4]

Susannah took Dalton to a Molly house on Butler Row, near Temple Bar, run by a man named 'Aunt Wittles'. Here, Dalton was introduced to 'Lydia Gough', 'Moll Irons' and 'Garter May', who offered him 'some sodomitical Civilities; but he being outraged as such effeminate Actions, took up a Quart Pot, and calling them "a pack of mollying Sons of B—s," swore 'he would drive 'em

---

4 James Dalton, *Grand Narrative*, p. 32.

all to the D—-l...upon which they very obligingly ask'd
his Pardon, and begged he would depart, since he was
not of their Profession'.[5] Throughout his criminal career,
Dalton entered into the world of the Mollies, and
although he reacted with homophobia and aggression,
what his account shows us is that there was a well-known
network of gay clubs and gay men who used them, across
London. Susannah remained in Dalton's employ as pick-
pocket for some time, until Dalton's sense of honour
got the better of him, 'I could never look at the nasty
Dog's Face, but I thought him neither a Man's Man,
nor Woman's Man, neither a Whore's Friend, nor a
Rouge's Confidant, but a Persecutor of the Party he falls
in with, and a Traitor to both Sexes' – it was not the
fact that Susannah kept the company of 'the Back-door
Gentlemen', but that he blackmailed them that angered
Dalton.[6] From Susannah's stories of gay life in the capital
we find a picture of a thriving culture that was creating
its own identity among the cellars, taverns and streets
of London.

Susannah Haws, being one day in a pleasant humour,
inform'd Dalton of a Wedding (as they called it) some
Time since, between Moll Irons, and another Molly, a
Butcher; and that one Oviat, (who sometimes stood in the
Pillory) and another Molly, a Butcher of Butcher-Row,
near Temple-Bar, stood as Bridesmaids, and that Oviat

---

5 James Dalton, *Grand Narrative*, p. 33.
6 Ibid., p. 35.

went by the name of Miss Kitten, the Butcher by the name of the Princess Saraphina; and that one Powell, who was call'd St Dunstans' Kate, pretended to be deeply in love with Madam Blackwell...[7]

These clubs offered their members the opportunity to meet, love and be themselves in an environment supposedly out of reach of the law. At Sukey Bevells, in the Mint, the club was renowned for its great extravagances: 'The Stewards are Miss Fanny Knight, and Aunt England; and pretty Mrs Anne Page officiates as Clark. One of the Beauties of this Place is Mrs. Girl of Redriff, and with her (or rather him) dip Candle-mary, a Tallow Candler in the Burough, and Aunt May, an Upholsterer in the same place, are deeply in Love.'

Reading these accounts, our modern understanding of gender and identity struggles to define how these people saw themselves – are they gay? Trans? Is this early drag culture? It is, perhaps, one and all of those things at the same time. Reading between the lines of Dalton's *Grand Narrative* – which exposed those whose lives had previously been carried out in secret – we find gay men from all walks of life. 'Kate Hutton', an old man who never wears a shirt; 'Orange Mary', an orange merchant near London Bridge; and 'Pretty Chris', a solider of the Second Regiment, were recorded alongside 'Hardware Nan', 'China Mary' and 'Flying Horse Moll'.[8]

---

7 James Dalton, Grand Narrative, pp. 37–8.

8 Ibid., pp. 39–40.

The feminised identity of some gay men in this period might lead us to identify this as an early trans culture, and while some may have indeed wished to have changed their sex, we must also understand the power of gender roles at this time. The binary identification of male and female heterosexuality created a cultural narrative that if you wanted to have sex with a man, you must be female, and if you wanted to have sex with a woman, you were masculine. This may go some way to understanding the performance of femininity that so often comes to light in early gay accounts.[9] *Hell upon Earth, or the Delectable History of Whittington's College*, written by an anonymous author in 1703, identified the use of female pronouns in the gay culture of Newgate Prison. 'Whittington's' was a slang name for the prison, and *Hell upon Earth* eagerly described the types of men who could be found within it: 'It would be a pretty Scene to behold them in their Clubs and Cabals, how they assume the Air and affect the Name of Madam or Miss, Betty or Molly, [...] and then frisk and walk away to make room for another, who then accosts the affected Lady, with "Where have you been you saucy Queen? If I catch you Stroulling and Caterwauling, I'll beat the Milk out of your Breasts I will so".'

At the start of the nineteenth century, an unusual case of child abuse led to the legal decision that fellatio between a man and an underage boy was not punishable by the

---

9 *Hell on Earth, or the Delectable History of Whittington's College*, 1703 (1729), p. 43.

Buggery Act of 1533. Rex *v* Samuel Jacobs, in 1817, established that a 7-year-old boy had not been raped, as forced fellatio was not defined as an act of rape by the law. Although this is shocking to us, what it does herald is a growing leniency in our legal system towards homosexuality, rising throughout the nineteenth century. Jeremy Bentham had written *Offences Against One's Self*, in 1785, a 60-page manuscript calling for the reform of England's sodomy laws, arguing that to be gay was not a crime or a danger to society, and should not be punishable by hanging. Fifty years later, in 1835, James Pratt, aged 30, and 41-year-old John Smith became the last men hanged for sodomy (under the older definition of the word, as an act simply outside heterosexual sexuality), who had clearly been engaging in consensual gay sex. Both men were married, and had met in rooms rented by 68-year-old William Bonill. Bonill's landlord had grown suspicious of the multiple male visitors he received, and on Pratt and Smith's arrival, he and his wife had spied on them through a keyhole. What they saw caused them to break down the door and call for the police. Both Smith and Pratt were sentenced to death by hanging, while Bonill was transported to Australia. Shortly before the men died, the magistrate who had committed them to trial, Hensleigh Wedgwood, wrote to the Home Secretary, Lord John Russell (grandfather of philosopher and historian, Bertrand Russell), arguing that their death sentences should be commuted. Wedgwood presided over many of the sodomy and assault cases and was becoming increasingly aware of the reality of consensual gay sex, and the unfair punishment the law was enacting on it.[10] He believed that it also often targeted those in the lower classes, as those who would have been tried from the upper levels of society were able to buy their freedom or the silence of their accusers:

> There is a shocking inequality in this law in its operation upon the rich and the poor. It is the only crime where there is no injury done to any individual and in consequence it requires a very small expense to commit it in so private a manner and to take such precautions as shall render conviction impossible. It is also the only capital crime that is committed by rich men but owing to the circumstances I have mentioned they are never convicted. The detection of these degraded creatures was owing entirely to their poverty, they were unable to pay for privacy, and the room was so poor that what was going on inside was easily visible from without.[11]

Even in the British Navy, where buggery was viewed as the most serious offence – more so than murder – by 1815, both accusations and convictions had entered a sharp decline.[12]

The records of the Old Bailey Proceedings have been digitised and are freely available to everyone. They

---

10 Charles Upchurch, *Before Wilde: Sex Between Men in Britain's Age of Reform* (University of California Press, 2009), p. 112.
11 Ibid.
12 Eugene L. Rasor, *English/British Naval History to 1815: A Guide to the Literature* (Praeger, 2004), p. 230.

provide us with an incredible source for research into historical attitudes towards gay men and the law in the UK. The most important courthouse in the British legal system, the Old Bailey has been our central criminal court since the late medieval period, and in 1834 saw its jurisdiction extended from London and Middlesex to cover the entirety of England. Trials held here were covered in great detail by the Victorian press, and so we have a wealth of first-hand testimony and case material from which to build a picture of gay lives in the nineteenth century.

Nearly thirty years after the trial of Pratt and Smith, in 1861, the death penalty for sodomy was finally removed, but what the records show us is that in the aftermath of their deaths there was a fundamental shift in how the courts dealt with cases of consensual gay sex between men. Discoverable under 'Sexual Offences: Other' in the Old Bailey Proceedings, we find the records of those men who were prosecuted, not for violent sodomitic assaults, but for consensual homosexual acts. And what is utterly unique about these cases is that of the twenty-five recorded at the Old Bailey between 1839 and 1903, fourteen of those were found to be Not Guilty, while for those convicted for consensual gay sex, the average punishment was for either six or twelve months.[13] This was most often due not to the sexual act itself, but to the fact that it had

---

13 To be exact, there are twelve 'Not Guilty' verdicts, one where the case was thrown out with insufficient evidence and one where the defendants are found not guilty of intent, but guilty on the second count of indecent exposure.

taken place in a public space, such as a park or a street. Charged with two counts of 'unlawfully and indecently assaulting each other, with a view to commit filthy and unnatural acts and practices', and 'indecent exposure in a public place', in 1875, Henry Harris, a 55-year-old labourer, and Nicholas Hartmann, 36 and a tailor, were found only guilty of indecent exposure, and given twelve months in Holloway Prison.[14]

	Offence	Defendant	Verdict	Sentence
1839	SO/Other: indicted for a misdemeanour of an indelicate nature	Thomas Powell (30), John Murray (45)	Guilty	Confined six months
1843	SO/Other: indicted for certain unlawful and indecent practices	James Lyon (37), Robert Cordell Allpress (37)	Guilty	Confined 12 months
1844	SO/Other: indicted for unlawfully meeting together for certain indecent purposes	Joseph Harradine (29), Robert Richards (17)	Guilty	Confined six months
1846	SO/Assault With Sodomitic Intent: indicted for unlawfully assaulting each other, with intent to excite, &c.	Thomas Davis (26), William Stepney (20)	Guilty	Davis: 12 months, Stepney: 6 months

14 Calendar of Prisoners, HO140, 31: 5, National Archives, findmypast.com

	Offence	Defendant	Verdict	Sentence
1846	SO/Assault With Sodomitic Intent: indicted for unlawfully meeting together, with intent to excite each other, &c.	John Smith (65), James Maslam (16)	Guilty	Smith (career criminal): 6 months, Maslam: 4 months
1848	SO/Other: indicted for diverse indecent acts	James Orchard, James Thurtell, Samuel Martis, Henry Ashley, Joseph Wilkinson, Thomas Clarke	Insufficient Evidence	
1853	SO/Other: unlawfully meeting together for indecent purposes	John Codey, Christopher Mollineux	NOT GUILTY	
1857	SO/Other: unlawfully meeting together in a public highway, and committing diverse indecent acts	Henry Jarvis (50), Fredrick Scott (19)	NOT GUILTY	
1865	SO/Assault With Sodomitic Intent: unlawfully and indecently assaulting each other, with intent, &c.	James Smith (30), Stephen Watson (19)	Guilty	Judgement Respited

	Offence	Defendant	Verdict	Sentence
1873	SO/Other: indicted for committing certain lewd and indecent acts	William Colney (20), William Ledger (30)	NOT GUILTY	
1875	SO/Assault With Sodomitic Intent: unlawfully and indecently assaulting each other, with intent, &c.	Henry Harris (55), Nicholas Hartmann (36)	Guilty of Indecent Exposure in a public place	12 months imprisonment each
1881	SO/Other: indecent exposure and assault	Edward Bellard (37), Robert Sullivan (27)	NOT GUILTY	
1881	SO/Other: unlawfully committing indecent practices. Second Count: for indecent exposure	William Jeffries (39), John Brocklington (25)	Guilty on Second count	12 months hard labour
1882	SO/Other: indecent exposure in a public place	George Stevenson (42), Joseph Tulley (18)	NOT GUILTY	
1883	SO/Other: indecently exposing the person of Gregory	Thomas Moore (45), Charles Gregory (29)	NOT GUILTY	

	Offence	Defendant	Verdict	Sentence
1884	SO/Other: unlawfully exposing themselves in a public place with intent	Frederick Self (17), Edward Wright Wild (35)	NOT GUILTY	
1885	SO/Assault With Sodomitic Intent: feloniously attempting to commit an unnatural offence	George Richard Stephenson (30), John Slater (21)	NOT GUILTY	
1886	SO/Other: For committing an indecent act with John Crawley	Henry Ernest Allan	NOT GUILTY	
1886	SO/Other: committing diverse acts of indecency with Gilbert Thomas	Edward Bryan Hodge (33)	Pleaded Guilty	8 months hard labour
1889	SO/Other: unlawfully committing acts of indecency with each other	John Sturgess (30), Walter Johnson (28)	NOT GUILTY	
1891	SO/Assault With Sodomitic Intent: unlawfully attempting to commit an unnatural offence	Louis Brace (29), Louis Kendal (24)	NOT GUILTY	

	Offence	Defendant	Verdict	Sentence
1902	SO/Assault With Sodomitic Intent	Prince Francis Joseph of Braganza, Henry Chandler (15), William Gerry (24), Charles Sherman (17)	NOT GUILTY	
1903	SO/Other: committing acts of indecency	Andrew Bohrer (37), Johnny Howard (14)	BOHRER: Pleaded Guilty	BOHRER: 12 months hard labour, HOWARD: placed under Father's care
1906	SO/Assault With Sodomitic Intent: with intent to commit an unnatural crime with Deric Goodhall, a male person; committing an act of gross indecency on and indecently assaulting the said Deric Goodhall	William Thomas Jacobs (26, painter)	Guilty	12 months hard labour

Here, Holloway Prison classed any inmate serving a sentence of longer than four months with hard labour as a 'Class V' prisoner. Those who were prosecuted for public indecency – often linked to consensual gay sex – served their sentences here. On Sunday, Tuesday, Thursday and Saturday their diet consisted of: one pint of oatmeal gruel and 8oz of bread for breakfast; and 4oz of cooked meat without bone, 1lb potatoes and 8oz of bread for dinner. On Monday, Wednesday and Friday, three meals were allowed: a pint of cocoa, made from two quarters of an ounce of flaked cocoa, or cocoa nibs, sweetened with three quarters of molasses or sugar, and 8oz of bread; dinner included a pint of soup, a pound of potatoes, and 8oz of bread, and supper saw a repeat of the next day's forthcoming breakfast: one pint of oatmeal gruel, 8oz of bread. Life in the prison population was monotonous, and rife with homophobia. As the anonymous author and reformed criminal of *Convict life: or, Revelations concerning convicts and convict prisons by A Ticket of Leave Man*, written in 1880, hinted, 'A very large proportion of the prisoners that belong to that class who "love darkness rather than light, because their deeds are evil" and these dark cells are a cover for all sorts of immorality and indecency, about which I cannot be more communicative'.

To trace more details about the lives of gay men who faced prosecution in the nineteenth century, the Newgate Register for prisoners often carries on the stories of those who appeared at the Old Bailey. In 1843, James Lyon, a 37-year-old clerk, was convicted alongside his lover, Robert Cordell Allpress, who had been born in St Ives, and at 44 was employed as a servant. They were convicted of 'only meeting together for the purposes of committing and committing with each other unnatural acts and practices' and were sentenced to one year in Newgate; they were released together on 20 August 1844.[15] Exploring the other criminal and court records gives us a chance not to misinterpret the archives of the Old Bailey, as some have done, seeing a conviction where none actually took place. When Stephen Watson, a 19-year-old carpenter, was convicted alongside 30-year-old traveller, James Smith, in 1865, their judgements were recorded as guilty of sodomitical assault on each other – a confusing attempt to define gay sex and criminality in the legal language of the period. However, the Central Criminal Court Calendar recorded that although they were convicted, their judgement was respited.[16] This term, 'Judgement Respited', delayed the act of sentencing in cases where the law was doubtful. Often, it led to no further action against those who had originally been convicted of an offence. Their sentences were simply not carried out. Writing in 1862, Henry Mayhew observed that 'those charged with the casual crimes of "lust, shame, and indecency", have likewise increased to a small amount, viz., 0.03 in each 10,000 of the population – the largest addition having occurred among those annually charged with rape, sodomy, &c.'[17] His statistics include not just gay men, and so it is indicated again that the imprisonment rate for homosexuals remained low throughout the nineteenth century.

---

15 Newgate Prison, London: Register of Prisoners. England & Wales, Crime, Prisons & Punishment, 1770–1935, findmypast.com
16 Central Criminal Court: After Trial Calendars of Prisoners, England & Wales, Crime, Prisons & Punishment, 1770–1935, findmypast.com
17 Henry Mayhew, p. 450.

In fact, counting all those who had their sentences respited, the two cases charged with 'indecent acts' and only prosecuted for 'indecent exposure', in every single case brought between 1848 and 1903 that attempted to bring about a prosecution for consensual gay sex between two males, the defendants received a sentence of Not Guilty. And during the height of the notorious Victorian Sex Panic of the 1880s, when almost half of all the cases were brought, the only case successfully prosecuted was that of 33-year-old Edward Bryan Hodge, who *chose* to plead guilty and was sentenced to eight months in Wandsworth Prison in 1886.

Hodge seems a peculiar anomaly among the rest of these cases. He is one of only two where the defendant admitted to their guilt – the other being the case of a 37-year-old school teacher and a 14-year-old boy – and the timing of his case comes in the direct aftermath of the Labouchere Amendment of 1885, the first criminalisation of homosexuality that ever occurred on our statute books, focusing, as it does, solely on homosexual relationships between men. Every other law before this point regarded buggery and sodomy to be an act that could occur between men, women and beasts. Nothing specifically targeted, alone, the relationships between men.

CONSIDERATION.

HC Deb 6 August 1885 vol. 300 cc1386–428

MR. LABOUCHERE: said, he rose to move a clause he had put upon the Paper—

MR. WARTON: (MP Bridgeport) rose to Order, He wished to ask whether the clause about to be moved by the hon. Member for Northampton, and which dealt with a totally different class of offence to that against which the Bill was directed, was within the scope of the Bill?

MR. SPEAKER: (Arthur Peel) At this stage of the Bill anything can be introduced into it by leave of the House.

MR. LABOUCHERE: said, his Amendment was as follows:—After Clause 9, to insert the following clause:— 'Any male person who, in public or private, commits, or is a party to the commission of, or procures or attempts to procure the commission by any male person of, any act of gross indecency with another male person, shall be guilty of a misdemeanour, and, being convicted thereof, shall be liable, at the discretion of the Court, to be imprisoned for any term not exceeding one year with or without hard labour.' That was his Amendment, and the meaning of it was that at present any person on whom an assault of the kind here dealt with was committed must be under the age of 13, and the object with which he had brought forward this clause was to make the law applicable to any person, whether under the age of 13 or over that age. He did not think it necessary to discuss the proposal at any length, as he understood Her Majesty's Government were willing to accept it. He, therefore, left it for the House and the Government to deal with as might be thought best.

New Clause (Outrages on public decency,)—
(Mr. Labouchere,)—brought up, and read the first and
second time.

1398

MR. HOPWOOD: said, he did not wish to say anything
against the clause; but he would point out that under the
law as it stood at the present moment the kind of offence
indicated could not be an offence in the case of any
person above the age of 13, and in the case of any
person under the age of 13 there could be no consent.

SIR HENRY JAMES: said, the clause proposed to
restrict the punishment for the offence dealt with to one
year's imprisonment, with or without hard labour. He
would move to amend the clause by omitting the word
'one,' in the last line of the clause, and substituting the
word 'two.'

MR. LABOUCHERE: had no objection to the
Amendment.

What the Labouchere Amendment did, for the first time,
was to single out consensual gay relationships as a specific
target, and more importantly to criminalise them not only
in the public space, but also in *private*. With Sir Henry
James' addition, it also doubled the penalty, two years'
imprisonment rather than one. It would be understandable
if in the aftermath of this law that conviction rates for gay
men would have skyrocketed, but, as the Old Bailey records

show, the opposite occurred. It is as if the courts were determined to resist the homophobia of the British Government. In this heady, hysterical aftermath of the passing of the Criminal Law Amendment Bill, alone, with no co-defendant beside him, Edward Bryan Hodge became the only man to admit, publicly and in court, that he was a homosexual.

Born on the island of Antigua in the West Indies in 1852, Edward Bryan Hodge came from a well-known West Indian society family. His father, Langford Lovell Hodge, had been born there in 1807, growing up as the son of a wealthy slave plantation owner. Hodge's grandfather, Langford Lovell Snr, held the position of aide-de-camp to Antigua's Governor, and the Hodge family dominated Antiguan society, owning a large estate known as Hodges Bay on the island's north coast.

Langford Lovell Jnr was 10 years old in 1817, when scandal engulfed his family on the island. The Hodges Bay estate held between thirty-five and forty-two slaves, of whom his father, Langford Lovell Snr, owned seven: George, Eloise, Castallia, Frederick, Sukey, Best and Lucretia. We only know their names because he left them, as property, to his wife in his will of 1817, dying not long after he had been internationally reviled in a pamphlet printed on the orders of the African Institution, for his treatment of a female slave.[18]

In England, John Hatchard (founder of Hatchards bookshops and then a renowned anti-slavery campaigner and printer) published a report by the African Institution that

---

18 https://www.ucl.ac.uk/lbs/person/view/2146639657, PROB 11/1591/248

alleged widespread torture and inhumanity among Antigua's society set towards their slaves, with Langford Lovell Snr singled out as a person of 'cruel and inhuman disposition' who had 'treated one of his slaves with great and unjustifiable severity and cruelty'.[19] Set out clearly in the pamphlet was an account that, in 1816, Langford Lovell Snr 'severely whipped a negro woman of his own, who was pregnant', and that when she had attempted to bring his treatment of her to the attention of the Governor, he had had her severely whipped again, for which he had been dismissed from the Governor's service. To add to the shame and horror of this story – and it was seen as deeply shameful by its British readers – was also the accusation that, due to Langford Lovell Snr's position in society, the case had been hushed up, which proved that there was no protection for those enslaved on the island under British law. It was a grotesquely sadistic story, one of many the African Institution exposed among the slave traders and plantation owners of the Caribbean in their fight to see slavery abolished.

Seeking to protect the reputation of Antigua's justice system and wealthy white inhabitants, a successful case for libel was brought against Hatchard, for unknowingly publishing a 'wilful and wicked fabrication'.[20] Much was

---

19 *A Complete Collection of State Trials and Proceedings for High Treason and Other Crimes and Misdemeanors: From the Earliest Period to the Year 1783, with Notes and Other Illustrations*, Volume 32, 1824, The Trial of John Hatchard, pp. 674–756.

20 'A Report of the Trial of the King V. John Hatchard: For a Libel on the Aides-de-camp of Sir James Leith ... and the Grand Jury of the

made of the fact that Langford Lovell Snr still, in fact, held his position in the Governor's service, and that the pamphlet had been published with the intention to enflame the tensions between slaves and the plantation owners during a time of widespread unrest and white fear of slave rebellions.[21] Little could be done to counter the government's arguments as the African Institution understandably refused to reveal the source of their information for the accusation against Langford Lovell Snr at the trial. He died shortly after.

Having witnessed his father's international shaming, Langford Lovell Jnr had grown up in an environment where protecting your reputation was everything. He trained as a barrister and was on his third marriage by the time his son, Edward Bryan Hodge, was born, having married Ellen Barwell in 1849. She had been born in Calcutta, in Bengal, and was twenty-one years younger than her husband, a man who had watched his family fortune crumble from tens of thousands of pounds to just under £300 at his death in 1862. It was a repeating family tragedy; Edward was 10 years old, the same age his father

Island of Antigua, as Published in the Tenth Report of the Directors of the African Institution. In the Court of King's Bench, Before Mr. Justice Abbott ... on February 20, 1817, Together with Mr. Justice Bayley's Address in Pronouncing the Sentence of the Court, Published by John Hatchard', 1817, p. 133.

21 *A Complete Collection of State Trials and Proceedings for High Treason and Other Crimes and Misdemeanors: From the Earliest Period to the Year 1783, with Notes and Other Illustrations, Volume 32*, 1824, The Trial of John Hatchard, pp. 674–756.

had been when his own father died, surrounded by scandal
and international revulsion. This international family, the
product of empire, colonialisation and the profits of
slavery, had decided to return to the motherland in the
late 1850s, and Edward's youngest sister, Ellen, was the
first in this family of immigrants to be born in England.
There were eight years between Edward and Ellen, and
four between him and his other sister, Alice, who had been
born in Antigua before the family emigrated back. They
had initially lived in Hove, where their father had died,
before moving to Camberwell. By 1881, Edward held the
position of clerk, at Trinity House, while the family lived
on Camberwell's Jasper Road. We don't know anything
more about Hodge until he was taken before the magistrate
at Lambeth Police Court on 27 February 1886. He had
been arrested on 13 February, and appeared at the Old
Bailey, charged with committing 'certain acts of gross
indecency with Gilbert Thomas', the following month.[22]
The only Gilbert Thomas who appears to be living in
London, and also in the Lambeth area, at this time, was
the 22-year-old son of the founder of the *Graphic* newspaper, William Luson Thomas.

So here we have the meeting of two worlds, the immigrant child of a slave-owning family, representing the
crumbling embers of a dying empire, and the artistic son
of the new modern media. We can't know what drew
Hodge to admit his guilt to the charge – Gilbert Thomas

---

22 HO140 90, A Calendar of Prisoners Tried At The General Quarter
Sessions Of The Peace, findmypast.com

doesn't appear in the Old Bailey records so he doesn't appear to have been charged and it does seem, given the pattern of zero convictions for this type of offence, that it was Hodge himself who was responsible for his own conviction. If he hadn't pleaded guilty, he would not have ended up facing an eight-month sentence in Wandsworth Prison. So why would someone risk prosecution by admitting to a misdemeanour, and the supposed public humiliation of being marked as a homosexual?

Describing the text among their 'New Books' on 19 January 1886, the month before Hodge's arrest, the *Birmingham Daily Post* summarised Robert Louis Stevenson's latest work as exposing '...a duality in man's nature, a better and a worse self, which are separable. Dr. Jekyll discovers a drug by means of which he can effect the change. As Dr. Jekyll he is learned, pious, good, respectable, and respected by everybody; then he takes his drug, becomes Edward Hyde, and goes out into the world, and indulges in whatever is vicious and wicked – cruelty, murder, &c., included. He escapes to his house, takes his drug, and becomes the exemplary Dr. Jekyll once more. But a new terror comes into his life, for the transformation which he had first effected by an effort of his will takes place involuntarily, and this involuntary change from the better to the worse self becomes more and more frequent.'[23]

It is not difficult to imagine the effect this story might have had on Edward Bryan Hodge, a young man raised on old traditions in the new world, who returned to the

---

23 *Birmingham Daily Post*, 19 January 1886.

old world only to find it thoroughly modernised. His sexual identity, that of a gay man, would have been unlikely to find support in the traditions in which he was raised. Perhaps he acutely understood this idea of duality in one's life as a gay man in the mid-1880s, now for the first time an identity that had been exposed and deemed criminal by the society around him. Did Edward Hyde represent the wicked indulgences – the sins – Edward Hodge was forced to commit simply to feel love, pleasure and a human connection? Had the hysteria of the Labouchere Amendment, passed only months earlier, worked its way into the heart and soul of Edward Bryan Hodge to such an extent that he now saw his own nature as wicked, a guilt to be confessed to? This could be the motivation behind his guilty plea. We are aware now that a socially conditioned, deep self-loathing and self-destruction is often suffered by those who grow up in a society that tells them to be gay, queer, trans, bisexual, or anything other than heterosexual, is wrong and morally corrupt. Although a gay culture existed in Britain for centuries, there was also widespread homophobia, and by the 1880s, science and medicine had begun its pathologising of sexuality that led to homosexuality being defined as a mental disease. Sentenced to eight months in Wandsworth Prison, shortly after this Edward Bryan Hodge vanishes from the historical record, only to re-emerge, unexpectedly, in 1906, again caught indulging in gay sex in public. 'SERIOUS CHARGE.—EVIDENCE BY A COPPER'S NARK', read the the *Hendon and Finchley Times* on 20 July 1906:

Edward Lovell, 48, of Packington-street, Islington, a well-dressed man, said to be very highly connected, and described as an artist and journalist, was charged on remand with committing a serious offence with a lad, aged 16, in a field near Highgate-woods.—Mr. Barker prosecuted on behalf of the police, and Mr. Weaver Bernard defended.— Detective Grosse, Y Division, said the prisoner, when arrested, said, 'I will give you anything. Don't press the charge against me.' A number of newspaper cuttings of reports of the Studio Murder were found in prisoner's coat pocket. —Detective Butters said he went to the prisoner's home and found a number of indecent photographs, and newspaper cuttings of indecent assault cases.—Richard Perks, painter, cross examination, said that he had his suspicions with regard to the prisoner, and therefore watched him. Witness had assisted the police for twenty-four years, and was known, he supposed, as a 'copper's nark'. He had not received money for giving information to the police. He had assisted the police in unravelling a lottery, and was rewarded for that. He had been engaged watching on behalf of the police, but had not been paid. He did it for the love of the thing. It was his hobby to try and assist the police all he could.—Mr. Bernard: A little Sherlock Holmes, eh. —Witness, continuing, stated that prisoner acted so suspiciously that he felt convinced something was going to happen.—Prisoner, who pleaded not guilty and reserved his defence, was committed for trial.[24]

---

24 The *Hendon and Finchley Times*, 20 July 1906.

Hodge was using his father's second name as his new surname, an attempt, perhaps, to escape the notoriety of his past. He was now 53, not the charitable 48 listed in the *Hendon and Finchley Times*, and had taken rooms on Packington Street, just off the Essex Road, in Islington. Having spent much of the twenty years after his last conviction in New York, Hodge had returned to London with determination. 'The Studio Murder Case', of which Hodge held clippings, was a sensational story that gripped the national press, as tales of lust and violence often did, the month before Edward's arrest. The victim, Archibald Wakley, was a young artist, 'a little over thirty years of age ... a quiet, reserved, well-balanced young fellow' whose painting *The Sleeping Beauty* had been shown at the Royal Academy earlier that year.[25] Wakley had been found brutally murdered and mutilated in his studio on Monmouth Road, Westbourne Grove, after returning home from a party late one night in the company of an unknown soldier. According to the *Edinburgh Evening News*, in the early hours of the morning of 24 May 1906, Wakley reportedly fled from his studio, pursued by an enraged soldier, who had battered him around the head with a hammer, and kicked him down the stairs.[26] The brutal and savage nature of the assault, and also perhaps the fact that its victim was a celebrated young talent, led to a mass police investigation where 600 soldiers from different regiments across the country were interrogated

25 *Sevenoaks Chronicle and Kentish Advertiser*, 1 June 1906.
26 *Edinburgh Evening News*, 1 June 1906.

in an attempt to find the culprit.[27] The scant evidence they had to go on was that Wakley had arrived back at his studio at 10.30 p.m., in the company of a tall man in the blue uniform of the Royal Horse Guards, and that the man was wearing spurs. This information proved vitally important to the investigation, as not only had Wakley suffered the most horrific and vicious hammer attack to his face and head, his thighs were covered in marks that could only have been left by a soldier's spurs. But the police were unable to find the murderer, and the inquest into Wakley's death took place in front of a nation gripped by this real life 'murder mystery'.

So it was not that surprising to find Edward with clippings of this sensational case in his coat pocket – he was now a journalist, after all. But there is perhaps a coded message at work here, because 'The Studio Murder Case' had done a highly unusual thing; it had opened a very public window onto what it was like to be a gay man in London. And as the case played out across the newspapers and breakfast tables of England, it became clear that Wakley had been the victim of a violent, homophobic murder. He was killed because he was gay.

Although the *Edinburgh Evening News* had some of their facts right, the reality of Archibald's death was far sadder. He had been found in his pyjamas, half in and half out of the shared lavatory that served Wakley and the two other artists who shared independent studios at Westbourne Grove – neither of whom had been home

---

27 *Edinburgh Evening News*, 1 June 1906.

at the time of the murder.[28] His body, covered by a coun-
terpane from his bed, was found by the studio's caretaker,
Mrs Mercer, who had come in to clean at 8 a.m. on the
morning of 24 May.[29] Although Archibald had most likely
been killed by the first blow of a hammer to his head,
over twenty other blows had followed and the inquest
was informed that 'great force had been used to inflict
the wounds: in fact, the assailant must have been in a
condition of absolute frenzy...nearly every wound had
caused a fracture of the skull'.[30] Archibald had been struck
once while he was standing, had stumbled back and hit
his head on the wall, falling to the floor, where the rest
of the blows were inflicted. His thighs also bore tiny
puncture marks that were later revealed to be caused by
the spurs of a soldier's boot, but no reason for their
appearance was offered to the court.

Scattered across Wakley's studio were numerous
sketches of soldiers, as well as multiple scraps of paper
scribbled with hurried addresses. After a witness stated
he had seen Wakley bringing back a soldier dressed in
the uniform of the Horse Guards, one piece of paper had
given the police a hopeful lead, written on it 'Trooper
J. T. Walker, D Squadron, Royal Horse Guards, Hyde
Park'.[31] John Thomas Walker, the Trooper in question,
was found to have a solid alibi for the night of the murder,

---

28 *West Somerset Free Press*, 2 June 1906.
29 Ibid.
30 Ibid.
31 *Western Times*, 8 June 1906.

but appeared and gave evidence at the inquest. He described meeting Wakley four months earlier, on an evening out in Hyde Park. They had smoked cigarettes and Wakley had invited him back to his studio for a drink, and while he was there, Walker had agreed to allow Wakley to paint his portrait at a later date. After an hour the Trooper had left, at around 1 a.m., a surprisingly short amount of time for two young men who seemed to be settling in for an evening of gentle comradeship. When pressed by the Foreman of the Jury, Walker revealed that they had passed the time by '...talking, and he was showing me some pictures. He proposed something which was distasteful, and that was the reason I did not keep the appointment'.[32] He had given Wakley his address, and after that had seen him again late at night in Hyde Park, although on that occasion they had not spoken.

The picture that was being painted for the inquest's jury and the press was one of Wakley as a young gay man who often frequented London's parks in the evening, as a hunting ground to pick up men. He found many of them among the military. Reporting on the inquest, the *Western Times* revealed to its readers two important pieces of evidence: firstly, that a bottle of port wine had been placed on the table, alongside some glasses with orange peel in them; and secondly, that a man was missing from one of the barracks and the police had been unable to find him. Although Wakley's rooms were searched, finger-printed and photographed by the police, no further clues

---

32 *Western Times*, 8 June 1906.

to his murderer were ever found, and the inquest recorded an open verdict of murder by persons unknown.[33]

A few weeks later, several newspapers ran reports that the murder had been solved. According to a story reprinted from *Reynolds's Newspaper*, Archibald had returned home with a companion, a soldier,

belonging to a certain regiment. They climbed the two flights of stairs, and reached the studio, situated just above the second landing. Wakley at once offered the trooper refreshment, an invitation which was accepted. The artist produced a bottle of port, filled a glass, and gave it to his guest. The soldier drank the contents of the glass, and, in a few minutes, collapsed, in a state of insensibility. When he recovered, the soldier levelled an accusation at Wakley, which he did not deny. Maddened by the thought of what had happened, the soldier rushed Wakley and tried to strike him. The artist dodged through the door towards the landing, snatching up a hammer to use in self-defence. The soldier dashed after him, caught him just as he was trying to find safety inside the lavatory, and wrenching the hammer from his grasp, struck him blow after blow with savage fury, battering him to death. Intoxicated with the passion for revenge, the soldier threw aside the hammer for a knife. With this he mutilated the body, and afterwards covered up the remains with bedclothes and made his way from the house. After seeking advice in a certain quarter, the trooper is said to have

---

33 The *Globe*, 25 May 1906.

caught, under another name, a boat to one of the most important of our colonies.[34]

Who knows how much of the *Reynolds's* report is true? They were certainly using the information given to them to paint a picture of the dangers of life as a gay man in London at this time. The murder suspect was depicted as a young new recruit, someone who was naive, who didn't understand the urban life of London, and who was insulted to the point of revulsion at the idea and existence of a gay man. For Edward Hodge, the brutality of those who hated and criminalised gay men was not merely an idea, it was his lived reality. The descriptions of his flat in 1906, after it was raided by the police, give the impression of a man who was investigating homophobic attacks and convictions in England. Was he planning an exposé? We may never know, and his arrest removed his ability to work and gather evidence undiscovered. Having been identified as a gay man by a police informant, Edward had left his rooms near the Essex Road and travelled to the well-known tavern, the Nag's Head, in Holloway. Here, he had picked up a 16-year-old boy, most likely a young rent boy, and they had taken a tram to Highgate Woods. After walking through a golf course, they had engaged in an 'indecent act', and Edward had been arrested. Unbeknownst to him, the police had followed him from the Nag's Head.

---

34 *Hartlepool Northern Daily Mail*, 18 June 1906.

When witness told prisoner that he would be taken into custody, he replied, 'My dear Sir, don't do that. You don't know what it means to me. You can have any amount, but don't lock me up.' On the way to the station the prisoner said, 'I told the boy I did not mean to do anything to him. I will do anything you want to do. Don't lock me up. You know it is not worth while [*sic*] to lock me up.' At the police station he said, 'I will give you anything. Don't press the charge against me. It was the boy who made the suggestion, not I.'—Prisoner, who protested innocence, was remanded. Bail was refused.[35]

Edward disappears again after this; perhaps he was convicted, perhaps he returned to America before he could be sentenced, but his offers of money and the press's hints of upper-class connections show that Wedgwood's fears of rich men being able to hide their gay lives behind money were still occurring. However, Edward's story shows us that this was no longer enough. The passing of the Labouchere Amendment in 1885, the exposure of a tele-graph rent-boy ring catering to politicians and the aristocracy in 1889, known as 'The Cleveland Street Scandal', as well as Oscar Wilde's high-profile libel trial in 1895, had shifted both popular and legal attitudes towards gay men. Convictions were now far harsher, and many lives were destroyed by a culture that demonised and shamed gay men. The Sexual Offences Act of 1957 finally decriminalised homosexuality in Britain, but the

---

35 *Barnet Press*, 7 July 1906.

legacy of the 1890s and the horrors suffered by gay men, from persecution to chemical castration, are a constant reminder of the brutality suffered by those whose consensual sexual identity is ignored or criminalised.

4

Loving Who You Want

'All of us are put in boxes by our family, by our religion, by our society, our moment in history, even our own bodies. Some people have the courage to break free.'
—Geena Rocero, 2014

Fluidity, of gender or sexuality, is not a modern concept. Bi and pan sexuality presents as an elusive history as those who cross-dressed, or sought to alter their physical sex. The existence of those of us who have relationships outside of the binary definitions is clear throughout history, and yet often those who lived these lives are portrayed with a singular sexual identity. The greatest struggle of understanding the history of our sexual culture comes not from identifying all the different types of sexuality, who belonged to what community at what time, but from simply accepting that the lines are and were blurred. Just as today, there were those for whom binary sexuality was an absolute, and there were those for whom it was not.

Although modernity has caused many problems of sexual identity and sexual expression, one of its important definitions has been the emergence of trans culture. Prior to the twentieth century there was a great deal of confusion among medical and social authorities about those who dressed and lived as the opposite gender, and had same or opposite-sex partners, and the biological examples of those whose genitalia developed in a markedly different way to what fitted the expected perception of male or female. Everyone who identified with even just one of these characteristics was termed a 'hermaphrodite', a blanket term that included all those who did not easily fit into two binary, clear-cut boxes. The confusion as to what and who could be termed intersex is made clear by the author of *ONANIA: OR THE HEINOUS SIN OF Self-Pollution AND ALL ITS Frightful Consequences (In Both Sexes) CONSIDERED* (1756):

I HAVE read, that in France there are a People who have a great Propension of the Clitoris naturally, and are equally able to make Use of those of both Sexes; and that the Laws there leave to their Choice which Sex to make Use of, after which the Use of the other are absolutely forbidden them. And we read, that in Florida and Virginia there is a Nation that have the Generative Parts of both Sexes... The following History, says an Author, made a mighty Noise, both at Paris and Toulouse. A certain young Woman at Toulouse had a Relaxation of the Vagina, resembling a Man's Penis ...

It gradually increased from her Childhood: she was searched by Physicians there, who gave their Opinion, it was a real Penis; upon which the Magistrates of the Town ordered her to go in Man's Habit. In this Equipage she came to Paris, where she got Money by showing herself, till, upon other Assurances that she was a Woman, and a Promise of being cured, she was brought into the Hotel de Dieu, where the Descent was soon reduced, and she [was] forced to resume her Female Dress, to her great Regret.[1]

To the author, all of those often termed the 'Third Sex' – anyone who was not a binary ideal of the male or female – was seen as a hermaphrodite. One important evolution out of this historical amalgamation has been the emergence of trans culture and identity. To be able to define oneself, and find others like you, as well as supporters and allies, has been of increasing importance for those who find they have been born biologically different to their identity. The twentieth century has given those facing this painful real-isation the chance to be able to live in the body they choose, rather than be held captive by its biology. The man responsible for pioneering the life-changing surgery chosen by some of those who identify as trans was Magnus

---

1 *ONANIA: OR THE HEINOUS SIN OF Self-Pollution AND ALL ITS Frightful Consequences (In Both Sexes) CONSIDERED:With Spiritual and Physical ADVICE to those who have already injured themselves by this abominable Practice. Eighteenth Edition, as also the Ninth Edition of the SUPPLEMENT to it, both of them Revised and Enlarged, and now Printed together in OneVolume.* London: Printed for H. Cooke, 1756, pp. 328–330.

Hirschfeld (1868–1935). He is one of the recognised founding fathers of the field of sexology, from which the study of sex in science, medicine, anthropology and history has come. Jewish and gay, Hirschfeld was born in Poland and earned his medical degree in 1892. He investigated gay cultures across the world, and was horrified to discover that many of his European patients were committing suicide – thanks to a widespread culture of homophobia and prosecution.[2] Hirschfeld's desire to stop this terrible consequence many felt, thanks to their society-inflicted feelings of shame and guilt, led him to open the Institut für Sexualwissenschaft, in Berlin, Germany in 1919. Here, he was determined to offer counselling, sex education, advice on birth control and to fight for the acceptance by society of all those whose sexuality was currently criminalised.

The Berlin of 1919, when the Institute first opened its doors, was one of liberation. In a backlash against the censorship that had dominated Germany during the First World War, movements arguing for a free and open German society, tolerant of all, and in the name of all, began to grow in popularity. Contraceptives were openly advertised in the newspapers, and films advocating for gay rights were screened in many of Germany's theatres.[3]

---

2 Heike Bauer, *The Hirschfeld Archives: Violence, Death, and Modern Queer Culture* (Temple University Press, 2017).

3 Laurie Marhoefer, *Sex and the Weimar Republic: German Homosexual Emancipation and the Rise of the Nazis* (University of Toronto Press), 2015, p. 33.

From here, Hirschfeld was able to advocate for those whose voices had not been heard before, and create an identity that – although it had long existed – had not been fully acknowledged before: what it meant to be trans.

The first person to receive surgery to reassign their gender was not a man, but a woman. Born Martha Baer in 1885, the German-Jewish author and suffragist Karl M. Baer was one of the first people to undergo gender reassignment surgery in 1906, as well as successfully having their birth certificate altered to correspond to their new identity.[4] A determined activist for women's rights, Baer had always carried a sense of being in the wrong body throughout their childhood. Although presenting as intersex, Baer had been forced into appearing as female for much of their early life. As they grew older, this identity, the restrictions and assumptions it placed on Baer, felt painfully alien. Seeking Hirschfeld's support to undergo surgery that would defeminise their body, Baer fought a legal case that resulted in an unequivocal and universal acceptance of their body and person as male. Hirschfeld provided medical documentation in support, which stated in no uncertain terms that Baer was '*in Wirklichkeit ein*

---

4 Standesamt Arolsen/N.O. Body: *Aus eines Mannes Mädchenjahren. Vorwort von Rudolf Presber. Nachwort von Dr. med. Magnus Hirschfeld. Reprint herausgegeben von Hermann Simon mit einer Vorbemerkung und einem abschließenden Beitrag: 'Wer war N.O. Body?'* Berlin 1993: Ed. Hentrich (Original Berlin 1907: Riecke), S. 178.
Geburt des Kindes Martha Baer am 20. Mai 1885, Geschlechts- und Namenskorrektur am 2. Feb. 1907.

Mann (in reality a man)'.[5] He also highlighted the deeply corrosive impact Baer's enforced femininity had on his mental state; Baer had procured cyanide and had twice intended to commit suicide as, inhabiting his female body, he was unable to marry the woman he loved.[6] After winning his legal case, with his new protected identity and birth certificate, Baer married that woman. In 1907, now 22 and a few months on from his surgery, Baer wrote the anonymously authored and semi-fictional *Aus eines Mannes Mädchenjahren* (Memoirs of a Man's Maiden Years), with a foreword by Hirschfeld, in the hope that others who were intersex would read it and learn that surgery was a possibility. The book was wildly successful, and went thought six editions in its first two years.[7] During the 1920s and 1930s, Hirschfeld performed a number of gender reassignment surgeries, not only on individuals who presented as intersex, but also on those born in the binary definition of biologically male or female. One of the earliest of these was Dora Richter (born Rudolph, 1891–*c*.1933). Believed to be the first person to undergo male-to-female surgery at Hirschfeld's Institute For Sexual Research in Berlin, Richter had come from rural poverty. She had found her way to Berlin, and to Hirschfeld, where she worked as a maid in the clinic. Prior to her surgery in 1931, she had been one of the many transsexuals

---

5 Magnus Hirschfeld, *Sexuelle Zwischenstufen*, p. 47.

6 John A. McCarthy, *The Early History of Embodied Cognition 1740–1920*, p. 237.

7 John A. McCarthy, p. 231.

Hirschfeld (and others) had argued to be allowed to wear women's clothes in public. In Berlin at this time, although cross-dressing was not illegal it often resulted in harassment in the street, either by the public or the police. Three years after Baer's surgery, in 1909, Hirschfeld successfully convinced the Berlin police to issue *Transvestitenschein* – passes for transvestites – which gave an individual permission to wear the clothing of the opposite sex in public.[8] Many of Hirschfeld's patients were registered as transvestites with the Berlin police, which, in a progressive and tolerant society, might seem understandable. Berlin, however, was heading for its darkest hour.

On 6 May 1933, the stomp of boots would have been heard through the windows of the Institute. Outside, young men in white shirts, rolled-up sleeves and open necks, with high-belted trousers, knickerbocker-style, tucked into the tops of socks like modern-day cargo pants and heavy boots, marched past. These were the members of *Deutsche Studentenschaft*, the German Student Union. A new youth wing of the Nazi movement, since 1931 the student union had aligned with the National Socialists. A few months earlier, at the beginning of 1933, Adolf Hitler, leader of the National Socialist German Workers' Party – the Nazis – had been appointed Chancellor of Germany, and quickly established the Third Reich, his totalitarian vision for state control of the German people. There was no place in the Nazi worldview for any form of sexuality or gender that

---

8 Robert Beachy, *Gay Berlin: Birthplace of a Modern Identity* (Alfred A. Knopf, 2015), pp. 191.

was not strictly binary and heterosexual. Although the
Nazi purge of non-heterosexuals had not yet fully begun,
the echo of the students' boots on the pavement outside
became a foreshadowing. Not long after their march ended,
these clean-cut young men returned to the Institute. They
smashed its doors and windows, destroyed its facilities
and raided its library and archives, seizing all the personal
records, documents and books, and setting fires in one of
the earliest of the Nazi public book burnings. Those delicate, meticulous records kept by Hirschfeld and his staff,
the private lives of those who had sought help and understanding for their sex and gender issues, were now in the
hands of the people most likely to do them harm. We do
not know what untold damage was inflicted at the hands
of those students during the raid, but at some point, Dora
disappeared. She was never heard from again and it is
believed that the bigots who destroyed the Institute also
took her life.

Berlin was not a lone refuge for those living trans lives.
On 30 April 1932 the *Airdrie & Coatbridge Advertiser*
reported the 'AMAZING STORY OF GLASGOW
WOMAN. LIVED AS MAN FOR MANY YEARS'.[9]

An amazing story of a Glasgow woman who has lived as
a man for many years and who went through a form of
marriage with another woman in 1917 has come to light.
The 'marriage' took place in Glasgow Sheriff Court, when
the 'husband' described herself as a widower. Since that

---

9 *Airdrie & Coatbridge Advertiser*, Saturday, 30 April 1932.

time the couple have lived together as man and wife, the 'husband' being employed in a city factory for several years as a man. Certain suspicions regarding the sex of the 'husband' were aroused recently, as a result of which she was examined by two doctors and certified to be a normal healthy woman. It is stated that since the 'marriage' the 'husband,' who is of a slim build, has gone about never attired in other than male clothing. She had many men friends, not one of whom suspected her real sex, and she was described by them as 'a fine little fellow'. One man who was acquainted with the couple has stated that he always regarded them as being very happily married. 'The "husband" was very fond of his "wife",' this man stated. '"He" was of the steady-going type, and kept "himself" to constant employment. His job was not one that demanded any great physical strength, otherwise I don't suppose "he" would have been able to keep it.'[10]

Although the paper's use of quotation marks makes the editor's attitudes clear, what articles like this show us is the undeniable existence of trans lives in our history. In the aftermath of the Second World War, the West had lost its understanding of trans rights, and it has only been in the last few decades that trans culture has become an acknowledged and accepted part of the human rights movement. We still have so far to go in protecting those in our society who are trans, and one way to combat the prejudice and bigotry that is often displayed against those

---

10 *Airdrie & Coatbridge Advertiser*, Saturday, 30 April 1932.

within that community is to understand that long before Hirschfeld and his Institute, trans bodies existed in our history. They may be harder to find, given the secrecy and erasure of previous known identity that many of those who changed their gender state went through, but they do exist, as long as you look for them. And what emerges out of our historical trans record is not a story of total degradation or horror, but society's awareness of the existence of trans people throughout time.

We find these records most often in our criminal and social archives. It would be easy to assume that this is due to a social disgust or rejection of those who are trans, but in actuality the laws used to attempt to prosecute trans individuals are never to do with immorality, but often much more simple matters, such as fraud or robbery. In other cases, they are simply recorded as matters of public interest.

'MAN-WOMAN' ran the *Nottingham Evening Post*'s headline, on 28 December 1910, 'Amazing Story of "Charley Wilson", a Workhouse Inmate'. Charley Wilson, it transpired, was well known to the papers of the Edwardian era. He had first appeared in 1897, in a story run by the *Chelmsford Chronicle*, of an elderly painter who had found himself desperately down on his luck in the West Ham Workhouse.[11] He had been a painter for forty-three years, a member of the Painters' Union, married twice, and now, after fracturing his leg in a fall, had been forced to seek help at the workhouse.[12] However, once

---

11 *Chelmsford Chronicle*, Friday, 22 October 1897.
12 *Lincolnshire Echo*, Tuesday, 5 October 1897.

there, admitted as a male ward and taken for the customary bath in order to remove any risk of lice and infection, there had been a surprising discovery. Charley Wilson was a woman. Giving the name of Catherine Coombes, Mr Wilson related his life story. He had been born at Axbridge in Somerset, in 1834, attending Cheltenham's Ladies' College until the age of 16, when he was married to his cousin, Percival Coombes, twenty-three years his senior. Wilson had always had the desire, or need, to dress in male clothing, and this led, he said, to grievous 'ill treatment' at the hands of his husband.[13] Trapped in a violent marriage with a man who cared little for him, Wilson had soon decided to run away and take refuge with his brother, who lived at Hill Top, West Bromwich. Here, he had met a man called Mr Tozer, a painter and decorator who agreed to teach him the trade. Wilson's new freedom was short-lived; discovered by his husband, he was forced to leave Hill Top and return to him. 'He said he would never leave me,' remembered Wilson. 'That decided the matter. I went to Birmingham again, took lodgings, [and] bought a suit of boy's clothes.'[14] Concealed here, Wilson changed into his new suit and then left for London, where he had lived ever since. Living as a man had never been hard, and he had worked for the Peninsular and Oriental Company for thirteen years, living at 7 Camden Terrace, Custom House.[15] He successfully married twice, the first time for

---

13 Ibid.
14 Ibid.
15 *Lincolnshire Echo*, Tuesday, 5 October 1897.

four years, the second for twenty-two, but was now a widower, and a Union man.[16] One might think that his outing in the national press in 1897 would have led to widespread rejection by his peers, but that was not the case at all. As the *Chelmsford Chronicle* reported:

> Those numerous kindly people who have manifested a personal and practical interest in Mrs Catherine Coombes who for 43 years passed in male attire as 'Charley Wilson', and worked as a painter, will hear with satisfaction that she was able to leave the West Ham Workhouse on Thursday night. Her working-men co-members of the Painter's Union have taken up her case with a vigour that does them great credit, and they hope, with the aid of their country branches, to raise enough in course of a few weeks to start her in some light business. Meantime, she has had an offer of employment, until Christmas at least, from a master house-painter and decorator.[17]

The *Daily Telegraph* reportedly received over £10 in anonymous and named donations for Wilson, while contributions also flooded into the workhouse itself; while the *Lincolnshire Echo* ran Wilson's story under the headline 'A Romantic Career: Woman's Life of Disguise'. You might be forgiven for assuming that the reading public, captivated by the fight for female emancipation, were responding to the idea of a victimised woman, rather

---

16 *Leamington Spa Courier*, Friday, 5 August 1904.
17 *Chelmsford Chronicle*, Friday, 22 October 1897.

than that of a trans man. But the problem is, Charley Wilson refused to go away. He didn't slink off, admonished or ashamed by his sudden appearance in the public world. He didn't assume women's dress and change back to Catherine Coombes. He went back to the life he had been leading for over forty years. In 1904, the papers were once again filled with stories about the life of Charley Wilson. He had been arrested and charged with drunkenness, appearing at the Westminster Police Court, once again dressed in male attire.[18] Interviewed by the *Express*, after escaping punishment thanks to the kindness of a gentleman who offered him employment, Wilson recounted even more of his life, only this time the journalists were concerned with one major aspect – Wilson's marital life:

'In my long life,' she said, 'I have met with a full share of love. I have loved much, and in return have been greatly loved. But because of the man's life I have led men have, of necessity, had no share in this, and also of necessity the love I had to give has been bestowed upon pure and true, good women. Of the love some other women, in their ignorance, would have given me I will say nothing. All through life in every place I have found someone who desired my love. Why, I have no idea. I have pondered over it often, but I cannot tell. One of them told me once it was because I was so kind, so gentle, so different from other men! My first 'wife', Annie Ridgway, was of the sweetest type of womanhood and she loved me so devotedly, purely,

---

18 *Leamington Spa Courier*, Friday, 5 August 1904.

and unselfishly that even had she discovered my secret, which she never did, I think she would have forgiven me. My second wife was as true to me as the first had been. She was so utterly devoted to me that I believe she would have laid down her life to do me a service.'[19]

Wilson's final appearance in the national press came in 1910. By this point he had been an inmate of the Chelsea Workhouse for over a year, and, now in his seventies, had been moved to a permanent bed in the infirmary. He was clearly a much-loved character among the workhouse staff, who told journalists that after every stay they had dressed Wilson in women's clothes, and every time he returned to them he was dressed as a man. This is a telling insight into how the moral guardians of London's poor attempted to force gender roles on Wilson, and yet also accepted that they were not going to be successful. In these final interviews, more of Wilson's adventurous life was uncovered, adding even more information to the earlier accounts of 1904 and 1897. He claimed his husband had cut his hair and sold it, and that was why he had kept it short all these years; that instead of coming straight to London to find work, he had first gone to Gloucester as a boy, and for three and a half years he had sailed the Mediterranean and Adriatic as a captain's clerk, without anyone guessing his secret.[20] It was after leaving the ship that he then apprenticed himself to a

---

19 *Gloucester Citizen*, Thursday, 4 August 1904.
20 *Nottingham Evening Post*, Wednesday, 28 December 1910.

painter, and worked as an ordinary house decorator at a shop on Kensington High Street. Here, he had fallen in love and courted a girl (Annie Ridgway) for four years, before eventually marrying her in St Margaret's, Westminster. For four years they had lived as man and wife, and then she had died. After that, while working in Huddersfield, he met and married his second wife, living together for twenty-two years; and after this, while working for the Peninsular and Oriental company on board their ships, he had made several journeys to Australia. Here ended the life of Charley Wilson.

Not all the trans stories that we can uncover in the archives are as clear-cut or kind as Wilson's. Some of them are simply tantalising, a brief mention, a line recording the existence of life and nothing more, such as with the 1850 prosecution of 20-year-old servant, Elijah Scott, 'a man known as Eliza', for assault with sodomitic intent. Although tried for an attack on a man named Bennett James Martin, Scott was eventually prosecuted and found guilty of common assault, but, as with so many cases surrounding men and sexuality in this period, his judgement was respited. We have no more information on him than those few lines. Perhaps more detailed is the case of James Tibenham, a 28-year-old groom prosecuted for stealing from his master, Francis Bailey, in October 1840. On the face of it, the case seems very clear-cut. Tibenham was discovered to have a bottle of ale and six yards of decorative fringe in his rooms, which the master believed he had stolen. Prosecutions between masters and servants were commonplace, but the trial text itself reveals a very different layer to this story, and we are left wondering if Francis Bailey attempted to bring a prosecution against his servant for a very different reason:

FRANCIS BAILEY: I live in Tavistock-place. The prisoner was my footman for about ten weeks. On the night of the 15th of September, at half-past eleven o'clock, after all the family had gone to bed, as I conceived, I looked out of the window, and observed the door which leads into the street, to be ajar—(my house stands back, and there is a covered way leading to the street)—I went down to fasten it, and saw a person in female attire, with a hand on the bell—I asked what she wanted, and was answered, 'I was ringing for one of the servants'—I turned round and saw that it was the prisoner, who is my footman, dressed as a woman—I called the police, and gave him in charge—the police-sergeant suggested the property of his boxes being searched, which they were—this fringe was found in his box, and the bottle of ale in a cupboard, locked up.

Cross-examined by MR. BALLANTINE: Q. I believe you had the prisoner with a three years' character? A. We had a character from a lady who knew him—not from the person he lived with—I am not able to identify this fringe—I am not quite certain that the ale is mine.

SARAH DAVIES: I am cook to the prosecutor, I saw this ale found in a cupboard in the footman's bedroom—the prisoner was the footman—he had got my bonnet, shawl, and apron, in the kitchen—he took them without my knowledge.

JOHN SUTTON: I belong to the house of Shoolbred and Cook—they supplied Mr. Bailey with some fringe on the 1st of September—I have seen the fringe found in the prisoner's box, and compared it with what was supplied to Mr. Bailey—it corresponds in pattern, weight, and colour.

Cross-examined: Q. I suppose you have a great variety of fringe? A. Yes, and a great deal of this sort—this might have been purchased in our shop without my knowledge.

MARY ANN RUSSELL: I am the prosecutor's house-maid—the prisoner had my gown-skirt on.

Although found on his master's doorstep, late at night, dressed in the maid's gown-skirt, the cook's bonnet, shawl and apron, and then discovered to have bought himself a large quantity of decorative fringe, Tibenham was declared 'Not Guilty'. We have no way of knowing the circumstances that led to his doorstep discovery – perhaps he had been returning from a visit to the Molly houses – and here is where the lines between modern definitions and historic lived experience begin to blur. Without a declaration by Tibenham that he felt he was born into the wrong body, we have no right to decide who he was. He could very easily be trans, or just as easily a gay or bisexual man inhabiting the Molly house culture that still existed in London at this time. But what his record, fleeting though it is, does tell us, is that diverse sexual and gender identities have always existed. Without question, trans identities and bodies emerge out of our archives the moment you acknowledge their existence. Our archives are full of trans bodies. Just as they are full of gay bodies, queer bodies, intersex and asexual bodies. Every sexuality identity and the body it inhabits has existed in our society since the dawn of time.[21] Take Eleanor (born John) Rykener, the fourteenth-century embroideress and sex worker. Arrested for prostitution in December 1394, Eleanor Rykener found herself brought to London's Guildhall to confess before the mayor and aldermen. It was quickly discovered that, although she dressed in women's clothing and lived as a woman, Eleanor's body was male. Her confession, first translated in 1995, makes clear she lived her life as a trans woman and shows us that to be trans is not a modern invention.[22] One of the biggest myths we need to expunge when we look at the history of sexuality is that human sexual expression has only ever found itself to be in one single box – heterosexuality – and that all other sexual identities were carried out in secret, by a tiny minority of people. That is not true. Any form of gender or sexual identity that exists today has existed throughout history. Our sexual landscape has always been a wild and untamed thing.

---

21 Barring, perhaps, those attractions that are based on specifically modern desires: cars, technology, AI and virtual worlds, although I am certain their historical equivalent could be found.

22 Kadin Henningsen, "'Calling [herself] Eleanor": Gender Labor and Becoming a Woman in the Rykener Case.' *Medieval Feminist Forum*, vol. 55 no. 1, 2019: 249–266

5
The Body

'The odour of her sex – pungent shell and sea odours,
as if woman came out of the sea as Venus did'
—Anaïs Nin, *Delta of Venus*, 1977

When you take a closer look at history, our genitals are everywhere. From the ninety-three penises littered throughout the Bayeux Tapestry, to Courbet's *The Origin of The World* in 1866, our genitals have always been an important part of cultural display. We've either idolised and revered them, or demonised and sanitised them. Our genitals have consumed us, just as we in turn consume them. Today, who has what genitals, and what this means to us, has become a global debate. Our cultural focus on identity and sexual obsession with the visual nature of pornography, bodily perfection and the rise of social media platforms like Instagram and Snapchat have given us a fixation with flesh in two dimensions. From body positivity to the gym obsessive, how we look, and how our genitals look, seems to be a modern obsession. But is that true?

Would Anne Lister have cared about vajazzling in the eighteenth century? Looking back over our history it is difficult to find a time when we were not, in some way, obsessed by our genitals. Their wetness, their softness, their changeability, their strength and their power. Their earliest depictions can be found in some of the world's oldest cave art, from Chalfant in California to the Vezere Valley in France. Iconography of vulva and phallus litters cave walls, while figurines and singular representations of the genitals themselves are continually altering our understanding of our prehistoric past. Here, devoid of the social rhetoric of diet and 'wellness' that so often disguises a culturally-shared and universal body dysmorphia, the human body was celebrated and eroticised, not sanitised. The Lion Man of the Hohlenstein-Stadel, found in Germany in 1939, is the oldest statue of a zoomorphic figure, depicting a man with the head of a lion. It is nearly 40,000 years old, and one of the few pieces of prehistoric carved art that depicts a male figure. Just like today, the visual culture we have so far uncovered from our primeval past is obsessed by the female figure.

The undeniable sensuality of the palaeolithic 'Venus' figures idolises the flesh of femininity: thighs, stomach and breasts that spread and roll across one another; a vulva, slit to make her sexuality clear, and a small head, hands and feet. The emphasis is placed on the largeness of her hips, buttocks and torso – areas of sex and reproduction, the creation of life and feeling. These figures represent women supreme, to our modern eyes they personify consumption and indulgence; a fertile carnality, happily unashamed in its excesses. This joyous ancient celebration of the female figure was first discovered in 1864, dug out of the palaeolithic rock shelters of Laugerie-Basse in south-west France. The 8th Marquis de Vibraye, Paul Hurault, christened them 'La Vénus impudique' – the Immodest Venus – and since his discovery, 144 figurines have been found across Europe and even as far as Siberia. Their popularity lasted for nearly 30,000 years. The oldest Venus figures date back to 40,000 years ago, while the youngest, the Venus of Monruz, is a sprightly 11,000 years young. The Venus of Hohle Fels, six centimetres tall and carved from a mammoth tooth, is the most ancient of these figures, and her design clearly influenced that of the most famous, the Venus of Willendorf. Discovered by a workman in 1908, the Willendorf Venus is carved from limestone and tinted with red ochre to accentuate her full, soft body. Since their discovery, the purpose of the Venus figures has created intense debate. Scholars have argued they represent a fetish for fertility, an idolisation of the mother and celebration of the power of reproduction. Others have described them as obese, with features that are exaggerated or grotesque. Neither of these attitudes allow for the simple fact that these ancient Venuses, are, without a doubt, sexy. They show a female body that, to our modern eyes, portrays a shameless lack of culturally imbibed self-hatred. They may be figurines of pregnant women, or they may be figurines of what we call fat women, but they are undoubtedly *women*.

By the time of the ancient world, the Romans and the Greeks, this celebration of women had begun to fall as empires grew. In the Roman town of Pompeii, destroyed by the eruption of Mount Vesuvius in AD 79, phalluses were everywhere. They were given wings, depicted on doorways, walls, as wind chimes and statues, a cornucopia of male virility. 'I am all in favour of encountering divinity in the genitals, male and female,' wrote Jane Caputi, in her excellent work *Goddesses and Monsters*, 'but the phallus is another matter'.[1] The rise of the phallus, given the form of a god in the Roman Priapus, has dictated Western culture for thousands of years. Priapus is cursed with impotency, and yet continually depicted as a man plagued by a gigantic, swollen erection from which he can never find release. He represents lust, carnality and primal urges, and his image held a long life in our historic sexual culture – appearing in Chaucer's 'The Merchant's Tale' as a linguistic trick to show the audience that January's motivations are not driven by the noble objection of love, but simply to sate her sexual desires. As 'the Phallus is deified, its female symbolic equivalent...which we might think of as "the cunt" – is everywhere stigmatised,' continued Caputi, and in the culture of the West this would certainly seem to be true. The vulva has only been depicted in rare moments of iconography since the rise of Christianity.

The Sheela-na-gigs of the eleventh and twelfth century – wild-eyed, howling women holding apart the

---

1 Jane Caputi, *Goddesses and Monsters: Women, Myth, Power, and Popular Culture* (University of Wisconsin Press, 2004), p. 373.

mouths of their vulvas as a gaping void – can be found squatting, defiantly, on the doors and windows of many of England and Ireland's old churches. Their presence, found also in Spain and France, perhaps represents an old belief that the sight of a woman's vulva would scare aware the Devil. This idea was famously represented in a beautiful engraving by the French painter, Charles Eisen (1720–1778), in his illustration for 'The Devil of Pope-Island', a tale originally published in a collection of folk stories compiled by Jean de La Fontaine (1621–1695). Eisen illustrated a publication of La Fontaine's poetical stories in 1762; in 'The Devil', a young woman named Perretta defeats the Devil by tricking him into looking at her vulva, the sight of which so terrifies him, he runs away.

PERRETTA at the house remained to greet
The lordly devil whom she hoped to cheat.
He soon appeared; when with dishevelled hair,
And flowing tears, as if o'erwhelmed with care,
She sallied forth, and bitterly complained,
How oft by Phil she had been scratched and caned;
Said she, the wretch has used me very ill;
Of cruelty he has obtained his fill;
For God's sake try, my lord, to get away:
Just now I heard the savage fellow say,
He'd with his claws your lordship tear and slash:
See, only see, my lord, he made this gash;
On which she showed:—what you will guess, no doubt,
And put the demon presently to rout,

Who crossed himself and trembled with affright:
He'd never seen nor heard of such a sight,
Where scratch from claws or nails had so appeared;
His fears prevailed, and off he quickly steered.

Eisen's illustration makes clear what it is that has frightened the Devil so much; Perretta stands with her back to the viewer, lifting up her skirts to her waist, as the Devil stares on in horror, both fascinated and recoiling at the same time. In a later illustration, c.1800, by Thomas Rowlandson (1756–1827), Perretta stands facing her audience, her 'hairy prospect', as he titled it, on display to the public as the Devil runs out of the door. This is how the vulva has come to be viewed by our sexual culture: it is a dirty, confusing, scary thing. Reality stars make money advocating vaginal douching – something that is absolutely unnecessary as the vagina is self-cleaning – and the earthy sensuality that is an entirely natural state for the human body is being culturally sanitised. But for a brief moment, in one part of late-medieval Europe, there was a time when all our genitals were celebrated, even venerated, by those in the Christian faith.

First discovered in 1848, hidden in the riverbed of the River Seine in France, a medieval badge, today often referred to as a 'pilgrim badge', changes our understanding of the place of genitals in religious and sexual culture at this time. Pilgrim badges were a popular amulet collected by those who visited holy Christian shrines and it is estimated that 'many millions' of badges, unique in design and identifying particular saints and shrines, were distributed across Western Europe. From the mid-fourteenth to early sixteenth century many of these symbolic and simple designs are astoundingly erotic. They included images of, among others, 'ambulant vulvas on stilts, winged and crowned pudenda pilgrims complete with pilgrims' staffs and rosaries, couples having sex, and ambulant winged phalli'.[2] Found most often in the Netherlands, these small metal tokens included images of phalluses with bells hanging from their testicles, vulvas with wings, and the fondly modern-day named 'Pussy Goes A Hunting' – a badge that depicts a vulva on horseback, firing an arrow from a bow. Little is known of the origin or meaning of these badges besides their bawdy nature, but it does tell us that the joy of genitals is something that humans have always attempted to express. In 1559, inside the pages of his *De re anatomica*, Matteo Realdo Colombo (*c.*1515–1559) became the first man to identify the clitoris as the 'seat of woman's delight'.[3] Although women, of course, had had them all along. The power of the clitoris, being one way to elicit the female orgasm, was central to the doctrines of sexual fulfilment that govern sexual culture up until the twentieth century. As the subject of ejaculation and the orgasm, both male and female, rightly deserves its own chapter, these can be found later on.

---

2 Lena Mackenzie Gimbel, 'Bawdy Badges and The Black Death: Late Medieval Apotropaic Devices Against the Spread of the Plague', thesis, p. v.

3 Victoria Pitts-Taylor, *Cultural Encyclopedia of the Body* (Greenwood Press, 2008), p. 80.

In the nineteenth century, the vulva became a thing to be coveted, although no longer as publicly as it had been in the past. It was not the property of the eroticists and pornographers, whose boundaries often overlapped in the worlds of art and literature. One of the most arresting images that portrays the old divinity of the prehistoric worship of the vulva is Gustave Courbet's *The Origin of The World*, painted in 1866. *L'Origine du monde*, to give it its original title, is a deeply sensual portrayal of a woman's sexuality. Up close between the spread legs of an uniden-tifiable woman, the viewer is given access to a picture that only a lover would normally see: the intimate intri-cacies of the tops of her thighs, meeting the soft curves of her vagina and abdomen, one breast displayed, with a nipple, hard, pink and erect, just visible under the folds of her shirt. The painting was commissioned by Halil Serif Pasha (1831–1879), an ambassador and diplomat of the Ottoman Empire, who settled in Paris and became an art collector in the 1860s. He compiled a wonderful collec-tion of erotic paintings from leading artists of the period, and for over a century the mystery of who posed as his 'Origin' has been left unsolved. In 2018, historian Claude Schopp uncovered what he believes is the solution: the Origin was Constance Quèniaux (1832–1908), a ballet dancer at the Paris Opera.[4] She had joined the ballet in 1847, at the age of 15; fourteen years later she had retired and was now the mistress of Serif Pasha. The revelation

---

4 Claude Schopp, *L'Origine du Monde: Vie du Modèle* (Editions Phébus, 2018).

of her identity as Courbet's model came from an angry letter about Courbet, sent to George Sand from the son of Alexandre Dumas in 1871, 'How dare he paint the most delicate and the most sonorous interior of Miss Queniault of the Opera,' wailed Dumas Jnr.[5] Courbet's staging of the Origin was not unique; a similar pose had been photographed by the erotic artist Auguste Belloc in 1860.[6] The faceless image, hairy, thin-thighed, and lacking the eroticism of Courbet's paintings feels familiar in its empty sex. Today we can consume pornography on any device we own, and the ability to create gifs – a short video clip on an ever-repeating loop – has allowed us to solidify sex into its most basic images, making them in ways simply sex-*less*. Why is it that Courbet's *Origin* maintains its connection to the erotic titillation of sexual desire, and yet Belloc's photographs feel flat and empty? Is this the moment in history where our sexual culture takes its first steps towards self-annihilation?

Our early disconnection with our genitals began in the nineteenth century, as the medical and scientific community – populated by quacks and a growing need for regulation – saw widespread self-publishing by anyone who claimed to have a medical degree. At the same time, theories and ideas swirled around in the universities and medical practices dominated by men, to create a new language and understanding of sex. By the end of the

---

5 'I thought I was in a strange dream' says author behind *The Origin of the World* discovery, euronews.com 3/10/2018
6 Claude Schopp, *L'Origine du Monde: Vie du Modèle*, 2018.

century, a primitive field of sexology would be born, focused on classifying and understanding what it defined as sexually deviant behaviour – where masturbation and homosexuality found themselves classed alongside rape and paeodophilia. Describing the role of a woman's sexual organs during sex, the 1860 *Medical Adviser and Marriage Guide, representing all the diseases of the genital organs of the male and female,* had this to say:

> In both sexes the act of coition is attended with pleasurable sensations, but their respective share in the act itself is very different. In the female there is but a partial expend-iture of the nervous power, when she fully participates in the sexual act, and none scarily when her feelings do not prompt her to return the ardor of the male; neither does she expend any nervous power in the production of erec-tion; no energetic rhythmic muscular contractions when the general excitement has reached its height, and no emission of semen; but merely an increased secretion from the vagina, excited by the impressions on the sensitive nerves of the female sexual organ, and serving to lubricate the passage to facilitate sexual commerce.[7]
>
> The man feels exhausted after the act; the woman simply yields herself up to the pleasurable excitement. The clitoris, which is known to be the part most susceptible of the pleasurable sensations in females, is not like the penis of the male, rendered by friction the seat of intense sensation

---

7 *Medical Adviser and Marriage Guide, representing all the diseases of the genital organs of the male and female,* pp. 73–4.

and nervous excitement during coition, and hence its excitability is found not to be wholly exhausted after the act is completed.

It is clear that the author had never satisfied, or understood how to satisfy, any woman in his life. One of the frustrations of understanding the role of sex in our historical past is that texts such as this have been taken as the dominant understanding of attitudes towards sexual interaction, when they are in fact outliers. Comments like this do not represent the cultural understanding of sex that existed in the Victorian era, or any era. To correct this, we turn to one of the most joyful expressions of interest in and love of our sexual organs – the slang we have used to describe them. Vulvas have been called 'Cupid's cloister' (1896), the 'altar' (1680) and 'nature's tufted treasure' (1827), while the clitoris is the 'cocktrap' (1888) or the 'purr-tounge' (1910), and the labia are the 'cunt-lips' (1888) or 'cockles' (1890). For men, the penis represents some of the most inventive word choices in the English language: if it's large, you were a 'lob-cock', a word that first appeared in 1682 and was still in use in 1896; if it was hard it was your 'spike' (1842) or your 'stiff-stander' (1650); while the testicles were 'oysters' (1762), plums (1618) and whirligigs (1698); and to be impotent was to be an 'apple-john' (1599) or a 'stuffed eel-skin' (1841). Our historic sexual past was also acutely aware that we didn't only have penetrative sex with our genitals, we had oral and anal sex too. 'Bum-fucking' first appeared in print in 1879, when the erotic magazine the *Pearl* published in its 'Nursery

Rhymes' section: 'His chere amie, who prefers bum-fucking to the old orthodox plan of coition'.[8] To 'suck' was applied to both fellatio and cunnilingus in the 1870s; 'gamahuche' appeared in 1788, to describe a man going down on a woman, and was still in use 100 years later, most memorably described by 'Walter' in *My Secret Life*: 'I gamahuched her ... She had never been cunt-licked before'.[9] And finally, 'cock-sucker' is now 130 years old, first appearing in 1890 to describe someone performing fellatio.

Today, our genitals, how they look, smell, taste and feel, seem to be becoming a universal obsession – not to protect and venerate their natural state, but to sanitise, manipulate and alter everything that makes them what they are, and what they have previously been celebrated for. In the 1890s, some women used Lysol – a household cleaning product – to douche their vaginal cavities, and its use became so widespread and popular in America that the company itself ran ad campaigns suggesting this practice to women throughout much of the twentieth century. Although often thought to be a coded way of marketing birth control, the language of the mid-century adverts played on female insecurity over the appearance of their genitals:

A man marries a woman because he loves her. So instead of blaming him if married love begins to cool, she should question herself. Is she truly trying to keep her husband

---

8 *Pearl*, 4 October 1879.
9 Walter, *My Secret Life*, IV 820 1888, 1966.

and herself eager, happy married lovers? One most effective way to safeguard her dainty feminine allure is by
practicing complete feminine hygiene as provided by
vaginal douches with a scientifically correct preparation
like 'Lysol'. So easy a way to banish the misgivings that
often keep married lovers apart. 'Lysol' has an amazing,
proved power to kill germ life on contact ... truly cleanses
the vaginal canal ... daintiness is assured, because the very
source of objectionable odour is eliminated.[10]

The reality, of course, was that dousing your intimate area
with what was akin to household bleach often resulted in
extreme pain, scarring and, in some instances, death.
Today, women are bombarded by images and news stories
of vaginal steaming, internal exfoliation, labiaplasty, and
operations to tighten, or even recreate, the hymen; while
pornography and the culture of women's magazines have
encouraged the removal of the entirety of a woman's pubic
hair – now so common that men expect this pubescent
performance as standard sexual practice. This begs the
question: if our genitals are on constant display, is their
power to consume and overwhelm us being lost? Not
content with obsessing about our own genitals, we now
obsess about the genitals of others – do they have the
'right' genitals to be able to be in our space, to share our
narratives, to sit at our table? When will this negative
fixation on our genitalia ever end? Perhaps this is an indicator of how unhappy our sex and gender culture is, and

10 https://timeline.com/sexist-history-douching-bcc39f3d216c

how far we have fallen from the unbridled, bawdy celebrations of the past. Because, as long as we are obsessing
over our genitals as abstract, modified things, we will never
be able to connect to that freedom and joy for them that
so clearly resonated in the past.

6

Masturbation

'As a sin against nature, it has no parallel except in
sodomy. It is the most dangerous of all sexual abuses
because the most extensively practiced.'
—John Harvey Kellogg, 1877

'While you never indulge in a woman's embrace,' wrote
the Roman poet, Martial (c.AD 40–101), 'but rely on your
whoreish left hand, And call yourself chaste, yourself you
debase, For a crime men can scarce understand.'[1] This,
in a nutshell, is the almost universal view of masturbation
in our history. From the ancient world to today, masturbation is the one sexual act that almost everybody does,
and yet somehow always gets us into trouble. For most
of us, our earliest personal experience of sexual pleasure
come from masturbation. It is how we teach ourselves
what feels good *to us*. It is also, historically, one of the
most well-documented sexual acts. Often seen as

---

1 Martial, *Epigram IX*, 41.

dangerous to your health by religious or medical authorities, the sheer proliferation of texts and source material
on this solo sex act goes back thousands of years. To
Victorian doctors, it was something that polluted and
damaged the human body, leading one eminent authority
to declare that it left a woman's vulva looking like 'the
ears of a spaniel'.[2] And yet, the multitude of sexual aids
and solo sexual acts recorded by medieval monks from
among their congregations proves that, for centuries, no
matter how dangerous self-pleasure may have been
portrayed, it did not stop us from doing it. From fears
that wet dreams were an indication of demonic posses-
sion, to how they became the first indication that someone
might be gay, masturbation allows us the freedom to
fantasise about sex, to transgress without actually trans-
gressing. Trying to understand his own body and also to
demonstrate a common ground with his patients who
came to him suffering from 'nocturnal emissions' – as
wet dreams were often called by the Victorians –
Dr Charles Knowlton remembered his earliest experience
of waking up to discover his body had responded to an
erotic dream: '[It] alarmed me exceedingly... I do not
think I ever met with one so mentally wretched as I was.
I think that onanism has much to do in causing this
disease...'[3] Knowlton blamed masturbation, or 'onanism'

---

2 Joseph W. Howe, *Excessive Venery, Masturbation and Continence*, 1888,
p. 72.

3 *The Boston Medical and Surgical Journal*, 10 September, vol. XLV,
no. 6 (1851), p. 112. Taken from 'The Late Charles Knowlton, M.D',

as it has been historically known, for his body's sexual responses. Writing in the 1840s, Knowlton's attitudes were shaped by a sexual culture that had been obsessed with the dangers of masturbation for just over 100 years. Prior to the eighteenth century, it simply wasn't that big of a deal – unless, of course, you were female. Between the sixth and twelfth centuries, wanking was simply not a grievous sin in the eyes of the early Church fathers, who rarely defined exactly what masturbation might mean. 'Masturbation,' writes Thomas W. Laqueur, 'was not, it seems, a category of sexual sin worth sustained precision of language'.[4] It did, of course, elicit some form of censure. In the tenth century, Buchard of Worms decreed that if a boy confessed to masturbating alone, he was required to do ten days of penance. If he masturbated with others, it was thirty days.[5] In the Penitential of Theodore, however, female masturbation was dealt with harshly; if a woman 'has coition alone with herself – *sola cum se ipsa coitum habet*' either with an object or her own hand, she was required to do penance for three whole years.[6] The fear of a woman deriving pleasure from a form of penetrative sex without a man was clearly far too dangerous.

To 'masturbate' first appeared in English in 1621, created

---

an obituary written by Stephen J.W. Tabor after Knowlton's sudden death at the age of 50. Tabor included the preface of Knowlton's unpublished Preface to his Case Book from 26 November 1840.

4 Thomas W. Laqueur, *Solitary Sex*, p. 141.

5 Ibid., p. 145.

6 Ibid., p. 141.

by Robert Burton in his *Anatomy of Melancholy*. Discussing the diseases caused by celibacy, 'mastupration' – most likely created from the Latin *mansus* for hand, and *stupro* for defile – featured high on his list of dangerous conditions.[7] Forty years later, the great seventeenth-century diarist, Samuel Pepys, was no stranger to wanking, preferring to do it in public. Sitting in his church congregation, Pepys took full advantage of the service to bring himself to orgasm on a number of different occasions in the late 1660s; most famously on Christmas Eve 1667, thanks to the sight of Catherine of Braganza, Charles II's Portuguese wife, and all her ladies of the court. 'God forgive me for it,' wrote Pepys, 'it being in chapel'.[8] Masturbation often allows us to act out our interior sexual fantasies, and to this Pepys was no stranger. A few years before his chapel salutation of the Queen, he recorded dreaming of Barbara Villiers, the Countess of Castlemaine. Villiers was the most powerful of Charles's mistresses, having become his lover in 1660, while he was in exile. Five years later, and after Charles had been restored to the throne, her presence at court was a source of intense gossip and daily observation, due in no small part to her incredible beauty. On 15 August 1665, Pepys spent a glorious daydream imagining himself as her lover:

Something put my last night's dream into my head, which I think is the best that ever was dreamt, which was that I

---

7 Ibid., pp. 160–61.
8 Samuel Pepys, 24 December 1667.

had my Lady Castlemayne in my armes and was admitted
to use all the dalliance I desired with her, and then dreamt
that this could not be awake, but that it was only a dream;
but that since it was a dream, and that I took so much
real pleasure in it, what a happy thing it would be if when
we are in our graves (as Shakespeere resembles it) we
could dream, and dream but such dreams as this, that
then we should not need to be so fearful of death, as we
are this plague time.[9]

Pepys using his masturbatory fantasies to stave off fear of
the plague is not necessarily a surprising aspect of a
person's sexual life. We all escape into our sexual fantasies,
some for pleasure, others to allow ourselves that which
we are denied in reality. But while masturbation was not
seen as a hugely difficult sin, there was a sudden and
unexpected shift in our sexual culture at the beginning of
the eighteenth century. The publication of *ONANIA: OR
THE HEINOUS SIN OF Self-Pollution AND ALL ITS
Frightful Consequences (In Both Sexes) CONSIDERED:
With Spiritual and Physical ADVICE to those who have
already injured themselves by this abominable Practice* in
1712 quickly caused what we could describe as the first
official sex panic of the mass culture/mass media world
in which we live today. *Onania* took its name from the
biblical story of Onan, whose tale has often been used to
justify fears of masturbation as the unwanted 'spilling' of
a man's semen in any act other than reproduction. For

---

9 Samuel Pepys: Tuesday, 15 August 1665.

the writer of *Onanism*, masturbation was a sin worse than sodomy, and those who indulged in it were betraying not only their bodies, but also their souls: 'Whilst yielding to filthy imagination, they endeavour to imitate and procure for themselves that Sensation which God has ordered to attend the Carnal Commerce of the two sexes for the Continuance of our Species.' That 'sensation' was an orgasm, and the reason the author was so worried about this specific sex act occurring outside of penetrative sex was that its sole purpose was to aid conception. Orgasms, you see, belonged to God.

The author of *Onanism* remained anonymous until 2003, when Thomas W. Laqueur published his magnus opus *Solitary Sex: A Cultural History of Masturbation*, arguing John Marten (1670–1737), a pharmacist's assistant and self-taught surgeon known for his creative 'cures' for venereal disease, was behind the text. Laqueur's claim is disputed by other historians, who believe that while passages of *Onanism* are lifted almost directly from editions of Marten's acknowledged *Treatise on Venereal Disease*, this is not conclusive evidence of his authorship.[10] But whoever the author, *Onanism* was written as a great piece of trash medicine. Circulating among the coffee houses of London, its reputation saw it published in over twenty-eight editions and translated into multiple languages across the eighteenth century. One of the text's biggest attractions was the inclusion of case studies and personal histories, added

---

10 Michael Stolberg, *Experiencing Illness and the Sick Body in Early Modern Europe* (Palgrave, 2011), p. 200.

to and increased with each subsequent edition. While it's important to question the authenticity of these case studies, they do offer us a unique window into the masturbatory life of men and women in the eighteenth century.

The following Letter, which came from a young married Lady, for its Remarkableness, and that it might be a Caution to others of the same Sex, I could not omit inserting.

To the AUTHOR of the Book called ONANIA. December, 18, 1731,

Sir,
SINCE it will be impossible for you ever to know from whom this comes, I can with Freedom relate my Case to you, which other ways I could not have Confidence enough so much as to mention one Tittle of it to any Physician living. My sad Case is, that when I was a young Girl of between fifteen and sixteen Years of Age, at the Boarding-School, being enticed and shewed the Way by three of my School-fellows, older than myself, which lay in my Chamber with me, two Beds being in the Room, I did as they did, which you can guess at, and your Book tell, and I thought it was pleasing enough: I followed it after-wards upon all Opportunities by myself; and so that by that Practice, and the lascivious Talk we had amongst us, and Play Books, and other Books, we used to read to another, I was to that Degree prompted thereby,

that I was resolved to marry the first Man that asked me the Question, and the more, because my Parents used to say it was Time enough for a Husband at four or Five-and-Twenty: In short, Sir, at Seventeen, I got me a Husband, unknown to my Parents; and though he was no unequal Match, for I had a considerable Fortune left me by a Relation, they turned me out of Doors, but soon after they were reconciled with us: I had three Children by my Husband in less than two years, for I had two at a Birth, but they all died, and also my Husband soon after. I remained a Widow two Years, and then I married with my Friend's Consent. But, alas! such was my Baseness during my Widowhood, I living in all Affluence and Plenty, meeting with nothing either to sour or ruffle my Temper, and having no suitable Offers of marrying, and being more inclined to the Delights of the Marriage-Bed than ever, with such vehement Desires, more especially just before and after the Course of Nature, I could not forbear returning to my former wicked Practice, and that so often, and with so much Excess, that I could hardly sometimes walk or sit with Ease, I was so sore: I indeed feared the ill Consequence, and now find it, but the Pleasure then would not let me hearken to that, for I had, and have now, a sad Bearing, and Forcing of the Womb, that I cannot stand long, and have another great Weakness follows me, so that I have not been so much as once with Child since I have been married, which is now about three Years, and is a great Trouble to myself, but

more does it discontent my Husband to have no heir
to leave what we have to: He would have me to take
Advice, but as I could not tell my Case to any Man
living, I spoke to my Midwife, and told her how I was;
she asked me some Questions, which I could not
answer, and she gave me something to take, but it did
me no Good, so that by my Husband's Order she went
to Sir David Hamilton for his advice, and he ordered
me several Things to take, and the Bath Waters, and
Injections, but nothing would do me any Good; and
she going to him from Time to Time and telling him I
was no better, she said he could do no more unless he
searched me, but I absolutely resolved against that; but
my Spouse said I should, and very angrily insisted on
it, so that to oblige him I said I would undergo it; and
he brought Dr. Hamilton to a Relation's House, where
he appointed, because he should not know us, and
there I let him search me, my Mask being on, and my
Midwife present; he told us that my Womb was very
weak and slippery, and that he was afraid I should
never have any Children, and wanted to ask me some
questions about the Cause by myself, but I told him I
could say nothing to the Cause, he knew that best as
he was a Physician; so that I believe he guessed at the
Cause ... I have now no Manner of Inclination to the
Act of Procreation, and very little Pleasure in the Act,
which I am thinking may be as much as any Thing the
Reason I can have no Children; but I have a good
Stomach, and sleep well; but it is strange that I that
used to be so amorous, and indeed so excessively

desirous of conversing with my first Husband, should
have no Inclination that Way at all to this Husband,
whom I love as my Life... Mrs E.O.[11]

Some might say it is difficult to know how true the letters
printed in *Onanism* were, but what they do tell us is that
masturbation was not seen as a male-only issue. Women
masturbated too, and their sexual self-knowledge was
something physicians were to become increasingly scared
of.

We know female masturbation was not simply a male
fantasy, to be feared and to be enjoyed, thanks in part to
the diaries of Anne Lister. Her graphic descriptions of her
sex life with her female lovers and their mutual masturbation and oral sex make clear the experiences and
knowledge late eighteenth- and early nineteenth-century
women had of their bodies. Writing in 1818, the same year
that Mary Shelley published *Frankenstein: or, The Modern
Prometheus* and *Northanger Abbey* and *Persuasion* both
appeared in print after the death of Jane Austen, Anne
Lister was attempting to elicit an orgasm from one of her
lovers: 'Tried for a kiss a considerable time last night but
Isabella was as dry as a stick & I could not succeed. At

---

11 *ONANIA: OR THE HEINOUS SIN OF Self-Pollution AND ALL ITS
Frightful Consequences (In Both Sexes) CONSIDERED: With Spiritual and
Physical ADVICE to those who have already injured themselves by this
abominable Practice. The Eighteenth Edition, as also the Ninth Edition of the
SUPPLEMENT to it, both of them Revised and Enlarged, and now Printed
together in One Volume.* London: printed for H. Cooke, 1756, https://
archive.org/details/b20442348/page/n5, pp. 152–4.

least she had not one & I felt very little indeed.'[12] Anne's experience of Isabella's 'dryness' was not metaphorical, but a clear indication of Isabella's lack of arousal. Two years and numerous lovers later, Anne's descriptions of her sexual methods leave little to the imagination and are a small indication as to why she may have occasionally found it difficult to make her lover come: 'I soon found out what was the matter, kissed and put my tongue in while I had three fingers of my right hand pushed as far as they would go up there ... she was ready and wide as if there was not virginity to struggle with.'[13] A delicate touch, clearly, was not Anne's preferred modus operandi.

Masturbation was also clearly present in the erotica of the nineteenth century, as much as in its early diarists' love lives. Created in 1825, *Les Charmes de la Masturbation* is a beautiful engraving depicting a nude heterosexual couple glorying in mutual masturbation. In *Phoebe Kissagen*, an 1866 novel by the eroticist Edward Sellon (1818–1866), his characters wonder, 'What shall we do?' said Chloe, 'shall we frig, or shall we gamahuche?' 'To 'frig', as Sellon's readers were well aware, was slang for masturbate. Writer, illustrator and translator, and son of a publican, Sellon had joined the army at the age of 16. After serving in India, he returned to England at the start of the 1840s, and, after a disastrous marriage, began to write faux-historical erotica for the well-known publisher of pornography, William Dugdale. He was a prolific author, but in the same year

---

12 *Gentleman Jack*, 18–19 September 1818, p. 61.
13 Ibid., p. 79, 11 October 1820.

as the publication of *Phoebe Kissagen*, and at the height of his creativity, Sellon took a room in Webb's Hotel (now the Criterion Theatre) and shot himself.[14] He was just 48 years old.

Throughout the nineteenth century, the hysteria over masturbation begun by *Onanism* added to the medical-isation of sex. It became the indication of a weak mind, body and spirit, and as the theories of Freud and Krafft-Ebing began to dominate our sexual culture's view of sexuality, our connection with our own sexual needs, our private fantasies and our own self-knowledge became shameful. Desire was not allowed to be self-evident, it had to be lured, coaxed and discovered between a loving couple. Innocence, or, more correctly ignorance, was what the medical community advocated, rather than a personal understanding of your own sexual self. To Freud, mastur-bation was the infancy of sex, an experience that was not required in adulthood but merely a developmental stage along each individual's sexual journey. His view of accept-ance, and then dismissal, was vastly different to that of the majority of the medical community, which still oper-ated on a lucrative fear of the act. Published in 1877, *Plain Facts for Old and Young: Embracing the Natural History and Hygiene of Organic Life* by John Harvey Kellogg made the near universal obsession with fears of masturbation clear: 'It is the most dangerous of all sexual abuses because [it is] the most extensively practiced. It is known by the terms,

---

14 Don Herron (ed.), *The Dark Barbarian: The Writings of Robert E. Howard, A Critical Anthology* (Wildside Press, 1984), p. 20.

self-pollution, self-abuse, masturbation, onanism, mastupration, voluntary pollution, and solitary secret vice. The vice is the more extensive because there are almost no bounds to its indulgence.'[15] Among his cures for men, Kellogg listed circumcision, electrocution, and a bag tied to the testicles 'as the continued pressure of the distended veins upon the testes, if unsupported, will ultimately cause degenerative changes and atrophy'.[16] For women, he recommended douching the vagina with 'three to five gallons' of astringent warm water, daily, and to combat the known side effects of masturbation – such as sexual apathy towards a partner – he suggested 'the application of faradic electricity to the vagina by means of a proper electrode is of great advantage. One electrode should be placed in the vagina, while the other, connected with the sponge, is passed over the lower portion of the spine, across the lower part of the abdomen, and along the inside of the thighs.'[17] Science and medicine, it seems, were terrified of self-enjoyment. By the nineteenth century, church orders were being replaced by the power of the state, and the state relied on those in medical authority to provide it with clear-cut doctrines for the sex lives of its citizens. Advice to state legislators in 1870s America outlined that the act of mutual masturbation between heterosexual couples should be seen as 'provoking

---

15 John Harvey Kellogg, *Plain Facts for Old and Young: Embracing the Natural History and Hygiene of Organic Life,* 1877, p. 231.

16 Ibid., p. 319.

17 Ibid., p. 321.

unsatisfied desires and incomplete sensations' that would only lead to 'profound perturbation in the genital apparatus'.[18] Replacing church with state now meant that sex no longer damned your immortal soul, now it just risked your health. Fear lay at the heart of both church and state decrees on the sex lives of their citizens. Because if you can create a climate of fear, then you have something to control. The influence of the qualified and certificated medical boards, which emerged in the nineteenth century across the Western world, and their influence on the state, dramatically altered our relationship with sex. Rather than being built from those who embraced sexual culture, education, birth control and pleasure, our governments have been advised by those who depicted sex as a moral danger. In 1848 a doctor's report on idiocy, requested by the state of Massachusetts, announced,

> There is another vice, a monster so hideous in mien, so disgusting in feature, altogether so beastly and loathsome, that in very shame and cowardice, it hides its head by day, and vampyre-like, sucks the very life-blood from its victims by night; and it may perhaps, commit more direct ravages upon the strength and reason of those victims than even intemperance; and that is, SELF-ABUSE.[19]

---

18 C. Bigelow, *Sexual Pathology: A Practical and Popular Review of the Principal Diseases of the Reproductive Organs* (Forgotten Books, 2018), p. 78.
19 Ibid., p. 50.

The scope of the report had been to judge mental insufficiency, but according to the will and beliefs of one doctor, state legislation was guided to recognise that masturbation was an indication of an unbalanced mind. This report was so influential that it was regurgitated and repurposed in books about sex and the sex organs by medical writers throughout the nineteenth century and across the English-speaking world. Bad sex advice always seems to spread like wildfire.

In our modern sexual culture, as fixated as it is on self-pleasure and individual gratification, it's surprising that masturbation doesn't have more of a central and acknowledged place. In 2018, the BBC created a new guide for women on their BBC Three website 'How to Masturbate: A guide to dating your Down Under', calling it a 'taboo subject', yet, in comparison, only three years earlier Sweden had created an entirely new word, *Kilttra*, specifically for women who wanted to wank.[20] Masturbation may have been demonised in the eighteenth century, but as the lives of ordinary people show – the Samuel Pepys and the Anne Listers – it was also a normal part of their sexual lives. Pleasure, and especially sexual pleasure, was about discovering what sex was, and, more importantly, what it could do for you. The next stop was discovering someone else to have it with.

---

20 https://www.bbc.co.uk/bbcthree/article/ef932792-17b5-4274-bba3-3452070c3e10

7

Flirtation

'Licence my roving hands, and let them go
Before, behind, between, above, below.'
—John Donne, 'To His Mistress Going to Bed', 1654

If masturbation is a solo pleasure, then flirtation is the first shared experience. Flirtation gives us the potential of sex, it arouses us, allowing our primal urges and instincts to rise from behind their intellectual restraints. To stay in a permanent stage of arousal would be an impossibility for most of us, but without it, sex lacks what we are all in pursuit of – pleasure. And while solo sex may have a chequered history, foreplay is something our ancestors have always been in favour of. From your very first kiss, to how to be a good lover, and, of course, how to have the best sex has always mattered. Tucked inside the pages of the *Bicester Advertiser* on 29 August 1863, an advert for the *HAND-BOOK OF COURTSHIP; OR, THE ART OF LOVE-MAKING FULLY EXPLAINED.*

A new work adapted for both Sexes offered to resolve the many mysteries around the art of flirtation for its apprehensive readers. Advising them to send thirteen stamps to 'Mr B.W. Edwards, Pontefract', the book's contents were outlined in detail:

CONTENTS :—How to choose a wife. Position and Qualities. Love at first sight. How to commence a courtship. Courtship of a lady with whom you are personally not acquainted. Courtship where the parties are acquainted. Courtship of a wayward young lady—of a domestic young lady—of a prude—of a proud young lady—of a bashful young lady—with an heiress—of a literary lady—of an actress—of a widow—an old maid—a shrew, &c., How to make a man propose. How to win a rich bachelor. How to make a declaration or 'Pop the Question.' Specimen Love Letters, written in a natural style, to meet the requirements of every supposable case. Twenty-one general rules for conducting a courtship, &c., &c. The work is indispensable to all engaged in, or contemplating commencing a courtship. No young man or woman should be without it.[1]

For the Victorians, flirtation was an artform, and what the *Art of Love-Making* shows us is that it was, undoubtedly, a shared pursuit. The book was marketed to both men and women, and understood that we all often lack confidence in our romantic endeavours, whether we are the

---

1 *Bicester Advertiser*, Saturday, 29 August 1863.

pursued or the pursuer. And flirtation guides were hardly a Victorian phenomenon. The twelfth-century *De Amore*, or 'The Art of Courtly Love', written by an unknown author under the pseudonym of 'André le Chapelain', set out a guide to the art of aristocratic flirtation. It advocated love, and the pursuit of flirtation – that may not always lead to physical consummation – as one of the most noble artforms. It also gave rules for how a love affair could be conducted, and with whom:

1. *Marriage is no real excuse for not loving.*
2. *No-one can be bound by a double love.*
3. *Boys do not love until they arrive at the age of maturity.*
4. *When one lover dies, a widowhood of two years is required of the survivor.*
5. *Love is always a stranger in the home of avarice.*
6. *It is not proper to love any woman whom one should be ashamed to marry.*
7. *A true lover does not desire to embrace in love anyone except his beloved.*
8. *A new love puts to flight an old one.*
9. *A man in love is always apprehensive.*
10. *Nothing forbids one woman being loved by two men, or one man by two women.*

Not only did it include these rules, and also a guide for speaking to women of a different class – both higher and lower – but it also defined love, how to deal with rejection, and believed all men were worthy and in need of instruction in the art of seduction. Even if that man happened to be a priest:

> a clerk cannot look for love, for on the strength of it he ought not devote himself to the works of love but is bound to renounce absolutely all the delights of the flesh, unspotted for the Lord whose service, according to our belief, he has taken upon him. But since hardly anyone ever lives without carnal sin, and since the life of the clergy is, because of the continual idleness and the great abundance of food, naturally more liable to temptations of the body than that of any other men, if any clerk should wish to enter into the lists of Love let him speak and apply himself to Love's service.[2]

One of the most famous love affairs of the twelfth century was that of the abbess Heloise and the monk, Peter Abelard. Heloise was a celebrity of her age. By her early twenties, her breadth of knowledge and learning was renowned across France and especially in Paris, where she lived as a ward of her uncle, Fulbert. In 1115, Peter Abelard, the new master of the Cathedral School at Notre Dame, moved into Fulbert's residence and offered to tutor Heloise. Abelard was a well-known and controversial teacher on theology and philosophy, whose reputation and ideas had seen him in regular conflict with many of Paris's great teachers, and his presence in Heloise's household – France's most learned young

---

2 *Bicester Advertiser*, Saturday, 29 August 1863, p.23

woman, and Paris's most exciting academic – was a match made in philosophical heaven. This was an age of ideas, debates, theory and argument; and Abelard's lectures drew hordes of attendants to Notre Dame, where Fulbert kept his residence. Not long after his private tuition began, Abelard became Heloise's lover, in an affair that many still see as legendary today. Her seduction soon resulted in a pregnancy, and, after discovery by Fulbert, Heloise was sent away to Brittany to give birth to their son in secret. Not long after this, and most likely to appease Fulbert, Abelard offered to marry Heloise, but with one condition – their union must remain a secret, or Abelard would be forced to leave the Church. His career would have been ruined by the exposure of a secret love child. Yet Heloise refused. She was living, disguised as a nun, in the convent at Argenteuil. Her letters to Abelard, some of the most famous love letters of all time, made her objection to the idea of marriage clear: '...the extreme unwillingness I showed to marry you, though I knew that the name of wife was honourable in the world and holy in religion; yet the name of your mistress had greater charms because it was more free.' For Heloise, marriage meant submitting. She would rather be a mistress, a woman who gave herself freely and expected nothing in return, than a wife, chained and chattelled. She believed in the ideology of courtly love – that it was glorious, a noble and beautiful thing. But like all stories of courtly love, there must also be a moment of tragedy. Either believing Abelard had forced Heloise to become a nun, or as revenge for his seduction of her, Fulbert had Abelard attacked and castrated. The scandal led to Abelard's public ridicule, and not long after he decided to take holy orders and become a monk, and also insisted that Heloise should become a nun. His defence against his shaming in society was to attempt to erase his sin of lust with celibacy. By 1129, nearly fifteen years after they had first become lovers, Heloise was now Abbess of a nunnery in Champagne. The community had been founded in 1122 by Abelard, himself now Abbot of Saint-Gildas-de-Rhuys, nearly 200 miles away. After years of silence, the lovers began a correspondence that created the myth of their legendary affair. Seven letters remain, published since the seventeenth century, that showcase Heloise's uncompromising sexuality, and the power of her own desires. She often addressed Abelard as 'Husband', as, before his castration, she had finally agreed to marry him in secret. But 'secret' was not how it remained, and their love affair became common knowledge. Nearly 300 years later, Chaucer referred to it in his 'book of wikked wyves', in 'The Wife of Bath's Tale':

676   *In which book eek ther was Tertulan,*
[In which book also there was Tertullian,]

677   *Crisippus, Trotula, and Helowys,*
[Crisippus, Trotula, and Heloise,]

678   *That was abbesse nat fer fro Parys,*
[Who was abbess not far from Paris,]

Throughout their correspondence, it is Heloise who is the most sexually charged; Abelard sounds only pompous and regretful. In one of her last letters, her passionate rejection of his indifference is powerful to read:

> You have not answered my last letter, and thanks to Heaven, in the condition I am now in it is a relief to me that you show so much insensibility for the passion which I betrayed. At last, Abelard, you have lost Heloise for ever. Notwithstanding the oaths I made to think of nothing but you, and to be entertained by nothing but you, I have banished you from my thoughts. I have forgot you. Thou charming idea of a lover I once adored, thou wilt be no more my happiness!

These love letters would be erotic enough without the added dimension of their existence winging its way back and forth over hundreds of miles of French country-side and from a beloved and respected Abbess to a powerful and well-known Abbot. These are two people who, supposedly, should never have considered sex – if our belief in historic sexual culture is one of prudish restraint and celibate indifference. But, throughout history, many sexual lives have been lived that contradict the supposed idea that sex has only ever been about repro-duction. For those living in the twelfth century, sex was about a deep, erotically noble love. A love that required the idea of flirtation to keep it alive. *De Amore* made clear that sex without love was not acceptable:

he who is so tormented by carnal passions that he cannot embrace anyone in heartfelt love, but basely lusts after every woman that he sees, is not called a lover but a counterfeiter of love and a pretender, and he is lower than a shameless dog. Indeed a man who is so wanton that he cannot confine himself to the love of one woman deserves to be considered an impetuous ass.[3]

This is a concept that was at the heart of courtship and sex guides for centuries. Flirtation was foreplay, it was the way of building a sexual attraction to someone who may become your partner, rather than a platonic attachment of friendship. But how do you flirt without the entire world seeing you? How do you form those attachments that are secret, and allow love to develop privately? Surprisingly, from the sixteenth century to the Victorian period, there was one common form of flirtation that appears to have been in use across Europe, and especially popular in England – the fan. Beginning in Spain in the sixteenth century, the use of the fan developed as a secret language, so that young courting couples would have a way to discuss, distract and deceive those around them – especially the supposed guardians of their virtue. This secretive Spanish code was 'set fourth in fifty different directions in a little booklet published in German by Frau Bartholomäus, from the original Spanish of Fenella', and in shortened, less complicated text in English by

M.J. Duvelleroy.[4] The code set out many of the problems young lovers face:

> *You have won my love (place shut fan near heart)*
> *When may I be allowed to see you? (the shut fan resting*
>   *upon the right eye)*
> *At what hour? (the number of the sticks of the fan indicate*
>   *the hour)*
> *Why do you misunderstand me? (gaze pensively at the*
>   *unfolded fan)*
> *Do not betray our secret (cover the left ear with the open*
>   *fan)*

By the eighteenth century, British fans had become a form of ingenious invention. Not trusting their owners (or the owners' paramours) to hold all of the different messages and codes of the fan in their heads, 'Conversation' or 'Speaking Fans' were invented. First advertised in the *Gentleman's Magazine* in 1740, these printed fans contained a handy guide not only to the code, but also how to use it. This dictionary of 'fanology' allowed lovers to communicate across the ballrooms and dance halls of all England's towns and counties.

> *A speaking fan! a very pretty thought;*
> *The toy is sure to full perfection bought:*
> *It is a noble, useful, great design,*
> *May the projector's genius ever shine!*

---

4 *History of the Fan*, 1910, pp. 137–8.

The fair one now need never be alone!
A hardship sometimes on the sex is thrown;
For female notions are of that extent,
Impossible, one I thought should give 'em
    vent.
New schemes of dress, intrigue and play,
Want new expressions every day.[5]

— *Gentleman's Magazine*, 1740

Although the *Gentleman's Magazine* marketed the conversation fans as a toy, their use required a great deal of commitment and patience. Exploring their history in 1910, this attempt to explain their use – and its supposed ease – from *History of The Fan* does little to decode their secretive messages:

Conversation- or speaking-fans are devices by which the different motions of the fan are made to correspond with the letters of the alphabet, a code being established by means of which a silent and secret conversation is carried on. Five signals are given, corresponding to the five divisions of the alphabet, the different letters, omitting the J, being capable of division into five, the movements 12345 corresponding to each letter in each division. 1. by moving the fan with left hand to right arm, 2. the same movement, but with right hand to left, 3. placing against bosom, 4. raising it to the mouth, 5. to the forehead. Example: - Suppose Dear [is] to be the word to be expressed. D

---

5 George Woolliscroft Rhead, *History of the Fan*, 1910, pp. 253–4.

belonging to the first division, the fan must be moved to the right; then, as the number underwritten is 4, the fan is raised to the mouth. E, belonging to the same division, the fan is likewise moved to the right, and, as the number underwritten is 5, the fan is lifted to the head and so forth. The termination of each word is distinguished by a full display of the fan, and as the whole directions with illustrations are displayed on the fan, this language is more simple than at first sight might appear.[6]

Nearly sixty years after the *Gentleman's Magazine* first marketed its 'toy for Ladies', the 'The Original Fanology, or Ladies' Conversation Fan' was created by Charles Francis Badini. Published 'as the Act directs by Wm. Cock, 42 Pall Mall, Aug 7, 1797', the Ladies' Conversation Fan was Badini's second attempt to create, publish and own the secret codes of Fanology. 'The telegraph of Cupid in this fan/ Though you should find, suspect no wrong/ 'Tis but a simple and diverting plan/ For Ladies to chit-chat and hold the tongue', read his fans, portraying them not as flirtation devices between lovers, but as a way for women to communicate in private. His earlier design had been published on 18 March, by Robert Clarke, Fanmaker, of No. 26 Strand, London. Both fans included motifs of Cupid, and a set of 'Answer and Question of that Lady to the Gentleman', to enable their owner to carry out her secret correspondences.[7] The Fine

---

6 George Woolliscroft Rhead, *History of the Fan*, 1910, pp. 253–4.
7 Ibid.

Arts Museum in Boston makes clear Badini printed his fans with two secret methods. Both involved a complex set of numbers, letters and movements to convey their holder's message, turning most 1790s dances or drawing rooms into arenas of semaphoric confusion.[8] They also place the agency of flirtation heavily in the hands of the women of the eighteenth century. Their communications were celebrated as secrets, and it was up to the men to decode and understand their messages without owning the fans themselves. Badini clearly created a craze, as in December 2001, Christie's 'Fine Fan' auction included Lot 90, a fan entitled 'The Ladies Telegraph, for Corresponding at a Distance.' Designed by Robert Rowe and published by M. Stunt, 191 Strand, opposite St Clement's churchyard, 20 April 1798, The Ladies Telegraph was a printed fan with twenty-six flaps, each corresponding to the letters of the alphabet, with one extra, the signal, to indicate the end of a sentence. By simply flashing each flap with its clearly printed letter, the owner could simply spell out words, or an instruction, with little confusion to its receiver. Ten inches long, and built of bone sticks with decorated handles, The Ladies Telegraph sold for £2,350.[9]

Eighty years later, and over 100 years since the *Gentleman's Magazine* printed its first advertisement,

---

8 https://collections.mfa.org/objects/123930/fanology-or-the-ladies-conversation-fan?ctx=36b31fbc-2a82-4286-b15c-ebad6bb12483&idx=0

9 https://www.christies.com/lotfinder/Lot/the-ladies-telegraph-for-corresponding-at-a-3829288-details.aspx

flirtation via fanology was still holding strong among the young – and old – courting couples of England. In 1869 the *Globe* declared,

> The fan, in the hand of a lady of fashion, has more to do with airs than air. It is the wand with which she weaves the magic spell around her victims; the sceptre with which she sways her subjects; the magnet, with the poles of which she attracts or repels the men who respond to her influence... The language of the fan is infinitely more comprehensive and full of expression than that of flowers... A girl who is especially gifted by Nature with the faculty of using a fan may be independent of training. With the same genius which guides a pencil of the heaven-born artist she will use her fan artistically. But for one girl so circumstanced there must be a score who stand greatly in need of instruction. To attract attention by adroit spreadings and closings of the instrument, to draw the gaze of a particular gentleman at a distance of, say, thirty or forty feet without appearing to notice him; to cover the one defective feature in a pretty face, and enhance the beauty of all the rest... to shut out the view, and shut up the stare of a too profound observer... to waft love in a particular direction...the girls of the period, so properly called [the nineteenth century], are wonderfully clever and successful in the use of their fans.[10]

Disappointingly, for those on the receiving end of such

---

10 the *Globe*, Wednesday, 21 July 1869.

magic, Rowe's clear designs of 1798 seem to have fallen out of fashion, and the complex hand movements of the 1740s had returned. These codes were now so accepted that the newspapers began to print guides to them, and courting manuals devoted pages to decoding, and instructing, young couples in the language of the fan.

Fan Flirtation: –

Carrying right hand in front of face – *Follow me.*

Carrying in the left hand – *Desirous of an acquaintance.*

Placing it on the right ear – *You have changed.*

Twirling it in the left hand – *I wish to get rid of you.*

Drawing across the forehead – *We are watched.*

Carrying in the right hand – *You are too willing.*

Drawing through the hand – *I hate you.*

Twirling in the right hand – *I love another.*

Drawing across the right cheek – *I love you.*

Closing it – *I wish to speak to you.*

Drawing across the eye – *I am sorry.*

Letting it rest on the right cheek – *Yes.*

Letting it rest on the left cheek – *No.*

Open and shut – *You are cruel.*

Dropping – *We will be friends.*

Fanning slow – *I am married.*

Fanning fast – *I am engaged.*

With handle to lips – *Kiss me.*

Shut – *You have changed.*
Open wide – *Wait for me.*

By 1886, a year after the age of consent was raised to 16, the *Manchester Courier and Lancashire General Advertiser* advised its readers that, '*it is much easier to flirt than to define flirtation…the use of fan flirtation has advanced from being an art to becoming a science.*'[11] This science took many forms. No longer were fans enough; flirtation could occur through movement of the eye, hand, or even the hat. From the coded conspiracies of the fan, flirtation was now becoming a science, a programmed form of behaviour that was supposed to secure you a mate through subtle linguistics and formatted responses. 'Vinegar Valentines' were the Victorian antithesis to the sentimentality of Fanology. Popular in the 1870s, these little Valentine's Day postcards – mass marketed and cheap – expressed in no uncertain terms the failures of flirtation. A fabulous collection now held in Brighton Museum illustrates their vicious and bitter nature. '*Why do they call you a nasty old cat*', reads one, depicting an unattractive woman holding a Valentine's Day card, '*And say many things a deal ruder than that, 'Tis from envy perhaps of your manifold graces / How would it not please you to claw in their faces*'. Men did not escape the ire of the Vinegar Valentines either; emblazoned on the front of a card showcasing a braying, overdressed young man, the message read: '*You're as vulgar*

11 *Manchester Courier* and *Lancashire General Advertiser*, Saturday, 8 May 1886.

a cad as I'd wish to meet | And yet you're devoured by pride and conceit | But I fancy before very long you'll find out | That everyone thinks you an ignorant lout.' How many of these were sent as jokes, rebuffs, or attacks is unknown, but the historian Annabelle Pollen believes the trade in Vinegar Valentines reached over 750,000 a year during the nineteenth century.[12]

Fanology made flirtation into an artform. It formed an intellectual connection to the object of your affection, to create a bond that would lead to true love, and, more importantly, great sex. Although we may no longer use fans, the coded flirtations of emojis at our fingertips show us that even though our society has little fixation on sex before marriage, we still like the subtle intricacies of sexual communication. The heritage of our sexual culture, from the bawdy song culture, to the slang of 'bull-dyking' and lives of those who defied gender and sexuality binaries, has always revelled in sexual self-expression, but also, more importantly, in connection. We flirt to make a unique language with the person we are attracted to, something that belongs to us and us alone. Even before we have taken someone to bed, we've often talked ourselves in and out of it many times over.

---

12 https://brightonmuseums.org.uk/discover/2014/09/08/love-letters-and-hate-mail-victorian-vinegar-valentines

8
Sex

'If our sex life were determined by our first youthful
experiments, most of the world would be doomed to
celibacy. In no area of human experience are human
beings more convinced that something better can
be had only if they persevere.'
—P.D. James *The Children of Men, 1992*

According to the thirteenth-century Bishop of Regensburg,
Albertus Magnus, there were five different types of sexual
positions. Ranked from those that were 'natural', to those
that were unnatural, immoral and certain to destroy your
soul, Magnus listed missionary, side-by-side, seated,
standing and *a tergo*, or, from behind. (This is unlikely to
mean anal sex, but instead what we colloquially refer to
as 'doggy style'.) You might be surprised to discover a
Bishop writing graphic descriptions of sexual positions at
the same time that spectacles were making their European
debut but the fascination and fixation on our intimate life
has been a preoccupation of both church and state since

their invention. From the act of sex itself, to the education of its existence and desire to treat any maladies it may inflict on you, sex has always been part of our historic sexual culture.

A century after Albertus Magnus, more medieval sexual positions can be found in the comic text of social morals known as *The Decameron*, written by the Italian Giovanni Boccaccio (1313–1375). Here, Boccaccio presents two sexual myths: firstly, that if a woman was on top it reversed the natural order of sexuality, and could result in the man becoming pregnant in her place; and secondly, that if a man had sex with a woman from behind, as the beasts do, he would succeed in transforming her into an animal. Boccaccio chose to depict a mare, showing us that the metaphor of riding during sex has little changed in over 600 years. These positions were not just dramatic invention; the Church was so worried about the idea of a woman being on top of a man during sex that the penitentials decreed a penance of three years for those who confessed to it. But just because the Church sought to tell people what to do with their sex lives, this didn't stop people from wanting and seeking pleasure. Sex feels good, and for those who embrace that connection little can be done to convince them otherwise. For many people, no matter what century you are in, how to have sex and what pleasure means has been a subject of great interest – no matter what a Bishop might have to say on the matter.

The aptly named *The School of Venus* or *The Ladies Delight* from 1680, is a well-thumbed seventeenth-century pamphlet depicting a discussion between two young women of practical, realistic and educational sex advice. First published in French as *L'escholle des filles*, the text had found a rapt audience among the English, including in our greatest diarist, the scandalised Samuel Pepys. Happening upon a copy of *L'escholle des filles* at his bookseller, Martin's on the Strand, on 13 January 1668, Pepys' horrified account recorded:

> ... I saw the French book which I did think to have had for my wife to translate, called 'L'escholle des filles,' but when I come to look in it, it is the most bawdy, lewd book that ever I saw, rather worse than 'Putana errante,' so that I was ashamed of reading in it.

Suitably shocked, it took Pepys nearly a month to pluck up the courage to buy a copy of this 'idle, rogueish book', which, after an hour of standing in the bookseller, he did on 8 February 1668.

> ... I have bought in plain binding, avoiding the buying of it better bound, because I resolve, as soon as I have read it, to burn it, that it may not stand in the list of books, nor among them, to disgrace them if it should be found.

A day later, settled in his bed on Sunday morning, Pepys found the time for 'reading a little of "L'escholle des filles," which is a mighty lewd book, but yet not amiss for a sober man once to read over to inform himself in the villainy of the world'. The delight Pepys seems to take in his own scandalisation at *The School of Venus* is no different to the playground squealing and dramatic cringing we do today when confronted by graphic, unashamed sexual discussions. Although it clearly set out to comically titillate its readers, *The School of Venus* also made the transmission and discussion of sex possible. Equally, it didn't portray sexual knowledge as the responsibility of men, or as something they alone owned. Presented as a dialogue between Katherine, 'A Virgin of Admirable Beauty', and her decidedly unvirginal cousin Frances, the text ranges from practical depictions of male and female genitals and their colloquial names, to how to experience the most pleasure during the sex act itself.

'The thing with which a man pisseth, is sometimes called a Prick,' opens Frances (now referred to by the diminutive 'Frank'), in the early pages, to the shock of her younger cousin. 'I must use the very words without mincing, Cunt, Arse, Prick, Bollocks etc,' she then insists, which gives us a unique example of the power words have always had in our sexual culture. These weren't secret or forbidden words; instead, they appear in the Old Bailey Proceedings and are printed in everyday literature.

Frank: Then let me tell you, the thing with which a man pisseth, is sometimes called a Prick, sometimes called a Tarse, sometimes a Man's Yard and other innumerable names, it hangs down from the bottom of their bellys like a cows teat, but much longer, and is about the place where the slit of our cunt is through which we piss.

Katy: Oh strange!

Frank: Besides they have two little balls made up in a skin something like a purse, these we call bollocks, they are not much unlike our Spanish Olives, and above them, which adds a Great Grace to this Noble Member, grows a sort of downey hair, as doth above our Cunts.[1]

Frances isn't shy of the language used for female genitalia either: 'In plain English it is called a Cunt,' she lists, 'though they out of an affected modesty mince the word, call it a Twot, and Twenty such kind of Names.' For those who got their hands on a copy of *The School of Venus*, it must have felt like discovering your first porn magazine or sex advice column. Here, in no uncertain terms, was a clear, helpful and encouraging guide to sex – and something that jumps off every one of its pages is an unbridled joy for sexual discovery.

Katy: So when the Man's Prick stands he thrusts it into the Wenches Hole.

Frank: I marry he does, but it costs him some pains to thrust it in, if the Wench be straight, but that is nothing if he be a true mettled Blade; by little and little he wilt get it in though he sweat soundly for it, by doing of this the Wench feels her Cunt stretch soundly, which must of necessity please her, seeing he rubs and tickles the edges of it in that manner.

---

1 *The School of Venus: or, The Ladies Delight*, 1680, pp. 13–14.

Katy: For my part I should think it would hurt.

Frank: You are mistaken, indeed at first it makes ones
Cunt a little sore, but after one is a little used to it, it
Tickleth and Rubbith in such a manner, as it yieldth the
greatest content and pleasure in the World.[2]

Texts like these are markedly different from the culture
of a century earlier. In 1581, a woman who shared sexual
knowledge publicly risked far more than being chided
for her use of language – she could be accused of witchcraft. At the Rochester Assizes, Reginald Scott, soon-to-be
author of *The Discoverie of Witchcraft* (1584), interviewed
Margaret Simmons, a married woman from the village
of Brenchley in Kent. She had been accused of witchcraft
by her parish vicar, the Reverend John Ferrall, who
claimed 'that always in his parish Church, when he
desired to read most plainly, his voice so failed him as
he could scant be heard at all.' Ferrall had accused
Simmons of enchanting him to cause this humiliation,
and now she was on trial for her life. From her cell,
Simmons told a very different story to Ferrall's grand-
standing complaint. One of male rage and impotence.
'You shall understand,' she told Scott, 'that this our vicar
is diseased with such a kind of hoarseness, as diverse of
our neighbours in this parish, not long since, doubted
that he had the French Pox and in that respect utterly
refused to communicate with him until such time as

---

2 *The School of Venus: or, The Ladies Delight*, 1680, pp. 15–16.

(being thereunto enjoined by M.D. Lewen the Ordinary) he had brought from London a certificate, under the hands of two physicians, that his hoarseness proceeded from a disease in the lungs. Which certificate he published in the Church in the presence of the whole congregation. And by this means he was cured, or rather excused of the shame of his disease.' We know little of Margaret's role in her community, but she was obviously a woman who understood what the term 'French Pox' – syphilis – meant, and that it was a sexually transmitted disease, a form of uncleanliness. Perhaps she had medical knowledge or had led the shunning of their vicar, but for some reason it was at her that Ferrall had levied his embarrassment at having to publicly declare to his congregation that he was not suffering from a disease linked to immoral sexuality.

Fear of bad sex, or sex that might damage your health, is as universal as the delight in sex itself. At the end of the seventeenth century, in 1690, Dr Thomas Kirleus, the 'Unborn Doctor', began to advertise his services in the printed proceedings of the Old Bailey. He chose his title due to his own birth having been by Caesarean section, making him an unnatural, or unborn thing.[3] Kirleus had been physician to the court of Charles II, as loudly and clearly stated on his advertisement, and practised out of rooms in Plow Yard, on Gray's Inn Lane. His speciality was the curing of venereal diseases, and any problems that might arise in a person's sex life. His unique remedy,

---

3 *The Tatler, vol 1,* 1822, p. 360.

available as either a pill or an elixir – with which he claimed to have cured over 500 people in London – was available at three shillings a quart, or one shilling per pill box. Kirleus also claimed that his remedy did not risk any danger to the lives of those who took it – a rarity in treatments at this time, which often killed the patient faster than any disease they had sought relief for. 'In all Diseases he gives his Opinion for nothing,' finished the advertisement, advising any reader to seek out the good doctor at his rooms.[4] Kirleus and his treatments had become a household name long before his advertisements began appearing in the Old Bailey Proceedings, and his death at the end of the seventeenth century was treated as a loss for London's sexually active community. Writing in his collection of erotic poems in 1700, the satirist, Thomas Brown, recorded:

> *On the Death of Dr. Kirleus:*
> *Ye Ghosts of Trigg, old Saffold, and Ponteus,*
> *Arise! arise! to meet the Great KIRLEUS:*
> *And ye kind Damsels of this sinful Town,*
> *Us'd to dispense Love's Joys for Half a Crown,*
> *Lament, for now your trusty Friend is gone.*[5]

What happened next was a little unexpected. The lucrative market for venereal disease that Kirleus had cornered needed to be continued by his family. His son John soon

---

4 Old Bailey Proceedings, 15 October 1690, a16901015-1.
5 Thomas Brown, *A Collection of Miscellany Poems, Letters, &c. 1700*, p. 9.

followed in his father's footsteps, advertising his family connections and the practice – still at Plow Yard in Gray's Inn Lane – in the *Flying Post* in 1702:

THE CRAFT OF MEDICINE
KIRLEUS CURES ALL

These are to give Notice,

That John Kirleus, Son of Dr. Tho. Kirleus, who was a sworn Physician in Ordinary to K. Charles II. many Years since, until his Death, but first a Collegiate Physician of London, with the same Drink and Pill (hindering no Business) cures all Ulcers, Sores, Scabs, Itch, Scurfs, Scurvies, Leprosies and Venereal or French Disease, and all such like Malignities, be the same never so great, at all times of the Year, in all Bodies (as his Father did) without Sweating, Smoaking, Fluxing, or any Mercurial Medicines, which are known to be dangerous, and often deadly: Of the two he hath cured many hundreds in this City, many of them after Fluxing with Mercury, which raiseth the Malignity, and all other Evils from the lower Parts, and fixeth it in the Head, which is not easily carried off, and so destroys many. Therefore take heed when you trust in these Cures, for there are but few that can cure any of these Distempers without the use of Mercury. He deals with all Persons according to their Abilities. The Drink at 3s. the Quart, the Pill 1s. a Box, with Directions. He gives his Opinion for nothing, to all that write or come to him, and as well to those afar off, as if they were present. He lives at the Glass-Lanthorn, in Plough-Yard, in Grays-Inn Lane.[6]

Two years later, John died, and here is where the story of venereal disease, women and female medical practitioners becomes interesting. *'KIRLEUS'S WIDOW CARRIES ON'* read the *Flying Post* in June 1705:

These are to give Notice, That Mary Kirleus, Widow of John Kirleus, Son of Dr. Tho. Kirleus, a Collegiate Physician of London, and sworn Physician in Ordinary to K. Charles II is the only Person that sells (exactly prepared) his famous Drink and Pill, which is eminently experienced to cure all Ulcers, Sores, Scabs, Itch, Scurfs, Scurvies, Leprosies, Venereal and French Disease, Running of the Reins, and all such Malignities, though never so Inveterate, in all Constitutions at all Seasons of the Year, hindering no Business, without Fluxing, or the Use of Mercury, which is generally Destructive. These Medicines are truly and faithfully prepared, as directed by her Husband, and as made and delivered to his Patients by her in his Life time (they being the only Persons then that sold it, and to whom the Secret was ever imparted.) Therefore beware of several late false Pretenders, for the daily certain and speedy Cures she performs will sufficiently recommend her excellent Medicines. She cures many after Fluxing, and in Compassion to the Distressed will deal with all Persons according to

6 *Flying Post*, 19–22 December 1702.

their Abilities. The Drink is three Shillings the Quart, the Pill one Shilling the Box, with Directions. She gives her Opinions for nothing, to all that write or come to her, to those afar off as if they were present.[7]

Mary was not content to give up the life she had known as the wife of one of the most famous medical men in London. She did not embrace the quiet solemnity of widowhood that was expected by those who believed women should be seen and not heard. Mary advertised her ability to practise as a Kirleus in multiple newspapers, pamphlets, and wherever she could. She became so successful that she features in the writing of Jonathan Swift, the author of *Gulliver's Travels* (1726). In *The Accomplishment of the First of Mr. Bickerstaff's Predictions*, Swift's satire on fortune-tellers printed in 1708, his leading character was visited by Mary on his deathbed: 'About two or three days ago he grew ill, was confined first to his chamber, and in a few hours after to his bed, where Dr Case and Mrs Kirleus were sent for to visit and prescribe him.'[8] This shows us that Mary was known across London for her ability to practise medicine, and that while women were shut out from the universities and unions that were becoming central to the medical world, they did not give it up easily. A year after Swift's portrayal of her, Mary found herself fighting a vicious and protracted battle with her sister-in-law, Susanna, who claimed that it was

7 *Flying Post*, 3 May–2 June 1705.
8 Jonathan Swift, Walter Scott, *The Works, Volume 10*, 1814, p. 172.

she who had been left Kirleus' original medications and instructions, and that it was to her only that those seeking Kirleus' remedies should apply.[9]

Susanna the Daughter of Dr. Thomas Kirleus, who was Sworn Physician in Ordinary to King Charles II. &c she having had above 20 Years Experience in the Dr. Life time, not only in making of Medicines, but knowing the true way of administring [*sic*] them; she with the same Pills and Drink hindring no Business, Cures all Ulcers, Sores, Itch, Scurf, Scurvies, Leprosies and Venereal Diseases at all times of the Year, which Medicines she makes as her Father did, without the dangerous use of Mercury that is generally used by others. She hath cured many in this City and Country after fluxing, which raiseth the Malignity and other Evils from the lower parts, and fixes it in the Head, and so destroys many. Take heed whom you trust in these Cures, for many pretends to it, but few can do it; she deals with all Persons according to their Abilities. The Pills 1s. the Box, the Drink 3s. a Quart, she gives her Advice Gratis to all that write or come to her. She still lives at her House at the Glass Lanthorn in Plow-yard in Grays-Inn-Lane, where she has lived above 20 Years.[10]

---

9 https://books.google.co.uk/books?id=wEoJAAAAQAAJ&pg=PA360&l pg=PA360&dq=thomas+kirleus&source=bl&ots=ZsKivD5yOY&sig=A CfU3U2iI112IPERXrFirKCh2-2a_oIaYw&hl=en&sa=X&ved=2ahUKE wjAx7yM7e7jAhWLYsAKHW_ADEkQ6AEwA3oECAcQAQ#v=one page&q=thomas%20kirleus&f=true *Tatler* no. 41.
10 7 December 1709 a17091207-1.

This pamphleteering battle between the two female Kirleuses raged on for years with no clear victor, but what it shows us is that women were far from shy or ignorant about the sexual problems or diseases that people encountered during their lives. And they were far from the only practitioners to be advertising their skills and knowledge at this time. For nearly a decade, from 1703 to 1711, Mrs Lilburn of Ludgate Hill advertised her practice in the pages of the Old Bailey Proceedings.

B. Lilburn, that formerly Lived on Ludgate-hill, next to the Kings-Arms Tavern near Fleet-Bridge, now lives at the Golden-Board, and Ball, next Door to Ship Court, up one Pair of Stairs, in the Great Old-Baily, near Ludgate-hill. Who maketh and selleth (and has done above 20 Years) the Water for taking away the Freckels, Pimple, Worms, Morphew, and red Marks of the Small-pox in the Face: With Elixir Salutis, Balsamum Vita, Tinctura Vita. Waters and Ointments for the Eyes, Powders, Dentrifices, Elixirs, Essences, Oils, Spirits, &c. both for Ornament, and Curing all Diseases incident to Humane Bodies; but more especially relating to the Female Sex, likewise Judgment upon Urine.

The Anti-scorbutick Pills, price 1s. 6d. the Box.
The Elixir for the Collick, and Gripes, 1s. the Bottle.
The Ointment for sore Nipples, and the Piles, 1s. the Pot.
An Ointment for Redness, Pustules, Heat, Scabs, Ringworms, Titters, Itch or breaking out in the Face, or else where, price 1 s. the Pot.

The Ointment for Aches, and Strains, 6d. the Pot.

The Water for the Freckles, Pimples, &c. The Author has for some Years past, left with several for Sale; who now doth understand, they have been abused by Counterfeits; which to prevent for the future, doth desire those that have bought from them – and not found the Effect-answer the Ends for which it is proposed, to acquaint her with it, and where they bought it – and likewise to take notice of the Seal, viz. The 3 Water-budgets, and B. L. on the top of the Seal. The Price of the half Pint-bottle 3s. That you be not imposed on, be sure remember her Name; and that it is the Person that formerly lived on Ludgate-hill.[11]

These were women treating women, and women treating sexual diseases without shame or embarrassment. This was the time of pill-poppers, and unctuous, foul-smelling elixirs, which often did far more harm than good. While men sought to legitimise the discipline of medicine, teaching anatomy and midwifery at universities, they also took steps to shut women out from the understanding of medicine itself. Both the church and the state had refused women access to the university system, and so, as medicine began to evolve as a science in the universities of Europe, women were often excluded from the debates and discoveries that were taking place. But while surgeries and books may have been the property of men, providing medicinal relief and healing advice was not

---

11 13 October 1703 a17031013-1.

something that women were ready to give up. Sex, and the problems we often encounter with it, was one of the most important areas of treatment for those seeking medical advice.

The medical men who emerged out of this period and into the early nineteenth century had some incredibly odd ideas about sex. It was always a danger, and always to be controlled. Writing in 1875, C. Bigelow M.D, the author of *Sexual Pathology: A Practical and Popular Review of the Principal Diseases of the Reproductive Organs*, went to great lengths to inform their readers of the dangers of the sex drive:

> A new power is present to be exercised, a new want to be satisfied. It is, I take it, of vital importance that boys and young men should know, not only the guilt of an illicit indulgence of their dawning passions, but also the danger of straining an immature power, and the solemn truth that the want will be an irresistible tyrant only to those who have lent it strength by yielding; that the only true safety lies in keeping even the thoughts pure... The instinct of reproduction, when once aroused, even though very obscurely felt, acts in man upon his mental faculties and moral feelings, and thus becomes the source, though almost unconsciously so to the individual, of the tendency to form that kind of attachment towards one of the opposite sex, which is known as Love.[12]

12 *Sexual Pathology: A Practical and Popular Review of the Principal Diseases of the Reproductive Organs*, pp. 20–21.

But sex was not a secret to the Victorians, and in fact, the idea that you should be able to have sex and *not* get pregnant was at the heart of the 1877 trial of birth control campaigner, Annie Besant. She was determined to provide birth control education and access to everyone within England in the 1870s, and took her case to court. Arguing that love was often thwarted by lack of financial security, Annie believed that contraception should be used by young married couples to help them have a happy and healthy sex life. Without this access, she believed the choice of celibacy or illicit, unprotected sex would only lead to social ruin and deeply unhappy people.

Let us now turn our attention to the case of Unmarried youth. Almost all young persons, on reaching the age of maturity, desire to marry. That heart must be very cold, or very isolated, that does not find some object on which to bestow its affections. Thus, early marriages would be almost universal did not prudential considerations interfere. The young man thinks 'I cannot marry yet, I cannot support a family. I must make money first and think of a matrimonial settlement afterwards.' And so he goes to making money, fully and sincerely resolved, in a few years to share it with her whom he now loves. But passions are strong and temptations great. Curiosity, perhaps, introduces him into the company of those poor creatures whom society first reduces to a dependence on the most miserable of mercenary trades, and then curses for being what she has made them. There his health and moral feelings alike make shipwreck. The affections he had thought to treasure up for their first object are chilled by dissipation and blunted by excess. He scarcely retains a passion but avarice. Years pass on — years of profligacy and speculation — and his first wish is accomplished, his fortune is made. Where now are the feelings and resolves of his youth? He is a man of pleasure, a man of the world. He laughs at the romance of his youth, and marries a fortune. If gaudy equipage and gay parties confer happiness, he is happy; but If they be only the sunshine on the stormy sea below, he is a victim to that system of morality which forbids a reputable connection until the period when provision has been made for a large expected family. Had he married the first object of his choice, and simply delayed becoming a father until his prospects seemed to warrant it, how different might have been his lot. Until men and women are absolved from the fear of becoming parents, except when they themselves desire it, they ever will form mercenary and demoralizing connections, and seek in dissipation the happiness they might have found in domestic life.[13]

Born just before the age of consent was raised from 13 to 16 in 1885, and less than a decade after Annie's famous trial, Nora Barnacle (1884–1951) was the muse, and later wife, of the Irish poet and author, James Joyce. They met in 1904, while Nora was working as a chambermaid in Dublin's Finn's Hotel. Their relationship was deeply erotic

---

13 Annie Besant trial text.

from the start, and although they spent much of their time in Europe, bringing up two small children, Nora and Joyce did not marry until 1931. Their lack of interest in a legal marriage and their libertine approach to sexual desire show us that sex was far from a reproductive act. Nora and Joyce embraced the pleasure of sex as if it was the most normal thing in the world. Their private desires, held so separately from their public lives, are the lives of true eroticists. Sex is not an artform or a performance between them, it is earthly, animal, and unashamed. And we are lucky enough to know this thanks to the letters they sent to one another while they were apart. On 8 December 1909, Joyce wrote Nora one of the most gorgeously graphic of all his letters:

My sweet little whorish Nora, I did as you told me, you dirty little girl, and pulled myself off twice when I read your letter. I am delighted to see that you do like being fucked arseways. Yes, now I can remember that night when I fucked you for so long backwards. It was the dirtiest fucking I ever gave you, darling. My prick was stuck in you for hours, fucking in and out under your upturned rump. I felt your fat sweaty buttocks under my belly and saw your flushed face and mad eyes. At every fuck I gave you your shameless tongue came bursting out through your lips and if I gave you a bigger stronger fuck than usual, fat dirty farts came spluttering out of your backside. You had an arse full of farts that night, darling, and I fucked them out of you, big fat fellows, long windy ones, quick little merry cracks and a lot of tiny little naughty farties ending in a long gush from your hole. It is wonderful to fuck a farting woman when every fuck drives one out of her. I think I would know Nora's fart anywhere. I think I could pick hers out in a roomful of farting women. It is a rather girlish noise not like the wet windy fart which I imagine fat wives have. It is sudden and dry and dirty like what a bold girl would let off in fun in a school dormitory at night. I hope Nora will let off no end of her farts in my face so that I may know their smell also. You say when I go back you will suck me off and you want me to lick your cunt, you little depraved black-guard. I hope you will surprise me some time when I am asleep dressed, steal over to me with a whore's glow in your slumberous eyes, gently undo button after button in the fly of my trousers and gently take out your lover's fat mickey, lap it up in your moist mouth and suck away at it till it gets fatter and stiffer and comes off in your mouth. Sometimes too I shall surprise you asleep, lift up your skirts and open your drawers gently, then lie down gently by you and begin to lick lazily round your bush. You will begin to stir uneasily then I will lick the lips of my darling's cunt. You will begin to groan and grunt and sigh and fart with lust in your sleep. Then I will lick up faster and faster like a ravenous dog until your cunt is a mass of slime and your body wriggling wildly.

Goodnight, my little farting Nora, my dirty little

fuckbird! There is one lovely word, darling, you have underlined to make me pull myself off better. Write me more about that and yourself, sweetly, dirtier, dirtier[14]

Joyce's words, and the insight letters such as this give us, showcase a shared sexual heritage from one century to another. There is little difference in tone from the joyful explorations of Katy and Frank in *The School of Venus* to Joyce and Nora's own private shared sexual self-education. What it does show us is that sex, and everything that goes with it, has always been cause for private celebration. Another of Joyce's erotic Noraisms went on sale in 2004. The auction of this letter attracted a huge amount of interest, given Joyce's known hatred of 'obscene jokes and swearing'.[15] For those to whom sex is a dirty or difficult thing, the vulgarity of Joyce's language was shocking. But for eroticists his joy and sexual self-expression is clear. Sex should never be confined by public morals. Between consenting adults it must be free, lusty and utterly devoid of shame. The sexual life Nora shared with Joyce, her independence and pleasure in their connection, has often been credited with inspiring his greatest works. This letter, so clearly filled with their shared creativity, was sold for £240,000, the highest price ever obtained for a signed letter from the twentieth century. These private words are perhaps the literary legacy we should be celebrating Joyce for, rather than the famous *Ulysses*.

---

14 James Joyce, *Selected Letters of James Joyce*.

15 http://news.bbc.co.uk/1/hi/entertainment/3877209.stm

Stripping out the romance of Joyce's words and looking instead at the acts he describes, we see nothing new in the sexual culture of the early 1900s. Here are descriptions of fellatio and cunnilingus, anal sex, foreplay and fantasy, as well as simple, ordinary penetrative sex itself. Written as the suffragettes were marching through London and Shackleton's *Nimrod* expedition had failed to reach the South Pole, Joyce and Nora encapsulate the true sexual culture that existed just before the outbreak of the First World War. In fact, wherever we look at sexual culture – not the attitudes of the church and state, but those held by ordinary people, living their ordinary sex lives – we see the same repeating ideas and experiences. People want to have sex. They want to enjoy pleasure. In April 2019, British rapper Stormzy debuted at the top of the singles chart with 'Vossi Bop', containing lyrics that included a clear-cut depiction of him ejaculating on a woman's face: *'gettin' freaky in the sheets, we're takin' body shots, then I finish with a facial just to top it off'*. This act is one that has little direct sexual gratification for the recipient, as journalist Rebecca Reid highlighted in her exposé of the expectation of 'facials' in modern sexual culture a year earlier.[16] 'I don't get any sexual pleasure from it – there are no pleasure receptors in my face,' pointed out one of her female interviewees. The idea of a sexual 'facial' itself found widespread condemnation from both anti-porn and sex-positive feminists, almost unique in its ability to unite

16 https://metro.co.uk/2018/02/23/time-talk-facials-kind-involve-semen-7 337371

these two warring factions in their belief that it signals nothing more than the degradation and submission of the (most often female) recipient. In contrast, male writers and sex educators have argued that the facial emerged out of the 1980s AIDs crisis, where the slogan 'cum on me, not in me' saw film-makers turn towards creating images of ejaculation that included female facial expressions as a way to reassure men that women were not afraid of their semen.[17] Almost forty years later, this act is now presented as something that is a normal part of sex for the single man. Stormzy's depiction of this act is not as part of a loving, lasting relationship, but purely as his own (or his fans' fantasised) sexual gratification from a casual encounter. But even this is hardly new to our sexual culture. The graphic poetry of John Wilmot, the Earl of Rochester (1647–1680), was no different, proclaiming male pleasure and laddish banter as a key part of his sexual experience. Throughout history, how we have had sex, and who we have wanted to have it with, has barely changed. It has always been about lust and love and intimacy. It has shown us, repeatedly, that the boundaries enforced by church or state on who to love, and how, have rarely succeeded. Over the course of hundreds, even thousands of years, human beings have still chosen to love who they love, and to experience pleasure over the fear of death or disease.

By the 1940s, new slang was being invented for the rock

---

17 https://jezebel.com/he-wants-to-jizz-on-your-face-but-not-why-you-think-5875217

'n' roll era. 'People think that rock and roll started in 1956, but they are wrong,' remembered Don Covey. 'In the late '40s and early '50s every other word was "rock".'[18] To Wynonie Harris, singer of 'Keep the Butter Churnin'', 'rock' was just a slang word for fuck. Two of his number one hits, 'Good Rockin' Tonight' (1947) and 'All She Wants To Do Is Rock' (1949), make the innuendo clear: *'I'm gonna hold my baby as tight as I can | Well, tonight she'll know I'm a mighty, mighty man | I heard the news: there's good rockin' tonight.'* The appeal of these lyrics across American culture is clear, and, quick to monopolise on the success of Harris (as well as many other black artists), less than a year into his career, the soon to be King of Rock 'n' Roll, Elvis Presley, released a cover version of 'Good Rockin' Tonight' in 1954.

But the identification of 'rock', or 'rock 'n' roll', with sex does not belong to Presley *or* Wynonie Harris. Twenty years earlier, the Black Swan Records single 'My Man Rocks Me (With One Steady Roll)' introduced this slang term for sex to our popular culture. The singer on this small, 75 cent recording was Trixie Smith (*c*.1885/1895–1943), an African-American college-educated, vaudeville and early film actress; and the Harlem-based Black Swan Records, created in 1921, was the first known music label to be owned by, run by, and marketed to black Americans. Smith recorded 'My Man Rocks Me (With One Steady Roll)' in 1922, and there is nothing covert about the sexual slang or innuendo within her lyrics. It

---

18 Tony Collins, p. 10.

is a song that celebrates the sexual stamina of her lover, who can keep going for hours without ceasing: *'My man rocks me with one steady roll | There's no slippin' when he once takes hold | I looked at the clock and the clock struck three | I said "Now Daddy, you a-killin' me!" | He kept rockin' with one steady roll.'* Adverts for Smith's music can be found across daily newspapers, from Kentucky to Texas.[19] And by 1943, avoiding the censorship of the 1930s, Smith's music had reached England; the West London Rhythm Club held 'very interesting and educational record recitals' at their headquarters (above the Bridgeway Club on Bradmore Lane, Hammersmith), where 'many famous jazz people were heard in the various recordings who included Bessie Smith, Trixie Smith, Louis Armstrong and Duke Ellington'.[20] Her sexually overt lyrics had found a new home among a country desperate to distract itself from the horrors of the Second World War – the club had formed that year and quickly acquired over 250 members who would meet to hear, talk and play jazz.[21]

Smith's life, as much as her music, shows us that while the authorities of the twentieth century fought to sanitise sex out of popular culture, it was impossible to do. There would always be those who fought to record and show

---

19 *The public ledger* (Maysville, Ky.), 1 April 1922; *The Dallas Express* (Dallas, Tex.), 16 Dec. 1922; *The Appeal* (Saint Paul, Minn), 20 May 1922.
20 *West London Observer*, Friday, 10 December 1943.
21 Ibid., Friday, 4 February 1944.

sexual culture in its entirety, free from social regulations enforced by governments and religious institutions.

In 1931, Smith appeared in a play, *The Constant Sinner*, written by screen icon Mae West and adapted from her 1930 novel *Babe Gordon* (also known as *The Constant Sinner*). Both West's book and the play depicted an inter-racial love/murder story between its anti-heroine, Babe, and 'Money' Johnson, a black, wealthy nightclub owner. It captured the sexual freedom and culture of 1930s Harlem, the same place populated by Claude McKay's 'bulldykes', where all races and all sexualities existed along-side one another. It was a brave novel for its time; interracial marriage was illegal in America until 1967, and the idea of a sexual relationship between a white woman and a black man would have been seen as equally criminal. Two years before West's novel, the Democratic Senator for South Carolina and white supremacist, Coleman Blease, had proposed an amendment that would require Congress to set a punishment for interracial couples attempting to marry, and for any person officiating at an interracial marriage. He was not successful, but his views were shared by many in America at this time.

Much like the salacious memoir of master thief, James Dalton, in the eighteenth century took readers into the sexual landscape of London, West's book took her reader into the heart of Harlem, a place where sex could be seen, instead of suffocated. It was vulgar and crude, but it was also unashamed. 'Babe was eighteen and a prize-fighters' tart,' opens the novel, 'picking up her living on their

hard-earned winnings. Her acquaintances numbered trol-
lops, murderers, bootleggers and gambling den keepers.'[22]
She secretly sells gangland morphine, heroin and cocaine
from her department store make-up counter in Baldwin's
Five and Ten, and spends her evenings enjoying the many
pleasures available to her in Harlem. West painted a racially
diverse nightclub scene that scandalised her critics, 'blasé
white society women gayly dancing with men of every
shade of colour from the cream of the creole to the char-
coal black of darkest Africa—negro girls with soft brown
eyes and fertile bodies filled with primitive fire, sitting
with their white lovers, happy to be seen with men of
social standing, wealth and culture'.[23] Here, in Harlem,
Babe navigates her three lovers: her discarded prize-fighter
husband, Bearcat Delaney; her long time African-American
lover, underground kingpin 'Money' Johnson; and her fling
with the wealthy, racist and obsessive Wayne Baldwin, the
heir to the Baldwin Five and Ten empire. When Baldwin
shoots Johnson dead, murdering him in a racist attack
(intimidated by the thought of a black man touching a
white woman), Babe covers up his crime. She convinces
her still-besotted, estranged husband, Delaney, to take the
blame, telling him that she shot Johnson in self-defence
as he raped her, seeking payment after she defaulted on
a gangland loan. In a further twist and to protect Babe,
Delaney then publicly claims *he* shot Johnson, after the
man lured Babe to an apartment to offer her a job, and

---

22 Mae West, *The Constant Sinner*, 1930, p. 9.
23 Ibid., p. 159.

instead attacked her. After a trial that showcases the worst of racial stereotyping, with a superstar lawyer secretly paid for by Baldwin, Delaney is acquitted, believing he is about to be united with a loving, grateful Babe. The reader, following Babe's journey, has been well aware throughout that her relationship with Johnson was entirely consensual, mutual and sexually satisfying, yet watches as the memory and reality of this man is corrupted by a white press and laws that only record him as a black rapist shot dead by a loving white husband. After the trial, a devastated Delaney is greeted with the shocking news that Babe has left him and is filing for divorce. She is in Europe, living with the racist Baldwin, who is still obsessed by the thought of interracial relationships:

> As for Baldwin, the frequent sight of black and white mingling together in Paris brings always the memory of Johnson's face when he had shot him. He cannot avoid thinking of Babe's white body and Johnson's black body, darkness mating with dawn. It is terrible, and yet it gives him a sensual thrill like the one he received when he first saw Babe and the black man in the Harlem Breakfast Club.[24]

West used Babe's relationship with Johnson to expose the reaction to interracial couples in black and white communities in the 1930s. The first time Babe is seen embracing Johnson by Baldwin, his reaction of disgust and desire

---

24 Mae West, *The Constant Sinner*, 1930, p. 312.

encapsulated the cultural racism and sexual fetishisation of black Americans, still prevalent today. Within the black community, which West held close ties to, Johnson's relationship with a white woman is met with both acceptance and anger. 'Money Johnson left a trail of broken hearts among the coloured women of Harlem,' wrote West, 'But what did he care as long as he had the most beautiful white woman a negro could ever dream of possessing?'[25] These racial and sexual tropes leak out of every page of West's novel, which became so popular it ran into its fourth edition within the first few months of its publication. The language and overtly racialised sexual tone will be difficult for modern readers, but it was supposed to challenge, to confuse, to arouse, and to horrify 1930s America, whether they were black or white. 'It is a trickster tale that uses racism to sabotage racism,' argues Jill Watts, biographer of Mae West, which 'dupes its audience into believing that it reaffirms their attitudes, no matter what they are, while at the same time opposing their firmly held assumptions'.[26] After the financial success of *The Constant Sinner*, West decided to turn her book into a play – the 1930s' equivalent of turning a successful novel into a film or TV series – and hired the biggest names in New York's African-American entertainment community. Trixie Smith, now an established singer and actress after the success of her 1922 hit 'My Man Rocks Me', agreed to take the role of

25 Mae West, *The Constant Sinner*, 1930, p. 175.
26 Jill Watts, *Mae West: An Icon in Black and White* (Oxford University Press, 2003), p. 134.

Liza, a brothel maid who gives evidence during the murder trial, for the performances during the play's initial run at New York's Royale Theater, in 1931.[27] The ideas within the book were shocking enough, but when West's financiers heard she intended to have Money Johnson played by a real African-American man – Lorenzo Tucker, 'the black Valentino' – they insisted she change the casting to a white man in blackface, who would take off his wig at the end of the show to prove to the audience that a black man and a white woman were not actually embracing on the stage in front of them.[28] The idea that a real interracial relationship would be physically presented on stage was harder for them to imagine than Mae West deciding to play the role of the 18-year-old Babe herself, at the age of 38. Although West agreed to the blackfaced actor during the show's Royale run, she demanded that Lorenzo Tucker take over the role of Money Johnson when the play went on its national tour. After sixty-four performances at the Royale, *The Constant Sinner* headed for the Belasco in Washington, D.C., with Tucker now in the leading role. They lasted two nights. On the second and final night, their performance was attended by Assistant District Attorney, Michael F. Keogh, who had been deluged by complaints since the curtain had fallen on the previous evening. He confiscated the script, calling it 'lewd and lascivious', personally horrified by what he saw as the

---

27 the *Brooklyn Daily Eagle* (Brooklyn, New York), 15 September 1931.
28 Jill Watts, p. 136.

'objectionable intermingling of race'.[29] The play was closed, and West was informed that a lynching mob had begun searching for Tucker. None of these events made it into West's autobiography, she only recalled the show's success at the Royale – 'We had two ticket offices take care of the crowds' – and that they continued to tour until the summer of 1932.[30] We don't know if Trixie Smith toured with the production after it left New York, but she starred alongside Lorenzo Tucker in the 1932 film *The Black King*, which parodied the life of black racial separatist, Marcus Garvey. What these lives show us is that words are paramount to our sexual culture. Whether spoken in slang, or graphic depictions in novels, plays and music, the sexual culture of the 1930s was determined to fight back against the pathologising and sanitising of sexual culture that the racism and sexism of the medical and scientific communities had attempted to enforce since the nineteenth century.

29 Jill Watts, pp. 141–2.
30 Mae West, *Goodness Had Nothing To Do With It: The Autobiography of Mae West*, 1959, p. 145.

9
Technology

'If your sexual fantasies were truly of interest
to others, they would no longer be fantasies.'
—Fran Lebowitz, 1992[1]

'Sex toys,' reads the introduction to a 24 carat gold, $15,000 dildo, the Lelo Inez, 'have long since graduated from the floppy rubber things you hide in your bedside table to beautiful works of interactive art.' Advertised on actress-turned-lifestyle-brand Gwyneth Paltrow's somewhat controversial website, Goop, since 2016, the Lelo Inez is supposed to represent the height of sensual luxury in female sex toys. We tend to think of these devices as part of modern sexuality, but ever since human beings figured out that they enjoyed sexual pleasure, they have also been attempting to figure out ways to have it more often, or increase the sensations of pleasure itself. Part of that has always included what today we call sex toys. In the past

---

1 'Sexual, Textual Madonna', *Washington Post*, 25 October 1992.

they were referred to as 'devices', 'instruments' or 'aids', the 'Widow's Consolation' or 'The Femme du Voyage'. For the moral authorities of church and state they were something to be criminalised, especially for their use among women. To be penetrated by anything other than the penis of a male partner was viewed as a grievous sin. It's a clear indicator that both our moral and secular authorities were well aware of the fact that sex, whether with oneself or others, regularly took place in our communities. The idea that sex has solely been about reproduction may exist if you view historical sexuality only through religious or medical doctrine, but those views do not represent the entirety of society, and, as we have often seen, do not even represent the views of some members of those organisations themselves.

So how do we define the technology of sex in the past? I believe it is anything that enables the sexual fulfilment of its user, that does not belong to the body of another consenting, living adult. With that in mind, we could call the printing press and the invention of the internet an important part of the history of technology of sex, but in this chapter I am going to focus specifically on the use of sexual aids, or sex toys, as part of our historical sexual culture. One of the earliest known forms of sexual aid is the dildo, the creation of an artificial penis for penetration either of its owner or their partner. They were known by many names: *godemiche, dildoe* and *consolateurs* are the most common in slang, while the word 'dildoe' itself is believed to have arrived either from the Italian *Diletto* to mean a 'woman's delight', or the English word 'dally', meaning a thing to play with. By 1785, Grose's *Dictionary of the Vulgar Tongue* defined the dildo as 'an implement resembling the virile member, for which it is said to be substituted, by nuns, boarding school misses, and others obliged to celibacy, or fearful of pregnancy'; however, by its revision in 1823, the definition was gone, leaving only the references to the word's origin in Italian and English, but no definition of the device itself. Today, we know historical dildos were commonly made from wood, ivory, metal, glass, wax or rubber. They could be used as strap-ons, or simply manually, and often appear in the discovery of trans or lesbian women and their partners, as much as they are in examples of use by heterosexual women. Havelock Ellis provided a rudimentary history of the European use of the dildo in his first volume of *Studies in the Psychology of Sex*, first published in 1897. Making note of their existence in the classical literature of the Romans and the Greeks, Ellis pointed his readership to view a vase held by the British Museum 'representing a *hetaira* holding such instruments', and also noted that the original objects themselves, made of leather, could be viewed in a museum in Naples.[2]

The use of an artificial penis in solitary sexual gratification may be traced down from classic times, and doubtless prevailed in the very earliest human civilisation, for such an instrument is said to be represented in old Babylonian sculptures, and it is referred to by Ezekiel (Ch. XVI v 17). The Lesbian woman is said to have used such instruments, made

---

2 Havelock Ellis, *Studies in the Psychology of Sex*, vol. 1 (1913), p. 169.

of ivory or gold with silken stuffs and linen … Through the Middle Ages (when from time to time the clergy reprobated the use of such instruments) they continued to be known, and after the fifteenth century the references to them became more precise … In Elizabethan England … Marston in his satires tells how Lucea prefers 'a glassy instrument' to 'her husband's lukewarm bed.' In sixteenth century France, such instruments were sometimes made of glass, and Brantôme refers to the godemiche; in eighteenth century Germany they were called Samthanse, and their use … was common among aristocratic women. In England by that time the dildo appears to have become common. Archemholtz states that while in Paris they are only sold secretly, in London a certain Mrs. Philips sold them openly on a large scale in her shop in Leicester Square. John Bee in 1835, stating that the name was originally dil-dol, remarks that their use was formerly commoner than it was in his day. In France, Madame Gourdan, the most notorious brothel-keeper of the eighteenth century, carried on a wholesale trade in consolateurs, as they were called, and 'at her death numberless letters from abbesses and simple nuns were found among her papers, asking for a "consolateur" to be sent.' The modern French instrument is described by Gamier as of hardened red rubber, exactly imitating the penis and capable of holding warm milk or other fluid for injection at the moment of orgasm; the compressible scrotum is said to have been first added in the eighteenth century.[3]

---

3 Havelock Ellis, *Studies in the Psychology of Sex*, vol. 1 (1913), pp. 169–70.

The artificial imitation of the male penis was not a surprise to Ellis, and far more examples than the few he listed in the early twentieth century have since appeared. Acknowledgement of the use of dildos by women, of course, emerges out of the fears of the early Church. The ninth-century archbishop Hincmar of Reims (806–882) wrote of his fears of 'women fornicating in their own bodies', with the use of 'machinas diabolica operationis' or 'machines of diabolical operations'.[4] 'They do not,' he wrote in *De divortio Lotharii et Tetbergae*, '...put flesh to flesh in the sense of the genital organ of one within the body of the other, since nature precludes this, but they do transform the use of the member in question into an unnatural one, in that they are reported to use certain instruments of diabolical operation to excite desire. Thus they sin nonetheless by committing fornication against their own bodies.'[5]

Claiming to follow the early penitentials often attributed (but not written by) Bede in the Anglo-Saxon era, the tenth-century writer Burchard, Bishop of Worms (*c*.950/65–1025) set out his views on the use of 'machina' by nuns – it was severe enough a sin to warrant seven years' penance.[6] By the sixteenth century the punishment had grown far more severe. In Spain and Italy, the use

4 Robert Mills, *Seeing Sodomy in the Middle Ages* (University of Chicago Press, 2015), p. 112.

5 Jacqueline Murray, 'Twice Marginal and Twice Invisible – Sexualities in History, 1200–1600', *Handbook of Medieval Sexuality* (Garland Publishing Inc., 1996), p. 198.

6 Robert Mills, p. 112.

of 'devices' or 'instruments' to penetrate the vagina during sex was punishable by death.[7] Such a discovery led to the deaths of two nuns, both burned alive in sixteenth-century Spain for using 'material instruments'.[8] In Fountaines, the publisher Henri Estienne recorded the death of a woman who was discovered to have disguised herself as a man and married another woman, in 1535. She was burned alive for the 'wickedness which she used to counterfeit the office of a husband – her use of a dildo to stimulate her wife'.[9] As England escaped the lesbian panic that engulfed much of Europe during the Early Modern Era, the use of dildos did not lead to the extreme punishments seen on the continent, and their use over the centuries is clear. The redoubtable Mrs Phillips, mentioned by Havelock Ellis, is the same Mrs Constantia Phillips who marketed her handmade regimental condoms, and also held a sideline in the sale of 'dil-dols' in the early eighteenth century.[10] Writing in her diary on 1 September 1823, Anne Lister recorded a fantasy over one of her latest crushes, 'In my mind, thought of her using a phallus to her friend.'[11] One of the fathers of sexology, Ivan Bloch, recorded that dildos were in

---

7 Kenneth Borris (ed.), *Same-Sex Desire in the English Renaissance: A Sourcebook of Texts, 1470–1650*, Routledge, 2015, p. 73.

8 Salvatore J. Licata and Robert P. Petersen (eds), *Historical Perspectives on Homosexuality*, Stein & Day, 1982, p. 17.

9 Ibid., p. 17.

10 Alan H. Mankoff, *Mankoff's Lusty Europe; the first all-purpose European guide to sex, love and romance*, Mayflower Books, 1972, p. 495.

11 *Gentleman Jack*, p. 105.

common use in the brothels of 1840s' London, as well
as by '...purveyors of erotic literature. They usually cost
£2. 10s and are made of india-rubber. There are different
kinds; one that can be used by two women at the same
time, another with appliances for several orificia corporis
[anal], a third with an attachment for the chin, etc.'[12]
Held by the Museum of London, a tiny advertisement
for the *'The Dildoe, or Ladies Syringe'* from the late nineteenth century demonstrated the utter ingenuity of the
sex toy makers of the Victorian era:

The grand desideratum accomplished by the Patentee, is
the substitution of Indian-Rubber for the shaft of this
article, instead of ivory, wood, silver, wax, or porcelain,
heretofore used, none of which substances could resemble
the real thing in effect, however beautiful they might be
shaped and painted. The Indian-Rubber shaft, when
dipped in warm water to bring it to blood heat, sufficiently
soft and elastic to titillate the female seat of pleasure,
without excoriating the vagina, or injuring the mouth of
the uterus.

The most complete article is made with a stomacher,
in order that one female may fix it firmly on herself so as
to operate upon another female. In this case, the ball, or
scrotum, is placed between the thighs of the Operator.
The upper strings are passed around her waist, and tied
in front; and the under strings round the thick part of the

---

12 Ivan Bloch, *Sexual Life In England Past and Present*, trans. 1936,
pp. 309–10.

thighs and tied behind. In this manner the machine will remain firm and effective through the 'soft encounter,' and the receiving female is wrought to that delightful pitch of burning ecstasy until she requires the balmy shower of love to consummate her bliss. She need only to say 'NOW!' and the Operator can instantly produce the exhilarating injection by nipping the scrotum with her thighs, because the ball being previously charged with water, only requires a slight pressure to produce that thrilling sensation so much desired at the critical moment.

This noble instrument may justly be entitled the Maid's Safeguard, the Widow's Comfort, and the Wife's Consolation. It will cure the virgin of the green sickness without the risk of impregnation. It will comfort the widow until she can make a suitable match. And it will be found a never-failing source of consolation to those married ladies whose husbands are impotent thro' age or debauchery.

Many elderly gentlemen, whose affairs have shrunk into their bellies, are in the habit of strapping these devices on, in order to administer due benevolence to the aged partner of their beds, because it is well known that a woman is never too old to relish enjoyment although age incapacitates the male from performing the operation.

Directions for use – Put a little soap and water into a jug, then take the article and dip its head in, pressing the ball with the thumb, when it will immediately fill. Before using put a lather of soap and water on the head; after using, squeeze out all of the contents, and hang it up to dry, with the head downwards. Use the water tolerably warm, and take care not to put pomatum, or grease of any kind upon it, as it softens it too much, and causes it to assume a white colour, which cannot be got out.

Price from £5 to £20.[13]

The idea of a dildo that ejaculates was not new – although the writer of the advert went to great lengths to expose the ease with which stimulating ejaculation would be possible thanks to the new material of Indian Rubber; in the 1784 French text *Le rideau levé ou l'education de Laure*, by eroticist Gabriel de Mirabeau, one of his principal characters, a young woman named Rose, becomes addicted to her ejaculating dildo and dies of exhaustion.[14] It might be easy to assume that such devices were merely the work of pornographic fantasy, but held in Blythe House, until 2020 the archive stores for many of London's largest museums, is an intriguing ivory dildo, believed to date from between 1800 and 1900. About eight inches long and carved with gentle horizontal ridges down the shaft, the dildo also contains a small cavity. It is accessed by removing an ivory plug at the base of the dildo, and could then have been filled with any liquid desired by the owner – milk, water, etc. was occasionally suggested. About an inch and a half above the base, extending out from the shaft itself, is a small metal screw, connecting

13 Museum of London Archive.
14 Rommel Mendès-Leite and Pierre-Olivier de Busscher, *Gay Studies from the French Cultures: Voices from France, Belgium, Brazil, Canada, and the Netherlands*, vol. 25, 1993, p. 81.

to an internal divider between the cavity at the dildo's base, and the small passageway that appears at its head, no wider than half a centimetre. Rotating the metal screw forces whatever would have been held in the cavity out and through the head of the dildo's shaft. It is designed to mimic ejaculation just as in the 'Ladies Syringe'. Today, devices like the POPDildo carry on this creative design. The sensation and image of ejaculation can be incredibly arousing for some women, and yet our modern sexual culture often presents the male orgasm as something negative. Testing a modern-day ejaculating dildo in 2017, *VICE* sex columnist, Maria Yagoda, declared, 'ejaculation is arguably the worst part about letting penises in you.'[15] The complications for women today around the idea of male ejaculation often stem from a rejection of the messages and images they receive from pornography. Being ejaculated on can represent a form of submission, rather than shared or even consensual pleasure. But we know that the idea of stimulating ejaculation has existed in our sex toys for centuries, so understanding and celebrating this part of our sexuality is important.

Ingenuity in designing sex toys was not limited to the Victorians. Published after the death of conman and counterfeit coin maker, William Chaloner (1650–1699), an account of his life revealed his early dabbling in London's sex toy trade: '[he] knew not what course to take for a Livelihood; but at length, the first part of his

---

15 https://www.vice.com/en_us/article/mbbk5n/i-tried-an-ejaculating-dildo-and-learned-a-lot-more-than-i-expected

Ingenuity shew'd it self in making Tin-Watches, with D—does, &c. in'em, which he hawk'd about the Streets, and thereby pick'd up a few loose Pence, and looser Associates'.[16] Sadly, no example of Chaloner's erotic watches remain, yet their existence, and his ability to sell them for mere pennies, shows that the trade in erotica was by no means restricted to the upper classes. And for those who could not afford to buy a dildo, candles, hair-pins, lead and slate pencils, leather thongs, sealing wax and many other objects are recorded to have been used by women as masturbatory aids. However, much like today, these home-made experiments in sex toys often resulted in personal injury and extremely awkward conversations with a doctor. Havelock Ellis recorded that in 1862 in Germany, a doctor found he was having to remove so many hairpins from the genitals of female patients that he 'invented a special instrument' for their extraction, while similar cases were recorded in Italy, France, England, Switzerland and New York.[17] None of the female patients offered any explanation as to how their accident had occurred.[18]

The marketing of sexual aids for ladies was not a clan-destine affair for the newspapers of Victorian Britain. Just as they marketed condoms on the front pages, inside,

---

16 Guzman Redivivus, *A short view of the life of Will. Chaloner, the notorious coyner, who was executed at Tyburn on Wednesday the 22d. of March*, 1698/9, with a brief account of his trial, behaviour, and last speech, p. 4.

17 Havelock Ellis, *Studies in the Psychology of Sex*, vol. 1 (1913).

18 Ibid.

within the advertisements, lay a veritable trade in sexual pleasure. One such device, seemingly innocent on first look, might be 'Vigor's Horse-Action Saddle', marketed from 1885. Available from Vigor & Co., at 21 Baker Street, Portman Square, London (just next door to the fictional detective, Sherlock Holmes), the 'Hercules' model of 'The Horse-Action Saddle' was presented as a cure for hysteria. 'The ADVANTAGES of this UNIQUE SUBSTITUTE for Horse-Riding are:' boomed the advert, 'It promotes health in the same degree that horse-riding does. It invigorates the system by bringing all the VITAL ORGANS into INSPIRITING ACTION. It acts directly upon the CIRCULATION and prevents STAGNATION OF THE LIVER. It is a complete cure for OBESITY, HYSTERIA, and GOUT.' Although presented as merely an exercise device for those who wanted to increase their appetite and improve their circulation, the mechanics of the Horse-Action Saddle leave its modern-day viewer with certain questions. The 1885 model depicted in its advertisement looks as if someone has placed a horse saddle on an upright packing case. It is not large, and the woman on top of it sits calmly, clasping what looks like a pair of bicycle handlebars attached to the front. Clearly evident along the side of the saddle is its three-speed setting – trot, canter and gallop. These were achieved by a motorised system inside the saddle, which both rocks and vibrates the section on which the woman is sitting. To make sure that they could not be accused of indecency, the saddle's sellers included a number of reviews from medical authorities; the *Lancet* apparently found the saddle very beneficial: 'both the expense and difficulty of riding on a live horse are avoided. The invention is very ingenious'; while *Field's* said, 'We have had the opportunity of trying one of the Vigor's Horse-Action Saddles, and found it very like that of riding on a horse; the same muscles are brought into play as when riding.' The final testimonial belonged to *World*, 'It is very good for the Figure, good for the Complexion, and Especially Good For The Health.'

Included in the advert's information was the important review by Ishbel Hamilton-Gordon, Marchioness of Aberdeen and Temair, who wanted it to be known that 'The Saddle has given her complete satisfaction', as well as the personal endorsement of Her Royal Highness, Alexandra of Denmark, The Princess of Wales. Alexandra had married Edward VII (known as Bertie by his family), the eldest son of Queen Victoria and Prince Albert, in 1863, two years after he experienced a horrific fall from family grace, from which he never recovered. As Prince Albert attempted to organise his son's marriage to Alexandra in 1861, Bertie was enjoying the charms of a number of London's premier ladies. A favourite of his was Nellie Clifton, and word shortly reached Albert of their entanglement. He wrote to his son in disgust:

With a heavy heart, on a subject which has caused me the deepest pain I have yet felt in this life... To thrust yourself into the hands of one of the most abject of the human species, to be by her initiated into the sacred mysteries of creation, which ought to be shrouded in holy awe until touched by pure & undefiled hands!...at your age the sexual passions begin to move in young men & lead them to seek explanation to relieve a state of vague suspense & desire. Why did you not open yourself to your father? ... I would have reminded you ... the special mode in which these desires are to be gratified ... the holy ties of matrimony.[19]

Albert's hopes of a restrained and sexually pure son were not to be realised. For Bertie, sex was an indulgence in which he took full and total pleasure. His tours of the brothels of Europe were frequent, with a particular favourite being the Parisian Le Chabanais. It was here, in 1890, that Bertie commissioned his *Siege d'Amour* or *chaise de volupté* to be built, a love seat that enabled him, now overweight and often out of breath, to have sex with more than one of Le Chabanais's women at once. Sex aids or toys were not unknown for men. Although most of the surviving examples are often clearly marketed to those in the upper classes – given their expense – it is not hard to believe that these were objects that those of a sexually curious nature might seek out and acquire. Although its publication date is currently unknown, for the discerning Victorian gentleman the privately circulated advertisement for the '*Femme De Voyage or Artificial Fanny*' might have sounded intriguing.

For the special use of Gentlemen on their travels. This can be packed up so as to be put in a hat, and when inflated, occupies the same space that the living object it is intended to represent would. They are made of all sizes,

---

19 RA VIC/z141/94, Albert to B, 16 November 1861. Jane Ridley, *Bertie: A Life of Edward VII*.

> from the full-length figure, with all its appurtenances, to the small quartering containing only the essential part wanted by man. Price from five to one hundred guineas.[20]

This is the Victorian version of a 'fleshlight', a male masturbatory aid, today often constructed from silicone and modelled from the bodies of well-known pornographic actresses. In the nineteenth century the possibilities of new technology and materials were seized on by the sex industry as much as they are in our modern lives. While manufacturers of condoms, douches and cervical caps could often be found in catalogues of 'Rubber Goods', there was also a trade in the use of rubber sex toys, marketed through the catalogues of manufacturers who sold 'Parisian Rubber Articles'.[21] The fantasy of the *Femme De Voyage* is clearly present in late nineteenth-century literature. The erotic novel, *La Femme Endormie*, which claimed to be authored by the mysterious 'Madam B', was published in Paris in 1899. The heroine is an artificial woman, who is introduced to her audience as being able to be 'employed for all possible sexual artificialities, without, like a living woman, resisting them in any way'.[22] Writing in 1909, Ivan Bloch reported that there was a market for 'fornicatory dolls', which allowed for 'fornicatory acts effected with artificial imitations of the human

---

20 Museum of London Archive.
21 Ivan Bloch, *The Sexual Life of Our Time in Its Relations to Modern Civilization*, 1909, p. 648.
22 Ibid., p. 649.

body, or of individual parts of that body. There exist true Vaucansons in this province of pornographic technology, clever mechanics who, from rubber and other plastic materials, prepare entire male or female bodies, which, as hommes or dames de voyage, subserve fornicatory acts purpose.'[23] These dolls were even capable of ejaculating or appearing to get 'wet', 'by means of a "pneumatic tube" filled with oil'.[24] In Bloch's description of these sex dolls there is little to discern them from the sex toys of today, and his description of the 'Hommes or dames de voyage' adds evidential weight to the existence of the actual object described in the tiny advertisement for the *Femme De Voyage* itself. Vastly out of the price range of the majority of people in England at this time, the cost suggests a circle of private and wealthy eroticists willing to finance their deepest sexual desires. The mass marketisation of sex dolls has been growing since the 1970s and the creation of the blow-up doll we recognise today, although this was banned in Britain until the late 1980s.[25] For many of us, the life-like representation of a man, but more commonly a woman, for a person to act out their unconsenting sexual desires on is deeply uncomfortable. Those in the sex doll community defend their right to this form of sexual expression, while some makers point to their work as aiding partners grieving over the death of a loved one, by recreating a doll in their image.

---

23 Ivan Bloch, pp. 648–9.

24 Ibid., p. 648.

25 Kate Devlin, *Turned On: Science, Sex and Robots* (Bloomsbury Sigma, 2018).

Technology should be an asset for our sexual experiences, enabling those with disabilities, trans bodies, and those whose bodies have been damaged by accident or war to experience sexual pleasure. And yet there is a much darker side to technology and modern sexual culture that our wider population is only just beginning to understand and acknowledge. One aspect of this is the ability to inflict sexual violence in computer games. This issue often leads to gut-reaction debates among those who feel 'it's only a game' and those who believe game creators have a duty not to allow illegal or violent gameplay within their worlds. As video games become more technologically advanced, allowing users to be almost totally emerged in worlds that are dictated by role-play and the gamer's own choices, where do we draw the line?

Technology and sex could be such a glorious unifying force; the creation of avatars and virtual worlds allows us to transcend corporal ideas of gender and sexuality. Anything becomes possible. In the adult fantasy online worlds like *Red Light Centre*, users are able to create an avatar that is hyper-customisable; this gives the user the opportunity to change the entirety of their sexual identity from the real world, and for those who are unhappy or unable to alter their outward appearance in real life, or unable to find others who share their sexual desires, the technology of the digital world has always offered the opportunity to find someone who understands.

10

Orgasms

'At last I felt the hot creme de la creme pouring down ...
and ... Fanny once more sank into my arms ...
thoroughly spent.'[1]
—*Randiana*, 1884

'To-morrow they told us should be acted, or the day after, a new play, called "The Parson's Dreame",' recorded Samuel Pepys, in his diary of 4 October 1664, 'acted all by women.' Although Pepys recorded the name of *The Parson's Wedding* incorrectly, his joy at a play being performed by a female cast remained absolute. 'What a bawdy loose play this "Parson's Wedding" is,' he remarked, a week later, 'that is acted by nothing but women at the King's house, and I am glad of it.'[2] To see women on the stage was a new and unusual sight for Restoration England. Four years earlier, Charles II had re-established the

---

1 *Randiana*, 64.
2 Samuel Pepys, 11 October 1664.

monarchy after the English Civil War and the murder of his father at the hands of Oliver Cromwell's Puritan Government in 1649. One of his earliest decrees was to bring back the theatre – outlawed by the Puritans – and, for the first time, instruct women to play female roles. For many centuries before this, women had been banned from the stage, and their roles played by men.

The King's Theatre – or house, as Pepys called it – had been built by Thomas Killigrew (1612–1683), author and director of not only *The Parson's Wedding*, but also the theatre, and The King's Company – those actors and actresses licensed by the new King to perform. Killigrew was a prolific playwright, having spent much of his life in exile with Charles II. *The Parson's Wedding* is one of his most 'bawdy' plays, written before the Civil War, and Killigrew's new staging in 1664 connected the old England of the past with its new royal future. Charles II's delight in women on the stage may have come from his mother Queen Henrietta Marie's love of joining in royal masques and plays at court. It is thanks to her that we have the word 'actress', used for the first time in 1626 by Sir Benjamin Rudyerd to describe a performance of hers at court.[3] However, until Charles II's Royal Proclamation, the right for any woman to act on the stage, in public, had been denied.

Among the new King's Company's male actors were a number of women, including the celebrated Nell Gywn,

---

3 Elizabeth Howe, *The First English Actresses: Women and Drama, 1660–1700* (Cambridge University Press, 1992), p. 21.

Margaret Hughes and Katherine Corey. *The Parson's Wedding* required at least thirteen different roles to be fulfilled, and Killigrew's 1664 performance called for every role (male or female) to be played by a woman. For those in the King's new Restoration England, the opening night of *The Parson's Wedding* gave them a play that depicted unfettered female sexual desire, and women speaking *as men*, talking about sex *as men*, and with a freedom, vulgarity and humour that had been restrained and criminalised during the decades of Puritan government.

So what has this to do with the history of the orgasm? As we know, language is one of the most important aspects for understanding our historical sexual culture, and *The Parson's Wedding* is packed full of bawdy, outrageous sexual slang. In it, we find jokes about the sexual needs of widows: '*If she hears thou keep'st a Wench, thou hadst better be a Beggar in her opinion ... for a Wencher, no Argument prevails with your Widow; for she believes that they have spent too much that way to be able to pay her due benevolence.*'; adultery: '*And what think you? is it not a sweet sin, this lying with another man's Wife?*', and almost as many words for sexual acts and sex itself as there are in the early dictionaries.[4] To be 'spent' was an early description of the orgasm, an act history has always known was shared by both men and women. The words we use to describe the feeling and act of orgasming have barely changed in nearly 600 years; both to 'come' and to 'spend' have remained in regular

---

4 T. Killigrew, *The Parson's Wedding* 1664, II vii.

use since the sixteenth century.[5] The pornographic novel *Venus in India*, published in 1889, used both, 'She seemed to do nothing but "come" or "spend!" I had heard of a woman "coming" thirteen or fourteen times during one fuck, but this woman seemed to do nothing else from beginning to end.'[6] Some words for the male or female orgasm were interchangeable, such as 'jelly' (1601), or 'cream' (1629), while words for vaginal fluids included 'curds' (1604) and 'wax' (1938), while men would 'spew' (1673) and 'shoot' (1837) just as they do today. 'This emission,' wrote 'Walter' in 1888, 'in popular language is called spending, or spunking, and is the period of the highest pleasure of the fuck'.[7] The idea of a man's semen being known as his 'seed' seems almost to be undatable. It is an ancient idea drawing on the image of a woman's body as fertile land to be sown, or impregnated, by a man. And yet, for much of history, from the ancient world to the early nineteenth century, people believed that man was not alone in having seed, women did as well, and a woman's orgasm – the spilling of her own seed – was one of the most important parts of the sex act.

The idea of male and female 'seed' dates back to the Classical world, when the second-century theorist Galen (one of the most important scholars of early medicine) argued that both men and women created a seed during

---

5 1546 [UK], J. Heywood, Proverbs II Ch. x: He brought the bottom of the bag cleane out. / His gadyng thus agayne made hir ill content, / But she not so muche as dreamd that all was spent.

6 1889 [UK], C. Deveureux, *Venus in India* I 39:

7 Walter, *My Secret Life*, 1888, V 959.

the moment of orgasm – the thick white fluid of male semen, and the milky, frothy fluid often released at the moment of the female orgasm – and it was the combining of this seed in the woman's uterus that led to the conception and development of a child. Galen's theories were incredibly influential; they were produced as an argument against the dominant theories of Aristotle, which believed female pleasure was unimportant to sex and that women were merely receptacles for male sperm. His focus on a 'two-seed' theory of conception saw Galen place the same interest and importance on the female orgasm as he did on the male, and from these theories a new doctrine of female pleasure was born. One thousand years later, Galen's theories had become one of the most important parts of medieval sexuality, shaping the attitudes, beliefs and sexual practice of many of those in the eleventh and twelfth centuries, whether they were aware of its heritage or not.

One of the most important sources we have for the impact of Galen's work on our sexual cultural history comes from the texts written by Hildegard of Bingen (1098–1179). Given into the care of the Benedictine monastery at Disibodenberg, Germany, before she was a teenager, Hildegard spent much of her early life living in the mixed monastic community of monks and nuns. Disibodenberg was entirely enclosed; for those within its walls there was no world outside. At the moment Hildegard was given to the monastery, the monks recorded it was 'in order to be buried with Christ and with him rise to immortality.'[8] The women who gave themselves, or, like Hildegard, did not consent but were given to a life of enclosure by their families, were expected to dedicate their lives and their bodies to God. If any nun attempted to leave or, worse, fell in love, they could expect the harshest of punishments. Passing judgement on a young nun who had requested to leave her convent after she had fallen in love with a man, St Anselm reminded her that she had previously attempted to leave to marry another man, who had died:

> Go now, sister, place yourself with him in the bed in which he now lies; gather his worms to your bosom, embrace his cadaver. Kiss his nude teeth, for now his lips have been consumed by rot. Certainly he does not now attend to your love to which he was delighted while living and you fear his putrid flesh which you then desired to enjoy.[9]

We might wonder how the child who was shut away from the world became the renowned composer, mystic, natural scientist and medical authority that we know Hildegard of Bingen to have been. As her biographer, Fiona Maddocks, points out, 'considering her lifetime's confinement in monastic institutions, Hildegard of Bingen had an impressive grasp of the heterosexual, sexually active life.'[10] She

---

8 Fiona Maddocks, *Hildegard of Bingen*, p. 25.

9 Sharon K. Elkins, *Holy Women of Twelfth-Century England* (University of North Carolina Press, 1988), p. 4.

10 Fiona Maddock, p. 163.

became an Abbess in her early forties, leaving Disibodenberg behind to found two communities of nuns, one at Rupertsberg near Bingen in 1150, and another at Elbingen in 1165. It was at Rupertsberg, between 1151 and 1158, that Hildegard wrote *Causae et Curae* (Causes and Cures), her handbook to the human body and the diseases it often fell victim to. From the abbey's quasi-clinic that treated not only the nuns, but also local women, midwives and prostitutes, Hildegard would have gleaned first-hand accounts of what her cloistered life experience did not allow – sex, and all the problems that came with it.[11] Her convent education, in Latin and classical texts, would also have exposed her to the ideas of Galen and many other scholars who wrote about the human body without censorship. These are not the cloistered, stereotypical, innocent nuns of popular culture, but educated women who used their skills to try and better help those around them. A large part of *Causae et Curae* was given over to Hildegard's discussion of sex, sexuality and conception, and it is here that we can see the power of Galen's theories. Hildegard's description of the orgasm was practical and also erotic, so much so that it could only come from a frank and open discussion of the sexual experience of other women:

When a woman is making love with a man, a sense of heat in her brain, which brings forth with it sensual delight, communicates the taste of delight during the act and summons forth the man's seed. And when the seed has

---

11 Fiona Maddock, p. 163.

fallen into its place, that vehement heat descends from her brain, draws the seed in itself and holds it, and soon the woman's sexual organs contract and all the parts that are ready to open up during menstruation now close, in the same way as a strong man can hold something enclosed in his fist.[12]

Here, Hildegard is describing the muscle spasms that often occur in the aftermath of the female orgasm; she also highlights the importance of both men and women achieving orgasm to aid conception. But that was not her only motivation. By the eleventh century there was a shared belief that if a woman did not come, or did not have regular sexual intercourse, it would lead to a build-up of 'seed', which could be deeply detrimental to her health. Again, this came from the Galenian school of thought, which had advised midwives to place hot poultices on celibate (or single) women's genitals to bring about an orgasm, to release that kept-in, decaying seed.[13] By the seventeenth century, the idea of the mutual orgasm was clearly depicted in the era's pornography and literary world, which added to a sexual culture that was heavily weighted on a man's ability to satisfy a female lover, and bring about her orgasm.[14]

The *Mercurius Fumigosus*, one of the earliest London

---

12 Fiona Maddock, pp. 163–4.

13 Jacqueline Murray, p. 201.

14 Sarah Toulalan, *Imagining Sex: Pornography and Bodies in Seventeenth-Century England* (Oxford University Press, 2007), p. 63.

quas-newspapers, published between 1654 and 1655 by John Crouch, gives us a clear depiction of sex leading to a mutual orgasm: 'But come (quoth he) let's swive and melt together, / Nor Bashfulness nor Modesty weighs a feather'.[15] This was a dangerous time to be part of the emerging journalistic scene. Crouch was a Royalist, and had found himself regularly imprisoned by Oliver Cromwell for the debauchery and bawdy nature of the two 'newsbooks' he had set up prior to *Mercurius Fumigosus:* the *Man In The Moon* and *Mercurius Democritus.* He had made his papers affordable to everyone, and throughout London Crouch's 'Mercury Women' stood on the street to sell them. In 1649, this had led to an outstanding battle between a Mrs Strosse, then selling the *Man In The Moon* outside the Salutation Tavern in Holborn, and some of Cromwell's guards. They had attempted to seize both her and the newsbooks, and in retaliation, Mrs Strosse had thrown pepper in their eyes, 'and with their own swords forced them to aske her forgiveness, and down upon their marybones and pledge a health to the King and confusion to their masters; and so honourably dismissed them.'[16]

Only ten years after the *Mercurius Fumigosus* suggested lovers needed to 'melt' together would come Thomas Killigrew's all-female production of *The Parson's Wedding* and depiction of an orgasm as being 'spent'. But although all of the cultural depictions of the orgasm show us its

15 1654, *Mercurius Fumigosus* 24, 8–15 Nov., 105.
16 Harry T. Baker, Early English Journalism, *The Sewanee Review.* vol. 25, no. 4 (Oct. 1917), pp. 396–411, 397.

importance to the sexual life of those living, was it something you were simply expected to know how to do? The simple answer to that, is no. Just as with the sex act itself, there was a large amount of literature available to instruct lovers in how to elicit an orgasm from their partners.

Published in English for the first time in 1709, *An Apology for a Latin Verse in Commendation of Mr Marten's Gonosologium Novum* contained an English translation of the supposed work of sixteenth-century surgeon, Ambroise Paré. Although today the *Apology* is recognised as 'an anthology of erotic and pornographic passages culled from a series of medical and paramedical works', its instructional ability is clear.[17]

> When a husband cometh into his Wife's Chamber, he must entertain her with all kind of dalliance, wanton Behaviour and Allurements to Venery; but if he perceive her to be slow, and more cold, he must cherish, embrace and tickle her, and shall not abruptly... break into the Field of Nature, but rather shall creep in little by little, intermixing more wanton Kisses with wanton Words and Speeches, handling her Secret Parts and Dugs, that she may take fire, and be enflam'd to Venery...[18]

17 George Sebastian Rousseau, Roy Porter, *Sexual Underworlds of the Enlightenment* (Manchester University Press, 1987), p. 48; Thomas Walter Laqueur, *Making Sex: Body and Gender from the Greeks to Freud* (Harvard University Press, 1990), p. 102.
18 *An Apology for a Latin Verse in Commendation of Mr Marten's Gonosologium Novum*, 1709.

Paré's sex advice was so influential among those seeking sexual knowledge that it was reprinted alone in 1860. The only known copy of the anonymous pamphlet *The Art of Begetting Handsome Children* lies glued into a scrapbook of pornography and erotica compiled at some point from the mid-nineteenth century onwards. The scrapbook's origin is unknown, and *The Art*'s uniqueness indicated that it might have been privately circulated, but the importance of its information is clear. Recommending that the knowledge within should be 'given at Marriage instead of gloves', *The Art* clearly modernised not only Paré's words, but their eighteenth-century reprint as well:

When the husband cometh into his wife's chamber, he must entertain her with all kinds of dalliance, wanton behaviour, and allurements to venery. But if he perceive her to be slow, and more cold, he must cherish, embrace and tickle her; and shall not abruptly (the nerves being suddenly distended) break into the field of nature, but rather shall creep in by little and little, intermixing more wanton kisses with wanton words and speeches, mauling her secret parts... so that at length the womb will strive and wax fervent with a desire of casting forth its own seed. When the woman shall perceive the efflux of seed to approach, by reason of the tinkling pleasure, she must advertise her husband thereof that at the very same instant or moment he may also yield forth his seed, that by collision, or meeting of the seeds, conception may be made.[19]

19 *The Art of Begetting Handsome Children*, 1860.

Here we see not only the still consistent idea of women having their own seed, but also the importance of and instruction in how to achieve a shared orgasm. The 'tinkling pleasure', as *The Art* called it, describes those feelings of stimulation and pre-orgasmic pleasure that women can feel as their body starts to experience an orgasm.

One of the joys of writing about the orgasm in the Victorian era is the opportunity to correct a myth about nineteenth-century sexuality that is often repeated and yet absolutely false: the vibrator was *not* invented so that Victorian doctors could rest their exhausted hands from masturbating their female patients to the point of orgasm as a treatment for hysteria. Since 2001, and the publication of Rachel P. Maines's book, *The Technology of Orgasm*, this myth has dominated newspaper articles, factoid lists, chat shows and even academic work. In *The Technology of Orgasm*, Maines claimed to have found evidence that the late Victorian medical fraternity would often treat women who had been diagnosed with hysteria to 'pelvic massage', to cause what she describes as a 'hysterical paroxysm' or orgasm. Maines believed that the popular vibration devices of the time, such as the 'VeeDee Vibrator', took the place of what had been manual labour on the part of the doctors, who were somehow unaware that the reaction they were provoking in their patients, by masturbating them to orgasm, was in any way linked to a sexual act. This has become a popular image for the press and media, resulting in the 2011 comedy *Hysteria*, starring Hugh Dancy and Jonathan Pryce. It is a brilliant film; however, the historical narrative it presents, often regurgitated in our popular culture, is completely false. We can see from the sexual culture, not only of the nineteenth century, but any century, that there was a clear understanding – both cultural and medical – that stimulating female genitals would often lead to an orgasm. On the one hand, stimulation of the female orgasm was acknowledged as a vital part of conception, and sex guides went to great lengths to point that out; on the other, the widespread fears about female masturbation and lesbian women (and also, the lived sex lives of lesbian women themselves where they...*orgasmed*) makes clear that knowledge and understanding of the female orgasm was part of our historical, shared sexual culture. There is literally no way to accept Maines's theory as a commonsense, rational argument when you look at the widespread historical evidence of how sex was seen, discussed and understood in the nineteenth century.

Writing my first book in 2013, I went through as many of Maines's original sources as I could access. Not a single one led to evidence of any physician using a vibrator to masturbate their female patients to a clitoral orgasm. Five years later, in 2018, Hallie Lieberman and Eric Schatzberg published their in-depth investigation into Maines, highlighting her work's influence not only in popular culture, but also on the academic field of nineteenth-century studies and sex history. They found that her arguments were often repeated unchallenged, and the myth of Victorian doctors inducing orgasms in their female patients was widely promoted, yet they too 'could find no evidence that physicians ever used electromechanical vibrators to induce orgasms in female patients as a medical treatment.'[20]

This myth took such a strong hold in our popular psyche because of our need to see the Victorian era as a time of paternalistic power. They are the eternal father figures against whom women must always rebel. And yet, the reality of Victorian sexuality was very different. For the average man and woman on the street, the idea of a sexual pleasure that was shared sat at the heart of their cultural understanding of sex. It is our recent history that has removed the strong and powerful messages surrounding the female orgasm. This lack of interest, alongside the widespread use of pornography and birth control – both important parts of our sexual culture – has laid the groundwork of individual consumption during sex, rather than sex as a shared and united experience. We make orders, demands on our sexual partners, expecting them to fulfil our fantasies often with little acknowledgement of their own. The communication *The Art* makes so clear, the mutual respect and care, can often feel as if it is being attempted by only one partner, or neither. Orgasms, too, have become weirdly fetishised; for men they are objectified in the pornographic image of the 'facial' or 'creampie', while for women pornography has introduced the orgasm as performance, and the Olympic gymnastics of 'squirting'.

---

20 A Failure of Academic Quality Control: *The Technology of Orgasm*, p. 25. This investigation also includes a detailed re-examination of Maines's source material and is a vital resource to anyone studying the history of the orgasm, medical or technological history.

Our non-pornographic sexual culture, too, has created different rules for how we perceive the male and female orgasm on screen. The 1933 Czech film *Extase* (Ecstasy) is often claimed to be the first non-pornographic film to depict a woman orgasming on screen. The actress, an 18-year-old Maria Kiesler, soon to be Hedy Lamarr, abandons her sexless marriage to a much older man, for a passionate love affair with a man she meets riding through the Czech countryside. Their love scene is delicately filmed; lying Maria on the bed, her lover moves slowly to the side as the camera focuses on her face. It is a deeply powerful and erotic scene, building to an intense crescendo marking the moment of orgasm with Kiesler's arching back and the string of pearls around her neck breaking to scatter across the floor. But *Extase* was not the first film to depict female sexuality. Four years earlier the film's director, Gustav Machatý, made *Erotikon* (1929), filming a similar scene with Ita Rina, the Slovenian beauty queen. Since then, the orgasm on screen has become a battleground, often censored if it involves a woman receiving oral sex, whereas a scene with a man receiving the same act is often accepted. Evan Rachel Wood publicly condemned the Motion Picture Association of America for removing a scene of her receiving oral sex in the film *Charlie Countryman* in November 2013. Writing on the social media platform, Twitter, Wood said, 'The scene where the two main characters make "love" was altered because someone felt that seeing a man give a woman oral sex made people "uncomfortable"... It is time for people to GROW UP. Accept that women are sexual beings, accept that some men like pleasuring women. Accept that women don't have to just be fucked and say thank you. We are allowed and entitled to enjoy ourselves.'[21]

Reclaiming the female orgasm seems to be one of the priorities for the twenty-first century. Far from being a central part of our historical sexual culture, today we are far more likely to discuss the female orgasm as something that is 'uncomfortable' to acknowledge, fetishised or ignored. Uncovering the attitudes to the female orgasm in the past may make us wish we could return to those older attitudes, but, disappointingly, there is a serious flaw to the 'two seeds' theory. For some authorities, it removed the ability for women to prove they had been raped. The belief that female pleasure was fundamental to conception, that without an orgasm a woman could not get pregnant, led some to conclude that if a woman conceived a child after rape then she must have enjoyed it; therefore, she could not have been raped. We are able to pinpoint the emergence of this theory to a little-known Latin text, *Fleta seu Commentarius juris Anglicani*, written towards the end of the thirteenth century. In *Fleta*, on the subject of rape and how to prove it in a court of law, the anonymous author claimed, 'If, however, the woman should have conceived at the time alleged in the appeal, it abates, for without a woman's consent she could not conceive.' For

---

21 Evan Rachel Wood, @Evanrachelwood, Twitter, 27 and 28 November 2013; https://www.cosmopolitan.com/entertainment/news/a16748/evan-rachel-wood-awesome/

those men who wanted to escape a charge of rape, if their victim had conceived a child during their attack they now had an airtight defence to use against her. It may, rightly, seem utterly illogical and stupid to us today, and yet there were several cases in the early 1300s where this defence was successfully used. In Cornwall in 1302, Justice Spigurnel, then hearing an accusation of rape, had recorded '…I asked the woman whose child it was, and she answered that it was W's; and I said that it seemed to me that a child could not be begotten unless both were consenting parties'.[22] He was not alone in his judgements. In Kent, in 1313, a woman named Joan attempted to bring a prosecution of rape, only to find the evidence of it, her child, would result in her case being thrown out:

> JUSTICE: You shall answer to the King for that you have ravished the maid Joan, who is thirty years of age and carries a child in her arms.

> The woman was asked who was the father of the child, and she answered that E. was. It was said that this was a wonderful thing, for that a child could not be engendered without the consent of both parties; and so it was said that E. was guilty of naught.[23]

The trauma and rage that this must have caused those

---

22 Corinne J. Saunders, *Rape and Ravishment in the Literature of Medieval England* (Boydell & Brewer, 2001), p. 73.
23 Ibid.

women who were brave enough to attempt a prosecution, only to be told that they must have enjoyed their rape, is unimaginable. Yet not all writers subscribed to the misogyny of this popular theory. Writing in the fifteenth century, Christine de Pizan (1364–1430) earned her living at the French court of King Charles VI. Although a prominent writer of love songs, it is her determined and passionate defence of the lives of women that she is most well known for in *The Book of the City of Ladies* (1405). Eager to disprove the many theories and judgements on women that the early male theorists were making, she argued against those men who believed women would enjoy rape, even if they initially said no.

> Yet it greueth me of that many men say that women wolde be rauyssed, and that it dyspleaseth them not though they saye the contrary with theyr mouthe.[24]

> [I am grieved that men say women want to be raped, and that they do not mind being raped even if they say the opposite.]

What this tells us is that, while some found obscene and grotesque theories surrounding rape and the female orgasm believable, there were educated and clever women determined to prove them wrong. No matter what century we find ourselves in, women were determined to fight for the right to their own bodies and their own lived

---

24 Corinne J. Saunders, *Rape and Ravishment in the Literature of Medieval England* (Boydell & Brewer, 2001), p. 30.

experience. Even in the stories of disappointment and tragedy stand women who were not going to take the violence enacted on their bodies quietly. They wanted justice. They knew what consensual sex was, and what female pleasure should be, and they were not going to let anyone tell them otherwise.

Perhaps one of the most frightening aspects of this bastardisation of the 'two seeds' theory is just how long it has held on for. Dr Vanessa Heggie, historian of medicine, has highlighted that it was still being presented as legal fact at the end of the eighteenth century. As Samuel Farr's *Elements of Medical Jurisprudence* (1798) set out: 'For without an excitation of lust, or the enjoyment of pleasure in the venereal act, no conception can probably take place. So that if an absolute rape were to be perpetrated, it is not likely she would become pregnant.' Farr's text was still being printed in the early 1800s, and we have a frighteningly recent example to show that, for some, these false theories surrounding rape and conception are still believable. During the 1970s, American anti-abortion activists seized on a (subsequently discredited) theory by the surgeon Fred Mecklenburg, that the sexual trauma of rape made conception unlikely. For those in the pro-life movement, 'trauma as birth control' gave them an argument against the rights of rape victims to abortions, strengthening their false beliefs that it was impossible for women who had been raped to become pregnant. In 2004, then American President, George W. Bush, nominated the Republican candidate James Leon Holmes to the Federal Court, much to the shock of many in the Senate. Known as an outspoken anti-abortion activist, Holmes had published an open letter backing a constitutional ban on abortion in 1980, stating, 'concern for rape victims is a red herring because conceptions from rape occur with approximately the same frequency as snowfall in Miami.'[25] In 2012, Todd Akin, then a Republican congressman for Missouri, having served for over a decade and now attempting to become a Senator, gave an interview to a local news station.

> Well you know, people always want to try to make that as one of those things, well how do you, how do you slice this particularly tough sort of ethical question. First of all, from what I understand from doctors, that's really rare. If it's a legitimate rape, the female body has ways to try to shut that whole thing down.

The idea that the female body 'has ways' to try and shut down conception shows that for over 800 years this false theory of how the female body works has held sway. It stretches all the way from a little-known legal text in thirteenth-century England, to the office of the American Senate today. Just as the death penalty for lesbians and gay men was exported to America from Europe in the seventeenth century, so too were the controversial false theories surrounding the female body and rape. What has been so dangerous about this theory is that it was seen as having scientific or medical authority. Rather than basing a

---

25 *Washington Post*, 7 July 2004.

judgement on what our sexual culture – the lived experience of those within it – can tell us about rape and the female body, this paternalistic, medical quackery has refused to give agency to women. It has become the property of those men for whom rape, abortion, and the woman's right to choose are about power, and never equality. It also demonised those women who had experienced an orgasm during their rape, by enforcing an ideology that this indicated that they wilfully enjoyed it, rather than it simply being a biological reaction to physical penetration.

Our orgasms are not a mystery, they are not a secret, they are simply a response to stimuli. Over many centuries human beings have attempted to perfect the art of the human orgasm. We have idolised it, declaring it the most fundamentally important part of sex; and we have demonised it, using it to betray women at times of great vulnerability. Today, popular culture is fixated on 'the orgasm gap', with new research claiming that men orgasm 85 per cent of the time in their sexual encounters, while heterosexual women only orgasm 63 per cent of the time.[26] For those who came before us, these figures would be inconceivable. The female orgasm was not elusive to our ancestors, it was a core tenet of their sexual interactions and perhaps it is high time we discovered their level of commitment to female sexual pleasure ourselves. Because what we can take away from the sexual heritage of our past is the importance of a shared pleasure in sex, and a belief that the experiences of all partners are of equal worth.

---

26 'How to close the female orgasm gap', the *Guardian*, 9 February 2018.

11

Contraception

'I say this is a dirty, filthy book'
—Trial of Annie Besant, 1877

Now that we've exposed all the intricacies of sex, from identity to orgasms, there seems to be one area, above all others, that demonstrates humanity's clear commitment to sex for pleasure's sake, and not reproduction. The history of contraception is probably as old as the history of sex itself – for as long as we have wanted to have sex, men and women alike have wanted to avoid two things: pregnancy and sexually transmitted diseases. For many of us today, birth control is a rite of passage. That first, surreptitious attempt to buy a packet of condoms, or an appointment with your nurse. The mortifying explanations of what to use, and how, delivered by someone in authority – or, at least, someone you consider to be knowledgeable. From older siblings and friends, to parents and teachers, anyone and everyone has advice to give. It can feel as if the eyes of the world are on you, judging your choices both in having sex, and how to do it safely. And whoever you are, whatever age, the public buying of birth control will always feel like an illicit activity. But 'Safe Sex' is hardly a new idea. From the ancient world to the modern, how we have sex *without* risking either pregnancy or infection – the two dangers of any sexual connection – has always been a priority. In fact, if there is any argument that *proves* sex has never actually been about reproduction in our culture, it is the existence of the wealth of ideas, inventions and attitudes that surround birth control.

Culturally, our modern birth control methods often fall into two main types: condoms and chemical birth control, most commonly taken in the form of the contraceptive pill. One of the flaws of these limited options is that contraception is not, and has never been, something that succeeds with a 'one type fixes all' approach. For many men and women, the accepted solutions available today do not cater to their diverse needs. Before this era of mass market pharmaceuticals, contraception was an individual choice, taken from many different options. But our understanding of this history has added to its limitations. Birth control, before the 1960s, is often believed to have been something that few would know about, and something many would disagree with. The battles fought by Marie Stopes and Margaret Sanger in the early half of the twentieth century to bring birth control to the masses are seen as sudden revelations, rather than women-led campaigns that were simply building on an active and long-standing culture that clamoured for birth control knowledge. Contraceptives have been an acknowledged part of our sexual culture for centuries, long before scientists focused their research on the manufacture of synthetic hormones. Their history is far longer and far more interesting than the last 100 years. And its simple existence shows us that sex as a human pleasure, done for its own sake, has always been a very human need – outside of the teachings of the church and state. Before the twentieth century, it was something that was shared between men and women, information passed through books and the oral tradition, spanning from the ancient world to our own. If we wonder what sex is for, birth control shows our capacity for, and pursuit of, pleasure without consequence, has often guided many of our sexual interactions. This, perhaps, is why birth control has been such an issue of social control for many of our state and religious bodies. If you dictate your citizens' attitudes and access to pleasure, you control the very essence of what makes us human. We are, at heart, at our most base level, pleasure seekers, and birth control is the ultimate licence for social rebellion.

The history of birth control in our most recent past has been incredibly dark, seized upon by the eugenics theorists and race scientists of the Holocaust, children of the ideas of selective breeding in humans first purported by Francis Galton in 1869. Throughout the twentieth century birth control has been marketed as a tool of emancipation for women, and yet it has allowed for the forced sterilisation and social control of minority populations, often without the knowledge of society as a whole. For seventy years, the American state of California performed over 20,000 sterilisations on its citizens, often without their knowledge or consent.[1] This state-sanctioned abuse was carried out from 1909 to 1979, and targeted men and women of colour, low income, and those who were disabled or simply labelled as 'undesirable'. In 1927, the US Supreme Court decreed that California, and the many states like it that were passing laws to allow forced sterilisation, had the right 'to segregate and systematically sterilize people to reduce the economic and societal burden they inflicted on the nation'.[2] America's policy for sterilising its citizens was incredibly influential. Writing in 1926, two years after America passed the Immigration Act of 1924 – which banned anyone from Asia and set quotas for those from southern Europe – Adolf Hitler saw the USA as an inspiration: 'There is at present one State where at least feeble attempts of a better conception are perceptible. This is not our German model republic, but the American Union…by principally refusing immigration to elements with poor health, and even simply excluding certain races from naturalisation'.[3] Hitler would have been well aware that those who had driven the Immigration Act into law were using it to force the deportation and sterilisation of those it believed to be 'pollutants' to the American race. Eugenics, as we call this form of social control and abuse, advocated sterilisation under its banner of birth control and contraception. Our

---

1 'The Politics of Female Biology and Reproduction', *The Current*, 6 April 2015.

2 'Op-Ed: It's time for California to compensate its forced-sterilization victims'. *Los Angeles Times*, 5 March 2015.

3 Adolf Hitler, *Mein Kampf*, 1941, New York, p. 699.

understanding of this movement in the 1920s and 1930s has, rightly, been dominated by those who used the limiting of conception to enact a grotesque barbarism on individual members of society. However, eugenics gives us a double-edged sword when trying to understand our historic sexual culture, for while it was responsible for the horrific actions of the Holocaust, prior to the Second World War it was also the only acceptable arena in which discussions advocating birth control could take place.

'Sexual intercourse is a very complex act,' wrote the author Michael Fielding, in 1928. 'It involves certain preliminaries of wooing and accumulation of tension; and it is not ended until the release of tension (called the orgasm)... an ideal contraceptive is one which never interrupts this complex continuous act...to accomplish itself as freely and spontaneously as if no contraceptive at all were being used. It must be, in other words, an unobtrusive contraceptive, one which never creates awareness of its existence. In addition to this, the contraceptive must be easy to apply, inexpensive and harmless ... There is no such perfect contraceptive.'[4] Michael Fielding was the pseudonym of Dr Maurice Newfield (1893–1949), and his work, *Parenthood: Design or Accident? A Manual of Birth Control*, became a popular and well-known guide to contraception throughout the 1930s and the Second World War. The idea that 'there is no such perfect contraceptive' is one many of us still deal with today – women who cannot take the contraceptive pill,

---

4 Michael Fielding, *Parenthood: Design or Accident? A Manual of Birth Control*, 1928, 5th edition, 1946, p. 45.

those who are allergic to, or have phobias of condoms, might agree with Newfield's declaration.

Maurice Newfield is a little-known figure in our history of the birth control movement, and yet within his life lies an understanding of the cultural attitudes towards sex and contraception, rather than the horrors of the scientific and medical communities. Born in 1893, Newfield had volunteered for active service at the outbreak of war in 1914, serving in both the British and Indian armies, contracting sandfly fever, cholera and malaria, and rising to the rank of Major before he was 26. Returning to England in 1919, he studied medicine at King's College and Charing Cross Hospital, qualifying in 1923 at the age of 30. He was a popular doctor for the British literary and intellectual elite, once spending a winter in Portugal as the private physician to H.G. Wells, another eager supporter of birth control. From 1933, he was the editor of the *Eugenics Review*, which bore as its motto 'Eugenics is the science which deals with all influences that improve the inborn qualities of a race; also with those that develop them to the utmost advantage', words uttered by the founding father of the movement, Francis Galton, in 1904.[5] Newfield represents the crossover between the now-controversial field of scientific eugenics, and those ordinary people who did not care about improving the qualities of the British race, but simply wanted to be able to have sex, for pleasure, without the risk of disease or pregnancy. In 1935 he had replaced Edith How-Martyn, a former suffragette, as the director

---

5 The *Eugenics Review*, Maurice Newfield, 1949, Oct. 41 (3) 102.2–116.

of the Birth Control International Information Centre (BCIIC) in London. Its President was Margaret Sanger, founded of what we now call Planned Parenthood. Based at 9 Parliament Mansions, the BCIIC was an active and exciting organisation to be part of. For many of the men and women who worked with Newfield, their interest was not in race science, but in simply alleviating the burden unwanted pregnancies placed on women. The BCIIC not only operated as a place where men and women could seek information, but also ran a network of female pamphleteers, who travelled across the capital and the country distributing leaflets on birth control and information about contraception to those who wanted it. Kitty Marion, militant bomber for the suffragettes and ex-music hall star turned birth control activist, was employed by the BCIIC in the 1930s as a pamphlet distributor. 'The surprise of most women when they heard of prevention instead of abortion, was an eye-opener,' Kitty recalled.[6]

Over all of this presided Newfield. He bridged the world between the medical community and the everyday normality of ordinary citizens' sex lives. It was to Newfield that the philosopher and historian, Bertrand Russell (1872–1970), turned in 1927, a year before the first publication of *Parenthood*, to save his marriage. Both he and his wife, Dora, had taken lovers, and yet Russell desperately wanted to recapture some form of conjugal harmony. 'What I

---

6 Kitty Marion, unpublished autobiography, p. 345., See also Fern Riddell, *Death In Ten Minutes: Kitty Marion. Activist. Arsonist. Suffragette* (Hodder & Stoughton),. 2018.

should like to hope,' he wrote to Dora, 'is that next summer Alice would leave us and you would possibly have had enough of Randall, and we could go away somewhere quietly together and begin again... I am sorry I have been so foolish about you these last years... There is of course no hope unless I can satisfy you sexually; for that, I will see any doctor whom Newfield recommends as soon as I get home.'[7]

The importance Russell placed on Dora's sexual satisfaction should not surprise us; he was a born Victorian, and would have grown up in that sexual culture that still idolised the female orgasm and pleasure in sex. Dora herself, although nearly twenty years his junior, had her own clear convictions and attitudes toward sex. Writing in 1925, at the age of 32, Dora outlined her views on birth control, dismissing the arguments led by the psychiatrists, doctors and clergy of the day that women had little to no sexual desire and sex should only be for reproduction:

> I'm quite aware that certain religious people are set as a moral principle that the purpose of sex-love is not mutual enjoyment but the perpetuation of the race. I am also aware that militarists enjoin on women the necessity of marriage and large families as a patriotic duty. Further, certain doctors have gone out of their way to try to prove that the use of contraceptives is contrary to health and nature...I'm

---

7 Letter to Dora Russell, 20 October 1927, *The Selected Letters of Bertrand Russell: The Public Years, 1914–1970*, vol. 2, Nicholas Griffin (ed.), Psychology Press, 2002, p. 269.

not concerned with the morals of convention or supersti-
tion, but with the morals of experience. It is the experience
of modern women that sex is an instinctive need to them
as it is to men, and further that the prevention of conception brings to them no loss of poise, health, or happiness.[8]

She had married Bertrand Russell in 1921, already pregnant with their first child, John, but it was to their daughter,
Kate, born two years later, that Dora dedicated *Hypatia*,
her answer to *Lysistrata, or Woman's Future and Future
Woman* (1925) by Anthony Ludovici. In *Lysistrata*,
Ludovici predicted that the availability of birth control
and contraceptives in society would lead to their use as
merely 'some kind of controlled and legalised infanticide',
whose sole purpose was for 'an improvement of the race'.[9]
He was, perhaps, capable of the foresight many of those
in the eugenics movement lacked; the fascism of the 1930s
co-opted the international birth control movement, now
irrevocably joined to eugenics by people like Newfield and
Margaret Sanger, using their theory as an argument
surrounding poverty and ill-health to create doctrines that
led to extermination and genocide. Looking back, we might
wonder why the race scientists and racist politicians of
this time were able to take hold of what is now, arguably,
understood to be one of the most important factors for
emancipation and freedom in our culture. Birth control

---

8 Dora Russell, *Hypatia: Or, Woman and Knowledge*, pp. 40–1.
9 Anthony Ludovici, *Lysistrata, or Woman's Future and Future Woman*,
1925, pp.115–16.

was not a new idea in the twentieth century; there was a long heritage of campaigns for access to birth control in England throughout the nineteenth century, and in the century before that, London was known as one of the contraceptive capitals of the world.

So how did eugenics take over the birth control movement? As the field of sexology began to emerge at the start of the twentieth century, science and medicine – the background fields of many of the eugenicists – lent a respectable cloak to those who wanted to discuss sex. However, this desire for respectability, placing sex not in the domain of culture, but of science and medicine, sanitised and stripped out the innate connection of birth control to sexual pleasure. Since the 1930s, science has controlled our understanding of both our bodies and birth control. As our sexual lives became the commonplace property of sexologists and psychiatrists of the twentieth century, the innate physical understanding of our ancestors of sexual pleasure, which existed right up to this era, began to be lost. This dialogue, one of science and sex, has dominated our knowledge and understanding of both the history of sex and of contraception. Because science and medicine are not culture. They may impact on it, but culture builds itself from many things, including medicine, science and politics. For those who were not subscribing to the idea of turning humanity into its own master race, contraception represented individual freedom in a world that was vast and populated, and where democracy demanded you gave your voice to support a single idea.

Dora Russell and Maurice Newfield were linked not

just by Dora's husband's sexual problems; they were both prominent members of the Workers' Birth Control Group (WBCG), where Dora held the position of secretary and Newfield was the Vice-Chairman. At 43 years old, the President of the WBCG, Miss Dorothy Jewson, was no stranger to radical politics. She had been one of the first female MPs elected by Labour in the 1923 General Election, securing almost 20,000 votes and defeating a popular ex-minister to become MP for her home town of Norwich.[10] The daughter of a local coal and timber merchant, she studied classics at Girton College, Cambridge, and became an active member of the early Labour Party. During the First World War she had organised the training and employment of working women, even taking a job as a housemaid 'in the squalid servants quarters of a luxury hotel, so as to study their grievances firsthand'.[11] Not only an ardent protector of the rights of working women, Dorothy was also dedicated to the dissemination of birth control literature among the working classes, especially working mothers, having witnessed the strain and destruction poverty wreaked on those with too many mouths to feed. In 1924, as she was serving her first (and only) year in office, Dorothy founded, alongside Dora Russell and Maurice Newfield, the Workers' Birth Control Group. She served as President of this radical-left policy pressure group from 1924. They outlined their aims and called for members in cheap and widely available pamphlets:

---

10 *International Woman Suffrage News*, Friday, 4 January 1924.
11 Ibid.

The Membership is open to men and women who are members of the Labour Party and its affiliated bodies or the Co-operative Guilds.

Annual Subscription, 1/-

The Objects of the Group are—

(1) To strengthen public opinion among workers as to the importance of Birth Control in any scheme of social progress.
(2) To bring within reach of working people the best and most scientific information on Birth Control.
(3) To bring pressure to bear through Parliament and otherwise on the Ministry of Health to recognise Birth Control as an essential part of Public Health work, and therefore to allow information to be given by the local Health Authorities at the Maternity and Child Welfare Centres. Meanwhile to help the promotion of Birth Control Clinics.

The Group feel that the time has come for a vigorous Propaganda Campaign among the workers of the country who, while their need of Birth Control information is very great, are denied the opportunity afforded to the well-to-do to obtain it.[12]

Dorothy was determined to use her voice and power as an MP to raise the issue of access to birth control, not for eugenics, but simply for cultural reasons, in Parliament,

---

12 https://wdc.contentdm.oclc.org/digital/collection/health/id/1712

and to its new Labour Government. This she did on 30 July 1924, in a combined attack on the Minister of Health, John Wheatley, with one of the WBCG's Vice-Presidents, Ernest Thurtle, Labour MP for Shoreditch:

Mr. THURTLE: Asked the Minister of Health if he will consider the desirability of allowing local authorities to impart to people who wish to obtain it information as to birth control methods without penalising such local authorities by withdrawing their maternity and child welfare grants?

Mr. WHEATLEY: My view is that the institutions provided by local authorities at the cost of public funds should not be used for purposes such as that referred to in the question, which are the subject of controversy, without an express direction from Parliament.

Mr. THURTLE: Is my right hon. friend aware that a very large conference of Labour women passed unanimously a resolution in favour of this course?

Miss JEWSON: Is the Minister aware that many working-class women attending these welfare centres are unfit to bear children and to bring up healthy children, and the doctors know they are unfit, and yet they are unable to give this information, which any upper or middle-class woman can obtain from a private doctor; and will he consider the bearing of this on the question of abortion, which is so terribly on the increase in this country?

> **Mr. WHEATLEY:** I submit that these are all sugges-
> tions and arguments which might be put to Parliament
> if it were considering new directions, but it is only my
> business to carry out the instructions received.[13]

Dorothy's use of the word 'unfit' was not a hint at a eugenic motivation, but rather an economic one. She hated the idea of children born into poverty, and working women losing their livelihoods due to continual pregnancies. Her enemy in legalising the commonsense dissemination of birth control literature was the Labour Minister of Health. John Wheatley had been born in Ireland, his family moved to Scotland when he was a young child, and before his career as an MP he had been a miner, a publican and later ran a printing press that gave a voice to the radical left. He was a member of the Independent Labour Party, and a deeply committed Roman Catholic. His staunch opposition to birth control was on both moral and reli-gious grounds, yet was seen by Dora, Dorothy and those within the soon-to-be-formed WBCG as a betrayal of the workers themselves, a betrayal of class, and a betrayal of hope.[14] Writing of the numerous meetings those members of the WBCG had with Wheatley both before and after the group's creation, Dora recorded the forceful spark that his refusal of support gave them: 'Mr Wheatley

---

13 HC Deb 30 July 1924 vol. 176 c2050 https://api.parliament.uk/historic-hansard/commons/1924/jul/30/birth-control#S5CV0176P0_19240730_HOC_155
14 Sarah Toulalan, *Sexual Politics: Sexuality, Family Planning and the British Left*, p. 52.

had stirred a hornets' nest: all through 1924 we buzzed and stung'.[15]

It was Labour's fear of losing the Roman Catholic vote that saw them refuse to openly back any campaign on birth control, even though it was widely, if not unanimously, supported by the party's female membership. Identifying Labour's 'failure to champion birth control and abortion at the highest levels', the historian Martin Francis writes that 'support for local authority provision of family planning advice contributed to Dorothy Jewson losing her Norwich seat in 1924', a backlash, Francis believes, from her Roman Catholic constituents.[16] Dorothy's bravery was astounding given the fact that only three female Labour candidates were elected to Parliament in 1923. That first unique moment in history, after the 1918 Representation of the People's Act – allowing some women the right to vote if they were aged over 30, and yet, perversely, any woman over the age of 21 the right to stand as an MP – saw only eight women elected to serve among the total 615 MPs. By 1926, the pressure of the WBCG led the editors of *Labour Women* to issue an editorial line stating that questions surrounding access to birth control were 'not party political' and would only 'impede the progress of the Party' itself.[17] So here, in one of the

---

15 Dora Russell, *The Tamarisk Tree*, p. 174.

16 *Labour's First Century*, p. 210.

17 Birth Control and the Labour Party Executive, *Labour Women*, 14/10 (October 1926), p. 151; Stephen Brooke, *Sexual Politics: Sexuality, Family Planning and the British Left*, p. 58.

most crucial moments in our history of birth control and democratic access to it, as well as a well-informed and unashamed sexual education, the Labour Party turned away from supporting women, and *everyone's* access to contraception, out of fear of alienating religiously motivated voters. Their refusal to support the freedom that access to fair and safe birth control creates in society paved the way for darker forces to instead seize on the theories and arguments formed by those early activists, who saw contraception as a way to promote freedom and reduce social strains. It is unsurprising that the prudish, conservative, taboo-ridden sexual culture advocated by the Catholic Church continued to have such a strong hold on our sex lives. This cultural manipulation saw the arrival of a new form of politics, one which promoted workers and women for the first time, yet still subscribing to the old ways, the old narratives, that used the fear of birth control as a way to stay in power, even by subtle and covert means. It still exerts such a control today.

'Poverty,' writes Melinda Gates, 'goes hand in hand with powerless women. If you search for poverty, you will find women without power. If you explore prosperity, you will find women who have power and use it... Quite simply, contraceptives are the greatest life-saving, poverty-ending, women-empowering innovation ever created.'[18] Now most well known for co-founding the world's largest charitable foundation, Melinda Gates joined Microsoft in 1987,

---

18 *Daily Mail* interview, taken from Melinda Gates, *The Moment of Lift: How Empowering Women Changes the World* (Bluebird, 2019).

shortly after graduating with an MBA from Duke University, North Carolina, USA. She worked hard at the company, becoming General Manager of Information Products until the early 1990s, when she left to start a family with her husband, Bill.[19] Acutely aware of the luxury she enjoyed as a stay-at-home mother, who had also worked hard at a committed career, Melinda has advocated for the freedom she has as a modern woman to choose when to start her family, arguing constantly that it was only possible due to her access to and ability to use birth control. In 2012, via the foundation she co-founded with her husband, Melinda Gates committed $560 million to an eight-year project designed to increase women's access to contraception, especially in the developing world.[20] It earned her a sharp reprimand from *L'Osservatore Romano*, the official newspaper of the Holy See, the heart of the Catholic Church, which accused her of being a Catholic who spread 'disinformation' about birth control, directly contradicting the Church's teachings prohibiting the use of contraception among its members. It is laughable to find such attitudes in our modern world, and yet they still exist.

Well over a century before Melinda Gates and the Catholic Church locked horns over the right of women to have access to birth control, in the 1890s the *Christian World* had supported the rights of men and women everywhere to access and use birth control. This is not actually

---

19 Bill Gates, principal founder of Microsoft, married Melinda in 1994.
20 https://catholicherald.co.uk/news/2012/08/01/vatican-newspaper-says-melinda-gates-off-the-mark-on-contraception

as surprising as it may sound. The Victorians cared deeply about birth control, and their ability to access it. Far from being a dirty secret, birth control could be found at the breakfast table. Throughout the 1890s, newspapers such as the *Illustrated Police News* carried multiple advertisements for the sale and distribution of condoms or 'French Remedy'. This was birth control in plain sight, not hidden away on the back pages, but often clearly advertised on the front page itself. 'To MARRIED LADIES,' read the advertisement, at the top of the front page of the *Illustrated Police News*, on 21 January 1899, 'TRY THE FRENCH REMEDY – Not a dangerous drug, but a WONDERFUL SECRET INVENTION. Never Fails. Particulars free to all applicants on receipt of a stamped addressed envelope. Apply to M.D., 217, Graham Road, London, N.E. PLEASE NAME PAPER.' The mysterious 'M.D.' advertised their 'Remedy' in papers across England, throughout the 1890s. Always addressed to 217 Graham Road, their advertisements can be found in (among others) *Pearson's Weekly*, the *Penny Illustrated Paper* and the *Sheffield Weekly Telegraph*. But who was the mysterious M.D.? Our first clue comes from an 1891 advertisement they ran offering a cure for baldness:

Moustachios In A Month, on the smoothest faces, are produced by using HIRSUTINE, the French formula for forcing hair growth…failure impossible… Sent free from observation on receipt of 1s to Madame A. DUMAS, at the Laboratory, 183, Graham Road.[21]

---

21 *Pearson's Weekly*, 13 June 1891.

M.D.... Madame A. Dumas! The change of address was
not due to a move of location, but to the London County
Council renumbering the houses in Graham Road in
1893:

> To Married Ladies. M.D. 217 Graham Road, London N.E
> (late 183) NOTICE: owing to re-numbering of GRAHAM
> ROAD by the London County Council, all appliances for
> particulars of that wonderful Secret Invention known as
> the FRENCH REMEDY should in future be addressed
> as above.[22]

From this address, the mysterious Madame Dumas (M.D.)
ran her business of supplying condoms, cures for baldness,
and many other objects that we would recognise as being
part of the artifice of love and flirtation. 'TO LADIES,'
read an advertisement in the *Sheffield Weekly Telegraph*,
'...English wives should send at once for a Special Treatise
and Price List of Surgical Appliances. Advised by the
Medical Faculty throughout the world.'[23]

Armed with Madame Dumas's address, we turn to the
census records for London in 1891 and 1901. And from
here, a surprising story emerges. Living at 183 Graham
Road, Hackney, in 1891 was 41-year-old author and journalist, George C. Dixon. Born in London, he shared his
home with his young wife, 20-year-old Catherine Dixon,
who was listed as a 'Patient [Patent] Medicine Dealer'.

---

22 *Penny Illustrated Paper*, 28 January 1893.
23 *Sheffield Weekly Telegraph*, 28 January 1893.

Operating on the boundaries of quack medicine, Catherine was peddling tonics and tinctures under the pseudonym of 'Madame Dumas' at a young age. A decade later, the census return lists both her and George (now in his fifties) as 'Surgical Appliance Dealers', and looking after their two nieces, 8-year-old Catherine and 16-year-old Elizabeth Howard, who worked as a housemaid. We have no way of knowing who got who into the condom business – was it George, or was it Catherine – but what is clear is that they were highly successful at it. Their business ran for over a decade, and earned enough for a weekly advertisement campaign in multiple newspapers, as well as looking after two young dependants. More importantly, given that it is Catherine whose background most closely connects to the medical world, what we have here is a young woman involved in the trade and sale of birth control in the 1890s.

And the Dixons were far from alone. The sudden explosion of birth control advertisements across the 1890s, from multiple suppliers, can be directly connected to the public support it gained in 1893 from the *Christian World*. This journal, seen as 'the representative organ of orthodox Christian Protestantism', ran an unexpected editorial arguing for the 'right and duty' of every man and woman to have access to, and use of, birth control.[24] The article caught the eye of long-standing birth control campaigner, Annie Besant (1847–1933), who recorded it in her autobiography:

---

24 Annie Besant, *An Autobiography*, Chapter IX.

And now, in August, 1893, we find the Christian World, the representative organ of orthodox Christian Protestantism, proclaiming the right and the duty of voluntary limitation of the family. In a leading article, after a number of letters had been inserted, it said:—

'The conditions are assuredly wrong which bring one member of the married partnership into a bondage so cruel. It is no less evident that the cause of the bondage in such cases lies in the too rapid multiplication of the family. There was a time when any idea of voluntary limitation was regarded by pious people as interfering with Providence. We are beyond that now, and have become capable of recognising that Providence works through the common sense of individual brains. We limit population just as much by deferring marriage from prudential motives as by any action that may be taken after it ... Apart from certain methods of limitation, the morality of which is gravely questioned by many, there are certain easily-understood physiological laws of the subject, the failure to know and to observe which is inexcusable on the part either of men or women in these circumstances. It is worth noting in this connection that Dr. Billings, in his article in this month's Forum, on the diminishing birth-rate of the United States, gives as one of the reasons the greater diffusion of intelligence, by means of popular and school treatises on physiology, than formerly prevailed.[25]

---

25 Annie Besant, *An Autobiography*, Chapter IX.

Just before its editorial, the *Christian World* had published a letter from the wife of a Methodist minister, detailing the many anxieties 'so typical of the harassed and economically struggling professional family of that time – too many children and too little money, physical exhaustion resulting from too frequent childbearing, lack of opportunity for outside interests or recreation, endless household chores, the selfishness of husbands.'[26] This had been immediately followed by a flood of sympathetic and commiserating letters to the journal, from other wives and interested parties. Birth control was a hot topic, and even the most reserved of moral campaigners wished to educate themselves about it.

Mary Gladstone (1847–1927), daughter of Prime Minister William Gladstone, found herself seeking out an awkward but determined correspondence with her father about birth control in 1888. She had married two years earlier, at the somewhat late age of 38, to the curate of Hawarden, Reverend Harry Drew, who was ten years her junior. Expected to fulfil the duties of a clergyman's wife, Mary found herself constantly required to hold opinions on subjects she had never expected.

Dearest Father: I saw that a book called Ethics of Marriage was sent to you, & I am writing this to ask you to lend it me. You may think it an unfitting book to lend, but perhaps you do not know of the great battle

---

26 Birth Control and the Christian Churches Author(s): Flann Campbell Source: *Population Studies*, vol. 14, no. 2 (Nov. 1960), pp. 131–147, p. 134, the *Christian World*. Editorial entitled 'A Marriage Problem', 15 June 1893.

we of this generation have to fight, on behalf of morality
in marriage. If I did not know that this book deals with
what I am referring to, I should not open the subject at
all, as I think it sad & useless for any one to know of
these horrors unless they are obliged to try & coun-
teract them.

For when one once knows of an evil in our midst, one
is partly responsible for it. I do not wish to speak to
Mama about it, because when I did, she in her innocence, thought that by ignoring it, the evil would cease
to exist. What is called the 'American sin' is now almost
universally practised in the upper classes; one sign of it
easily seen is the Peerage, where you will see that among
those married in the last 15 years, the children of the
large majority are under 5 in number, & it is spreading
even among the clergy, & from them to the poorer
classes. The Church of England Purity Society has been
driven to take up the question, & it was openly dealt
with at Church Congress. As a clergyman's wife, I have
been a good deal consulted, & have found myself almost
alone amongst my friends & contemporaries, in the line
I have taken ... everything that hacks up this line
strengthens this line, is of inestimable value to me, &
therefore this book will be a help to me ... It is almost
impossible to make people see it is a sin against nature
as well as against God. But it is possible to impress them
on the physical side. Dr. Matthews Duncan, Sir Andrew
Clark & Sir James Paget utterly condemn the practice, &
declare the physical consequences to be extremely bad.
But they have little influence. If you quote them, the

answer always is 'They belong to the past generation'.
They cannot judge of the difficulties of this one.

I would not have dreamed of opening the subject,
only that as you are reading the book, you cannot help
becoming aware of the present sad state of things. It is
what frightens me about England's future.[27]

The Ethics of Marriage was an anti-birth control text
that had been published that year by the American
H.S. Pomeroy. It was from here that Mary drew her
understanding of contraception as the 'American sin'; it
was something invasive, a new idea to her that risked the
ruination of England. What this shows us is not the prudish
anti-sex attitude of Victorian England, but the vast, gaping
divide between those who lived in the practical reality of
those, like Mary Gladstone, who did not. Established in
1850, the offices of the American suppliers, Constantine
& Jackson, stood on Wych Street, just off the Strand in
London, 'a few doors west of the Law Courts'. From here,
they distributed their 'Specialities', set out in an illustrated
collection of 'Ladies and Gentlemen's India Rubber
Surgical Appliances'. The catalogue from 1882, now held
by the Wellcome Collection, contains not only a vaginal
douche, 'The Constantine Syphon Enema' (with elas-
tic-gum vaginal tubes), but also a wide variety of condoms,
or, as they called them, 'Letters'.

27 Anne Isba, *Gladstone and Women*, 2006, p. 145; S. Harris, *The Cultural
Work of the Late Nineteenth-Century Hostess: Annie Adams Field and Mary
Gladstone Drews*, p. 70.

The increasing demand of late for 'Letters', owing in a great measure, to the pamphlets issued by various Malthusian societies, renders almost imperatively necessary the following instructions for the proper and safe use of these useful articles: — a 'Letter,' — or 'Capto Anglaise', as it is termed by the French – is a long circular sheath, or tube, closed at one end, worn by the male during coition, for the guarding against either conception or disease…preventing semen from entering the vagina… encompassing the whole male member so that there is no actual contact between the skin surface of the generate organs, and it is, therefore, impossible that the mucous membrane can become contaminated with the syphilitic virus. There are several varieties of Letters: - the French, the American, the Spanish, Dr Hay's Paterson's 'Circular Protectors' and the same eminent Medical Specialist's 'Malthusian Caps'. The 'French Letter' is made of skin; the 'Blue Ties' as one of the qualities is termed, are somewhat corse [*sic*] in texture, but thoroughly effective; the 'Second Whites' are thinner, whilst the 'Best Whites' are the thinnest and finest manufactured. The 'Spanish' also made of very fine skin, are extra strong and large in size, and are curved in shape at the closed extremity. India-Rubber 'Letters' are, as their name indicates, made of that material, and are shaped like the ordinary French ones. When rolled up this variety is termed 'American' and they are then most portable and lasting.

Constantine & Jackson went to great lengths to point out they were the sole agents for the Parisian condom manufacturers Ferimer Freres, who made skin condoms, and the Brooklyn-based rubber condom maker, Dr Henry Paterson. Also contained within their catalogue were handy instructions for how to use them:

> Before using either of the skin descriptions it is necessary that the 'Letter' should be thoroughly moistened both inside and out by immersion in water. It is then turned inside out, nearly to its whole length, like you would a sock, leaving about two inches at the closed end. It is now placed with its inner end over the glans, or upper end, of the male member, and the remainder of the sheath pulled gently down until it covers the whole of the organ. Care should be taken to leave about an half-inch, or so, of its length to overlap at the top, as a receptacle for the male semen. Were this precaution not taken, the wearer would receive a severe shock... Being rolled up, there is a great facility in putting them on, which is done by placing the 'Letter' over the glans and unrolling it on the male member until the whole is covered. No water is required with those made of India-Rubber, but, if the dry lubrication is objected to, a little glycerine or vaseline (both easily carried whenever the occasion may arise) can be rubbed over about a couple of inches of the top or closed end of the 'letter'.

To ensure that their readers were left in no doubt as to the efficiency and quick supply of their condoms, Constantine & Jackson also included a fair and in-exorbitant price list:

Skin Letters

French Blue Ties		...5s
"	2nd Whites	...6s
"	Best Whites (Superfine Quality)	...9s
Spanish, Best Quality		...10s

India Rubber Letters

Long Elastic, French Make		...4s
American, Rolled		...3s
"	Best quality	...6s
Dr Paterson's Circular Protectors		...5s
"	Extra superfine	...8s

For the convenience of those who take the precaution to carry 'Letters' about with them or, at any rate, keep a supply at home, and whose female relatives may be extra inquisitive, we have introduced 'Circular Protectors' done up in the form of cigarettes, with tobacco inserted at each end. These are indistinguishable from real cigarettes and are supplied in handsome pocket cases at 6s per dozen.

As a final line, to aid their authenticity and reputation, the catalogue states, 'Mrs Annie Besant speaks very favourably' of their goods. Eleven years prior to Mary Gladstone's fears of the 'American sin', British society had been gripped by the trial of birth control campaigner, Annie Besant, and her publication of *The Fruits of Philosophy*, in 1877.

Annie Besant is possibly one of the most important female campaigners in our historic sexual culture. Born into the Wood family, in London, in 1847, her father died when Annie was only five years old. This unexpected tragedy plunged the family almost into poverty, and, unable to care for her, Annie's mother sent her to live with a family friend who would provide her with a strong education. This upset so early on in life forged a determined, passionate and independent young woman. She became engaged in the summer of 1866 at the age of 19,

...to the young clergyman I had met at the mission church in the spring, our knowledge of each other being an almost negligible quantity. We were thrown together for a week, the only two young ones in a small party of holiday-makers, and in our walks, rides, and drives we were naturally companions; an hour or two before he left he asked me to marry him, taking my consent for granted as I had allowed him such full companionship—a perfectly fair assumption with girls accustomed to look on all men as possible husbands, but wholly mistaken as regarded myself, whose thoughts were in quite other directions. Startled, and my sensitive pride touched by what seemed to my strict views an assumption that I had been flirting, I hesitated, did not follow my first impulse of refusal, but took refuge in silence; my suitor had to catch his train, and bound me over to silence till he could himself speak to my mother, urging authoritatively that it would be dishonourable of me to break his confidence, and left me—the most upset and distressed little person on the Sussex coast... Looking back over twenty-five years, I feel a profound pity for the girl standing at that critical point of life, so utterly, hopelessly ignorant of all that marriage meant, so filled with impossible dreams, so unfitted for the role of wife....out of sheer weakness and fear of inflicting pain I drifted into an engagement with a man I did not pretend to love.[28]

Frank Besant, the 26-year-old brother of the celebrated author, Walter Besant, was determined that he had found himself a suitable wife. By the autumn, Annie apprehensively agreed to a betrothal, although she attempted to break off the engagement soon after, 'but, on my broaching the subject to my mother, all her pride rose up in revolt. Would I, her daughter, break my word, would I dishonour myself by jilting a man I had pledged myself to marry?' Fourteen months later, Annie was married.

In December, 1867, I sailed out of the safe harbour of my happy and peaceful girlhood on to the wide sea of life, and the waves broke roughly as soon as the bar was crossed. We were an ill-matched pair, my husband and I, from the very outset; he, with very high ideas of a husband's authority and a wife's submission, holding strongly to the 'master-in-my-own-house theory,' thinking much of the details of home arrangements, precise, methodical, easily angered and with difficulty appeased. I, accustomed to freedom, indifferent to home details, impulsive, very hot-tempered, and proud as Lucifer. I had never had a harsh word spoken to me, never been ordered to do anything, had had my way smoothed for my feet, and never a worry had touched me. Harshness roused first incredulous wonder, then a

28 Annie Besant, *An Autobiography.*

storm of indignant tears, and after a time a proud, defiant resistance, cold and hard as iron. The easy-going, sunshiny, enthusiastic girl changed—and changed pretty rapidly— into a grave, proud, reticent woman, burying deep in her own heart all her hopes, her fears, and her disillusions.

One of the greatest disillusionments Annie experienced in those early days of marriage was her introduction to sex. 'Many an unhappy marriage dates from its very beginning,' she remembered, in her autobiography, 'from the terrible shock to a young girl's sensitive modesty and pride, her helpless bewilderment and fear…I had been guarded from all pain, shielded from all anxiety, kept innocent on all questions of sex, [it] was no preparation for married exist-ence, and left me defenceless to face a rude awakening.' Determined to create a life of value, Annie began to write a year into her marriage, first publishing on the lives of saints, and then, more successfully, short stories.

It was the first money I had ever earned, and the pride of the earning was added to the pride of authorship. In my childish delight and practical religion, I went down on my knees and thanked God for sending it to me, and I saw myself earning heaps of golden guineas, and becoming quite a support of the household. Besides, it was 'my very own,' I thought, and a delightful sense of independence came over me. …I did not understand that all a married woman earned by law belonged to her owner, and that she could have nothing that belonged to her of right…it was rather a shock to learn that it was not really mine at all.

Under British law, all Annie earned belonged to Frank, who believed taking his wife's earnings was both his legal and moral right. Two children followed, Arthur and Mabel, while Annie and Frank's relationship worsened. Unable to see any escape, she began to contemplate suicide.

> All my eager, passionate enthusiasm, so attractive to men in a young girl, were doubtless incompatible with 'the solid comfort of a wife,' and I must have been inexpressibly tiring to the Rev. Frank Besant. And, in truth, I ought never to have married, for under the soft, loving, pliable girl there lay hidden, as much unknown to herself as to her surroundings, a woman of strong dominant will, strength that panted for expression and rebelled against restraint, fiery and passionate emotions that were seething under compression.

At her wits' end, in 1873 Annie did the unthinkable; she left Frank, and returned to London.

> My dear mother was heart-broken. ...She recognised far more fully than I did all that a separation from my home meant for me, and the difficulties that would surround a young woman, not yet twenty-six, living alone. She knew how brutally the world judges, and how the mere fact that a woman was young and alone justified any coarseness of slander. Then I did not guess how cruel men and women could be, how venomous their tongues.

An ugly battle was quickly initiated, as Annie's brother fought to gain her legal separation from her husband. Although she does not include the details of the petition, it appears Annie was able to provide evidence of some form of brutality – most likely sexual – that enabled the law to find in her favour: 'when everything was arranged, I found myself guardian of my little daughter, and possessor of a small monthly income sufficient for respectable starvation. With a great price I had obtained my freedom, but—I was free. Home, friends, social position, were the price demanded and paid, and, being free, I wondered what to do with my freedom.'

Within a year of her divorce, and now aged 30, Annie had joined the Free Thinking Society, becoming close friends with social activist, lawyer, and soon-to-be MP, Charles Bradlaugh (1833–1891). Bradlaugh had separated from his wife in 1870 and although we do not know the extent of their relationship, in 1877, 'Bradlaugh and Besant' became the names on everybody's lips.

The year 1877 dawned, and in its early days began a struggle which, ending in victory all along the line, brought with it pain and anguish that I scarcely care to recall. An American physician, Dr. Charles Knowlton...—wrote a pamphlet on the voluntary limitation of the family. It was published somewhere in the Thirties—about 1835, I think—and was sold unchallenged in England as well as in America for some forty years... The book was never challenged till a disreputable Bristol bookseller put some copies on sale to which he added some improper pictures, and he was prosecuted and convicted. The publisher of the National Reformer and of Mr. Bradlaugh's and my books and pamphlets had taken over a stock of Knowlton's pamphlets among other literature he bought, and he was prosecuted and, to our great dismay, pleaded guilty. We at once removed our publishing from his hands, and after careful deliberation we decided to publish the incriminated pamphlet in order to test the right of discussion on the population question, when, with the advice to limit the family, information was given as to how that advice could be followed. We took a little shop, printed the pamphlet, and sent notice to the police that we would commence the sale at a certain day and hour, and ourselves sell the pamphlet, so that no one else might be endangered by our action... We were not blind to the danger to which this defiance of the authorities exposed us, but it was not the danger of failure, with the prison as penalty, that gave us pause. It was the horrible misconceptions that we saw might arise; the odious imputations on honour and purity that would follow. Could we, the teachers of a lofty morality, venture to face a prosecution for publishing what would be technically described as an obscene book, and risk the ruin of our future, dependent as that was on our fair fame? To Mr. Bradlaugh it meant, as he felt, the almost certain destruction of his Parliamentary position, the forging by his own hands of a weapon that in the hands of his foes would be well-nigh fatal. To me it meant the loss of the pure reputation I prized, the good name I had guarded—scandal the most terrible a woman could face.

Born in Massachusetts, Dr Charles Knowlton was a
well-respected family clinician. Responding to what he
discovered to be a local need for sex education, in 1832
he wrote and privately distributed *Fruits of Philosophy: or
The Private Companion of Young Married People*, a helpful
guide to all aspects of sex – including birth control – for
his patients. Unsurprisingly the book was incredibly
popular, arriving in Britain within the next two years,
where it was continually published with a yearly circulation
of 700 until the stupidity of the Bristol printer.[29] Having
now fallen foul of the UK's Obscenity Act, Knowlton's
practical guide to sex and birth control had been banned.
This was not something Annie would allow. With
Bradlaugh's help, she went on the attack, determined to
'publish and be damned' or, at least, publish and be
arrested, and fight for *Fruits of Philosophy* in court.

The day before the pamphlet was put on sale we ourselves
delivered copies to the Chief Clerk of the Magistrates at
Guildhall, to the officer in charge at the City Police Office
in Old Jewry, and to the Solicitor for the City of London.
With each pamphlet was a notice that we would attend
and sell the book from 4 to 5 p.m. on the following day,
Saturday, March 24th. This we accordingly did, and in
order to save trouble we offered to attend daily at the

---

29 Charles Knowlton, *Fruits of Philosophy: or The Private Companion of
Young Married People*, USA, 1832. (London, Third Edition, J. Watson,
1841) Rosalind Mitchison, *British Population Change since 1860*, London,
1977, p.28, and Annie Besant, *An Autobiography*, 1893, Chap. IX 'The
Knowlton Pamphlet'.

shop from 10 to 11 a.m. to facilitate our arrest, should
the authorities determine to prosecute. The offer was
readily accepted, and after some little delay—during which
a deputation from the Christian Evidence Society waited
upon Mr. Cross to urge the Tory Government to prosecute us—warrants were issued against us and we were
arrested on April 6th. Letters of approval and encourage-
ment came from the most diverse quarters, including
among their writers General Garibaldi, the well-known
economist, Yves Guyot, the great French constitutional
lawyer, Emile Acollas, together with letters literally by the
hundred from poor men and women thanking and blessing
us for the stand taken. Noticeable were the numbers of
letters from clergymen's wives, and wives of ministers of
all denominations... After our arrest we were taken to the
police-station in Bridewell Place, and thence to the
Guildhall, where Alderman Figgins was sitting, before
whom we duly appeared, while in the back of the court
waited what an official described as 'a regular waggon-
load of bail.' We were quickly released, the preliminary
investigation being fixed for ten days later—April 17th.

The trial began on the 18th of June, and it was Annie
who made the arguments for the defence. For three days,
she stood before the court, defending the right to distribute
information about birth control to the masses. In one
stunning paragraph she offered an astounding critique of
Darwin and Francis Galton, and against the theories of
natural selection that so corrupted the later eugenics
movement:

Among the brutes the weaker are driven to the wall, the diseased fall out in the race of life, and the old brutes, when feeble or sickly, are killed. We all know and have read of instances in which wounded stags have been set upon by their companions and killed. If that were the case amongst men — if the drunken and the improvident were over-ridden in the struggle for existence by those who were careful and temperate — the result might be to improve those who survived, and Mr. Darwin's position might be true. If men insisted that those who were sickly should be allowed to die without help of medicine or of science — if those who were weak were put upon one side and crushed — if those who were old and useless were killed — if those who were not capable of providing food for themselves were allowed to starve, — if all that were done, the struggle for existence among men would be as real as it is among brutes, and would doubtless result in the production of a higher race of men; but are you willing to do that, or to allow it to be done? If not, you are taking away the natural checks instead of keeping them; and instead of improving the race of human beings in the midst of a struggle for existence, you are perpetuating that which tends to the deterioration of the race.[30]

Although they were found guilty, the court made clear that they believed their publication was not done 'to

30 Text from Annie Besant's trial at the High Court 1877. Original Source: https://archive.org/stream/queenvcharlesbra00brad/queenvcharlesbra00 brad_djvu.txt

corrupt the morals' of the British public, and Bradlaugh launched an immediate appeal, which was successfully won a year later. 'Mr. Bradlaugh carried the war into the enemy's country,' recalled Annie, '…and commenced an action against the police for the recovery of some pamphlets they had seized; he carried the action to a successful issue, recovered the pamphlets, bore them off in triumph, and we sold them all with an inscription across them, "Recovered from the police."' The success and attention of the trial had brought the demand for *Fruits of Philosophy* to an almost feverish height, its circulation was now over 125,000. 'Victory was finally won all along the line. Not only did we, as related, recover all our seized pamphlets, and continue the sale till all prosecution and threat of prosecution were definitely surrendered… Since that time not a copy has been sold without my knowledge or permission…the pamphlet had received a very complete legal vindication.'

Annie had secured the right of everyone in England to access and enjoy sexual knowledge, and more importantly, knowledge of how to have safe sex. But her joy was short-lived. In 1875, Frank had attempted to kidnap their daughter, Mabel, while she had visited him for the summer, and Annie had had to resort to legal action to have her returned. In January 1878, Frank made an application to the High Court of Chancery to deprive Annie of custody of Mabel, but the petition was not filed till the following April. His petition read:

> The said Annie Besant is, by addresses, lectures, and writings, endeavouring to propagate the principles of Atheism, and has published a book entitled 'The Gospel of Atheism.' She has also associated herself with an infidel lecturer and author named Charles Bradlaugh in giving lectures and in publishing books and pamphlets, whereby the truth of the Christian religion is impeached, and disbelief in all religion inculcated... It further alleged against me the publication of the Knowlton pamphlet.

This proved too much for the court, which judged Annie to be an improper guardian for her daughter, and removed Mabel from her care. It is hard to imagine what the pain of this private loss, coming so soon after a public victory, must have been like for Annie. But her grief was not to last long – within two years Mabel turned 18 and immediately returned to her mother. By 1893, Annie felt all her battles had been justified, 'we find the Christian World, the representative organ of orthodox Christian Protestantism, proclaiming the right and the duty of voluntary limitation of the family... Thus has opinion changed in sixteen years, and all the obloquy poured on us is seen to have been the outcome of ignorance and bigotry.'[31] She published her autobiography, and, far from retiring into obscurity, continued to be a passionate campaigner across the world. Yet even the remarkable Annie Besant was not the first Englishwoman to determinedly bring contraception to the masses.

---

31 Annie Besant, *An Autobiography*, Chapter IX.

The honour of being the first sex shop in London most likely belongs to The Green Canister, situated on Half Moon Street (now Bedford Street), in Covent Garden.[32] Run by the exceptional 'Mrs Phillips', The Green Canister sold both contraception and sex aids. One contemporary authority recorded that 'her shop is unique in the world. It consists of wares which are never sold publicly, which indeed can hardly be found at all in ordinary towns, and are only made and used in London and Paris. In Paris they are sold secretly in fancy shops; in London this woman has a shop near Leicester Square with them as her only wares'.[33]

Teresia Constantia Phillips (1709–1765) was one of the eighteenth century's most famous women. God-daughter of the Duchess of Bolton, she was beautiful, educated and a bigamist. In 1732 she opened The Green Canister, which specialised in 'Bandruches Superfines', her handmade condoms of sheep's or goat's gut, delicately fashioned on glass moulds, eight inches long, and either pickled or scented. Those of her best quality were 'secured round the neck with ribbon, which could be in regimental colours'; while for the gentleman determined to avoid either pregnancy or disease at all costs, her 'Superfine Double' were made from 'two superimposed and gummed caecums, the blind end of the sheep's bigger gut'.[34] Her

---

32 Dan Cruickshank, *The Secret History of Georgian London: How the Wages of Sin Shaped the Capital* (Windmill Books, 2010), p. 169.

33 Ivan Bloch, p. 309–10.

34 Lucy Inglis, *Georgian London*; Richard Gordon, *The Alarming History of Medicine*, p.p 144–5.

designs were so well-known that they feature, strewn across the floor, in the third plate of Hogarth's *Rake's Progress* of 1736. Scandalising high society with her memoirs, *An Apology for the Conduct of Mrs T.C. Phillips*, published in eighteen different parts in 1748–9, Mrs Phillips left England for Jamaica in 1751. Here, her life of glorious renown continued, and she became the only woman to hold a governmental post, 'Mistress of the Revels', given to her by the Governor Henry Moore.[35]

Looking back at this history of contraception you might be forgiven for thinking that we have become more prudish in the wake of the scientific breakthrough of the pill, rather than less. The lives of the women who marketed and promoted birth control in the eighteenth and nineteenth centuries seem far more understanding of the concept of pleasure and its importance to sex. The twentieth century, and today, only appear to be a desperate fight for the reclamation of those attitudes towards both birth control and sex itself. Contraception gives us permission to seek pleasure in our sexual lives. It is a blatant, overt admission that we desire an intimate physical connection with another human being, without the risk of pregnancy. This simple action defies the teachings of God, the Church, and any other moral authorities, acknowledging a very human need to lose ourselves in sensation, in the flesh of another human being.

---

35 Trevor Burnard and John Garrigus, *The Plantation Machine: Atlantic Capitalism in French Saint-Domingue and British Jamaica* (University of Pennsylvania Press, 2018), p. 74.

12

Sex Work

'The most interesting class of womanhood
is woman at her lowest degradation'.[1]
—William Acton, 1860

On 17 November 1982, fifty women from the English
Collective of Prostitutes (ECP) occupied the Holy Church
in King's Cross for twelve days. They were protesting
against police violence and racism, and a legal state that
often took away the children of women arrested for solici-
ting. Their demands were as follows:

1. *An end to illegal arrests of prostitutes.*
2. *An end to police threats, blackmail, harassment and racism.*
3. *Hands off our children – we don't want our kids in care.*
4. *An end to arrest of boyfriends, husbands, sons.*
5. *Arrest rapists and pimps instead.*
6. *Immediate protection, welfare, [and] housing for women who*
   want to get off the game.

---

1 'The Literature of the Social Evil', *Saturday Review*, 6 October 1860.

They were supported by the Labour MP Tony Benn, the only MP to publicly declare sex work as a form of industry that needed regulation and protection of its workers, just like every other industry operating in the UK. Little has changed for those in the sex industry since the ECP's protests. Sex work is still viewed by the majority of those in society as a dangerous and vulgar profession, and there is a constant and disappointing refusal to listen to those within it. Public women, from history to today, are supposed to be seen and not heard.

A history of sex work is complicated. Not morally, but because...well, where do we begin? There is a reason why we refer to it as the 'world's oldest profession' – the selling of sex, the trading of the commodity of one person's body for another's pleasure, is something that has existed for a very, very long time. In Dijon, in France, during the fifteenth century prostitution was a licensed trade. Most of the towns across the region ran public brothels, and some were even funded or administered by the town council. The women who made their living from sex were licensed as *'femmes publique'* – public women – a definition that started the long-held cultural assumption that believes women in public have given up their sexual agency. They are acceptable targets for male lust and rage, and invite sexual harassment by their audacity to exist in the world alone. In our modern world, sex work has become a battleground for feminism. On one side, we have those who believe that sex work is an abuse of women and should be criminalised, and on the other, we have those who believe it should not. For those against, the threats and horrors of sex-trafficking, child and drug abuse, coercion and stigmatisation make compelling cases against the sex industry; but for those who operate within it, the right to earn their money with their bodies, to be safe and protected within their industry, and to live in a world without the shaming of sexual culture is equally, if not more, justified. The voices of those who work in the sex industry, the majority of whom are female, are often ignored or silenced by the moral majority who judge sex work to be a degrading and damaging industry for its practitioners. The desire to fit sex work into a moral code, rather than a sexual culture – which is what it has always been part of – often exposes the base prudery of those who desire to 'save' sex workers, and their own inhibited attitudes to sex.

On 1 January 1979, Carol Leigh created the term 'sex work' to describe what is commonly referred to as prostitution, to reflect the agency of those who choose to work within it. Her definition came at a time of global activism by sex workers, especially in the Western world. Throughout the 1970s, across Europe and America, women-led collectives were set up to protect the rights of those working in the sex industry. Beginning in France in 1972, collectives and quasi-unions were founded in Sweden, Italy and England, while COYOTE (Call Off Your Old Tired Ethics) began to set up branches across America. These women were seeking protections for themselves and others at a time when feminism had made prostitution itself a target. But the regulation of prostitution is hardly new; it has occurred at various moments across our history, and every time has showcased the worst of our sexual culture. Because for some reason, consent, whether in our private sexual lives, or the public nature of sex work, is a concept that many seem to struggle with. The relationship between men, women, sex and sex work has created problems for our sexual culture. It has divided women into two categories – whore or virgin, good or bad, chaste or immoral. This binary view of womanhood has changed little over the centuries. And we have built it, in totality, on our view of sex work. This is a flawed system, not only because our cultural reaction to sex work has become intensely prudish in the last two centuries; but also because, prior to that, sex, and all that went with it – semen, pleasure, the orgasm – was viewed by our laws and religious codes as a form of property. Prostitution was justified as a necessary 'evil', an outlet for men's sexual lusts to stop them from attacking the pure, virginal women who would become their brides. The idea that men are unable to control their sexual natures has formed in relatively modern history, and yet is a core part of our modern sexuality. We use it to excuse street harassment, the idea that 'boys will be boys', and that sexual aggression is a sign of virility. For sex workers, their existence has been advocated, in part, by those who believe access to sex workers will reduce the danger of men raping 'ordinary women'. Edward William Latimer, a 61-year-old serial sex offender in Western Australia, was granted freedom from prison in the summer of 2019 so that he could visit sex workers. The Supreme Court Justice who passed this judgment, Anthony Derrick, said, 'Access to sex workers will not of itself resolve the issue of the respondent's ability to manage his sexual urges ... [but] the option for the respondent to engage in regular, albeit infrequent, sexual contact should serve as an additional protective factor.'[2] There is little in the Judge's decision that protects the sex workers he has now given a serial rapist access to from his attacks, which highlights a common cultural problem – the mistaken belief that sex workers cannot be raped. It also suggests that granting access to sex workers to those men who believe their right to sex does not require the consent of another human being will limit their offending behaviour. History, as ever, tells us this is not true. In fifteenth-century Dijon, where prostitution was regulated and controlled, over 125 rape cases were brought before the Dijon magistrates between 1436 and 1486. These were not the rapes of sex workers, but a statistical occurrence of one or two rapes per month, usually of unmarried, single or widowed women, as well as wives whose husbands were not at home. The cases normally described women who were abducted from their homes, dragged out into the town and gang raped by local young men.[3] Access to legitimate sex workers did little to limit this form of sexual violence from the townsmen, and was rarely punished. In Venice, which also had a thriving sex work community, the only rapes that were taken seriously were those where a man of lower status had raped a woman or child who belonged to a wealthier or more privileged social stratum.

---

2 https://www.theguardian.com/australia-news/2019/jul/09/sex-offender-released-from-wa-prison-and-given-conditional-access-to-prostitutes
3 Shani D'Cruze (1992), 'Approaching the history of rape and sexual violence: notes towards research', *Women's History Review*, 1:3, 377–397, DOI: 10.1080/09612029300200016, p. 381.

In England, across the sixteenth and seventeenth centuries, Nazife Bashar uncovered 274 cases of rape brought before the English Assize records of the home counties between 1558 and 1700.[4] Only forty-five of these cases, in just over 150 years, resulted in a guilty conviction. So the legitimisation of sex work does little to stop those men who believe rape is an acceptable part of their sexual culture, and sex workers who face this graphic form of sexual violence are often disbelieved and dismissed.

The British relationship to the sex trade has not always been one of such intense prudery. In London, the sex trade flourished wherever there was pleasure, most often around Covent Garden and alongside the theatres, pubs and bawdy houses of sixteenth- and seventeenth-century England. *The Wandering Whore*, a guide to the various 'Crafty Bawds, Common Whores, Wanderers' and 'Night-Walkers' found in the 1660s, ran to five different editions. Set out as a conversation on life in the sex industry in London, each edition moved the dialogue further along, and contained detailed instructions for the sex-seekers of London. 'If you fancy a variety of faces,' invited the second edition, 'the Cherry-garden, Hatton-wall, Bloomsbury, Drury Lane, Dog and Bitch Yard, Fleet-lane, Turn-ball-street, Rosemary Lane, Long Acre, Lincoln-in-fields, Spittle-fields, Wheeler-street, Mobb-lane, Smock-ally, the Row at the six Windmills, Petticoat-lane, Dunnings-ally, Lorg-ally, More-fields, Cheapside, Cornhill, Leaden-hall-street, &c.' were the

---

4 N. Bashar, 'Rape in England between 1550 and 1700', in London Feminist History Group, *The Sexual Dynamics of History*, pp. 34–5.

places to go. 'Where when you meet with a complete lusty Girl to your mind, say with the witty wanton Poet: "Let me thy naked parts feel without light/And with sweet sports protract the pleasing night".'[5] Fifty-three different women were listed under the directory of 'Common Whores', including Betty Cox, Green Moll, Mrs Diamond and Mrs Warren, while the cost of buying a woman's virginity was set at £5. In the last half of the eighteenth century, a new guide to all the various women in London who either sold sex, or had sold sex, was regularly published to inform its readers of a veritable 'Who's Who' of the London sex trade. *Harris's List of Covent Garden Ladies* was first published in 1757, a slim and delicate pocketbook that published an annual list of nearly 200 of London's sex workers until 1795. 'The lovely nymphs' contained within it 'share in their bounty, have hearts as large, as universal as their desires; and the whole race of mankind are the objects of their warm regards. Like true citizens of life, they scatter blessings with unrestrained munificence'.[6] What followed was a truly sensational breakdown of attributes, cost, addresses as well as the man you would answer to if you mistreated one of Harris's Ladies or refused to pay her. 'Miss N—wc—mb, at Mrs. Adams', King's Place' was a favourite of the list's 1788 edition:

Restraints of reason, ties of blood, marriage vows and prudential maxims, are all weak barriers, when Miss

---

5 *The Wandering Whore*, 1660, p. 9.
6 *Harris's List*, 1788, p. vii.

N—wc—mb appears, opens her arms, and excites to pleasure. Her teeth invite the burning kiss, her stature tall, but quite genteel. Her complexion pleases the eye; and her soft plump body rebounds from the close embrace, and demands repeated pressures. Her yielding limbs, though beautiful when together, are still more ravishing when separated. And when properly played between them, we may cry out with the poet Addison, 'I'm lost in extacy. How shall I speak the transports of my soul? I am so bless'd I fear 'tis all a dream.' Other beauties indeed, may give equal joys, but few like Miss N—b can continue them; others may forge chains, and put them on their lovers, but few like her can rivet them. Her great prudence, uncommon with the sisterhood, keep her admirers attached to her; and none can quit her but with regret. From strangers (who must be gentlemen) she expects a genteel compliment; but once acquainted, she abates in her demands, in proportion as she increases in her attachment. She has fine dark eyes, with light brown hair, and is about nineteen years of age. Has not been in the trade, more than a twelvemonth.[7]

The descriptions of the list range from fawning dedications to clearly delighted innuendo 'Miss Charl—tte C—ll—ns, Oxford Buildings, Oxford Street, was 'said to have not only a delicate hand at stroking, but great skill in the use of the churn, soon making love's butter from nature's cream.'[8] This was the same era as Mrs Philips, and just as

---

7 *Harris's List*, 1788, pp. 47–8.
8 Ibid., p. 53.

Anne Lister was about to begin writing her diary. This was a ribald, rowdy England, a place where sex was celebrated, accepted and proclaimed. Sex workers were celebrated, they were celebrities and idolised on the stage and in their famous memoirs. The public women were unashamed of their place in the limelight, and our sexual culture acknowledged their existence without attempting to remove it.

So what happened? In 1860, the *Saturday Review* remarked that society seemed 'to have arrived' at a moment when the 'most interesting' image of womanhood was one primarily concerned with its 'degradation'.[9] This is echoed by modern historian Kirsten Pullen, who argues that, although multi-defined, in all histories the identity of the prostitute 'structures understandings of female sexuality and is the extreme to which all women are compared'.[10] The *Saturday Review*'s acknowledgement of the extent to which prostitution – and, therefore, womanhood and its relationship to sex – had become a focus for Victorian society is not surprising. The 1860s heralded governmental attempts to control and regulate the sex industry under the Contagious Diseases Acts of 1864, 1866 and 1869, and introduced registers of prostitutes, while also forcing internal examinations and the treatment of sexually transmitted diseases on the women concerned.

The Contagious Diseases Acts allowed for any woman to be forcibly examined for symptoms of venereal disease if a

---

9 Lynda Nead, *Myths of Sexuality: Representations of Women in Victorian Britain* (Oxford, 1988), p. 1.

10 K. Pullen, *Actresses and Whores: On Stage and Society* (Cambridge, 2005), p. 5.

policeman suspected that she might be carrying the disease. Often, this was targeted at known prostitutes, but all that was needed for the examination to be carried out was the officer's belief that the woman 'might' be infected, whether or not she was known locally as a prostitute. Little or no evidence was provided, other than the policeman's word. The woman was then ordered to appear before a magistrate, who would decide whether or not the examination should take place; and, if he decided to allow it, he would order her to be examined by a doctor. If she was found to have any symptoms of the disease, or the doctor suspected she might show them later, the woman was immediately removed to a lock hospital, or locked ward. Here she would remain for three to nine months, with little or no contact with the world outside. Lock hospitals were exactly as their name suggests – wards specifically for the treatment of sexual diseases, from which there was no escape.

When the Acts were first enforced they were passed with little opposition, applying only to port and barracks towns, and heavily couched in the language of social improvement. It was for the benefit of the health of the population, protection against the social evil of prostitution, and, given that many of the women targeted were working class, little interest was taken in their welfare. But by 1869, when the boundaries of the Acts were extended to the civil population and stories of horrifying episodes – in which women seemed just to disappear from the streets – soon began to be published in the press, the terrifying realities of life under the Contagious Diseases Acts became apparent.

There was an immediate response: the Ladies National

Association for The Repeal of the Contagious Diseases Acts was founded, launching a frank and honest discussion on the relationship between men and women and the sex industry at its meetings, in pamphlets, and in the national press. 'An Englishwoman' wrote of the need and motivations of the Ladies National Association (LNA) in the *London Daily News*, published in 1869:

> Permit me to explain, in a brief but careful way, what the danger is in which we find our country and everybody in it involved, through the ignorance and carelessness of whole classes of our countrymen, whose duty it is to know better, the apathy of legislators who have permitted the destruction of our most distinctive liberties before their eyes, and the gross prejudices and coarse habits of thought of professional men who have been treated as oracles on a subject on which they are proved mistaken at every turn.[11]

The tone of her writing expresses the violent anger many women felt at the loss of liberties and double standards to which they were subjected under the Acts. This was not an attack on a class or profession of women; this was an attack on womankind. The LNA began a long and loud campaign to expose the truth of the Acts, from their basis in poor statistics to the punishment of women in what was – for the Victorians – a very male sin, that of physical sexual lust. For twenty years, one of the Ladies National Association

---

11 'The Contagious Diseases Acts', *London Daily News*, 28 December 1869.

founding members, Josephine Butler, was at the forefront of the campaign for the repeal of the Acts. She was one of the earliest female social investigators, heading into the towns and ports where the Acts were enforced in order to bring back the stories of the women who suffered under them. They were published in the *Shield*, as well as in the national press, and exposed not only the women's experiences, but also those of the common soldiers and naval men. Working-class men and women who did not seek a legal marriage, but who often lived in committed, lifelong, common-law marriages, were also targeted by the Acts' enforcers. Although they lived what society would have seen as 'respectable' lives, the lack of a legal marriage certificate meant that they were punished and degraded under the Acts, whereby enforcers could seize the women and remove them for months at a time. The risk of this happening to a woman who was not a prostitute was increased with the creation of a task force of special constables, sent down from London to oversee and enforce the Acts on the local populace. Josephine took her campaign to international levels, travelling across Europe to build international pressure on a government that refused to admit the Acts were the most 'conspicuous disgrace of our time'. After many years of vilification, in 1886 the repeal campaign was finally successful, owing much, if not all, to Josephine's tenacity and dedication. She was an exceptional woman, uniting women in the fight for their own freedoms and liberties long before the suffragette movement even began.

The creation of the Acts had brought the discussion of the sex act itself directly into the public gaze in ways that deeply challenged the constructed Victorian sensibilities of social reformers. It clearly demonstrated that sex outside of marriage was occurring, and that women – believed to be of a certain class – were actively engaging in it. Now, a woman's sexuality was to be defined by fear and immorality. For women of the middle and upper classes, they were protected from identification with these lower class 'markers' or masks. Targeting the working-class women also helped to create a divide between them and those in a position to help them – women in the upper and middle classes. Working-class women could be portrayed as diseased seducers – the maid, the nanny, the women of the street. The danger to your husband was not just out in the public world, but within your own home. The Acts also helped to create a rhetoric that saw the free enjoyment of sex – one that was not restricted to seeing it merely as a form of procreation – as something bad, associated with disease and sexual immorality. In the public world, sex for its own sake was now inherently linked to prostitution. Middle- and upper-class women claimed their respectability through sexual purity, and so suddenly sexual knowledge became unfashionable, immoral, and to be avoided.[12] And yet, it was the middle-class social reformers who went to great lengths to prove that the *working classes* were the ones with a limited understanding of the consequences of the sex act – arguing that while they were

---

12 There was also an instant backlash to horrors enforced by the Acts: Hamilton, Margaret, 'Opposition to the Contagious Diseases Acts, 1864–1886', *Albion*, 10.01 (1978), 14–27; Waldron, Jeremy, 'Mill on Liberty and on the Contagious Diseases Acts' (Cambridge, 2007), 19–20.

widely engaging in it, they did not comprehend the consequences of increased poverty and children.

Historians have struggled to separate female sexual
agency from perceptions of female victimhood in the
nineteenth century. Both our scholarship and the source
material from which it is drawn suffer from a fixation on
female victimhood. There is an inherent bias brought about
by the cultural construction of a working woman as prostitute, which inhibits our understanding of the reality of
sexual attitudes in the nineteenth century. Working-class
women were, and still are, identified as the main source
of illicit or immoral sex in Victorian society, 'the unskilled
daughters of the unskilled classes'.[13] This phrase, coined
by Dr Abraham Flexner in 1915, was repeated by Judith
Walkowitz in her important work, *Prostitution and Victorian
Society: Women, Class, and the State* (1982), and has become
so influential that it has been repeated across many texts,
even occasionally repurposed as a direct quote from historians themselves. Flexner had based his conclusion on
G.P. Merrick's 1890 text, *Work Among the Fallen*, which
identified 11,413 women engaged in prostitution who had
been incarcerated in Millbank Prison. Of this number,
'10,646 were the daughters of working men, or the equivalent; 544, of small shop-keepers; 128, of professional men;
82, of small officials; 13, of gentlemen'.[14] This 'class legislation even in harlotism' was derided in a letter to *Vox*

---

13 A. Flexner, *Prostitution in Europe* (New York, 1915), p. 62.
14 Ibid., p. 63; G.P. Merrick, *Work Among the Fallen, As Seen in The Prison
Cells* (London, 1890), pp. 23–4.

Populi, in 1871, printed by Josephine Butler as part of her campaign to repeal the Contagious Diseases Acts.

During the nineteenth century, 'moral reformers were unable to construct a cultural model that would make a poor woman's move into prostitution comprehensible within her social and cultural world'.[15] The works on the subject of prostitution in this period, in keeping with the emerging works advocating for social anti-sensualism, established the myth that it was a morally downward path, 'a narrative involving diseases, destitution and early death'; and this identity has been continually reproduced without examination by modern historians, who rely on an image of the 'fallen woman' taken from the constructions of nineteenth-century art and literature.[16]

Looking at the work of William Tait, Ralph Wardlaw, William Logan, William Bevan, Michael Ryan and James Talbot, the early attempts of nineteenth-century reformers struggled to understand prostitution in urban areas.[17] The

---

15 L. Mahood, *The Magdalenes: Prostitution in the Nineteenth Century* (London, 2013), p. 69.

16 Ibid., p. 1.

17 W. Tait, *Magdalenism: An Inquiry into the Extent, Causes and Consequences of Prostitution* (Edinburgh, 1840); R. Wardlaw, *Lectures on Female Prostitution: its Nature, Extent, Effects, Guilt, Causes and Remedy* (Glasgow, 1842); W. Logan, *An Exposure from Personal Observation of Female Prostitution in London, Leeds, and Rochdale, and Especially in the City of Glasgow; with Remarks on the Cause, Extent, Results and Remedy of the Evil* (Glasgow, 1843); W. Bevan, *Prostitution in the Borough of Liverpool* (Liverpool, 1843); M. Ryan, *Prostitution in London, With a Comparative View of That of Paris and New York* (London, 1839); J.B. Talbot, *The Miseries of Prostitution* (London, 1844).

identification of 'the life of a public strumpet' took many forms and early investigators sought to define the many 'different classes' and forms that prostitution took.[18] A common theme of these works is a significant shift in the tone used to discuss the women, which had, by the middle of the nineteenth century, moved away from earlier depictions of seduction as the root cause of prostitution, to the immoral choice and agency of the women in Victorian society to engage with this industry freely. Social reformers uncovered, to their surprise, that prostitution in urban areas was 'a trade to which girls served an apprenticeship in the same way they would have done when learning millinery… they grew up familiar with the language, the manners, and the "morale" of the brothel…and walked the streets of their own account'.[19] By 1870, William Acton's *Prostitution, Considered in its Moral, Social and Sanitary Aspects in London and Other Large Cities and Garrison Towns with Proposals for the Control and Prevention of its Attendant Evils* described the prostitutes of an East End music hall as the epitome of modern single women, independent from men and enjoying the freedom their economy gave. His fear of this woman who was 'free to exercise her calling, and to receive the profits of it for herself' was because of her proximity and interaction with the married women who inhabited public spaces in Victorian England.[20]

---

18 Wardlaw, *Lectures on Female Prostitution*, pp. 14–15.
19 L. Mahood, p. 69.
20 William Acton, *Prostitution Considered*, pp. 23–5.

My chief interest lay in considering the effect produced upon married women by becoming accustomed at these reunions to witness the vicious and profligate sisterhood flaunting it gaily, or 'first-rate', in their language – accepting all the attentions of men, freely plied with liquor, sitting in the best places, dressed far above their station, with plenty of money to spend, and denying themselves no amusement or enjoyment, encumbered with no domestic ties, and burdened with no children.[21]

Much of the middle-class reform of the 1860s to 1880s attempted to remove sex from the public sphere and place it in the realm of the domestic – to remove the potential for extramarital affairs and illicit sex by claiming that working women were being used or manipulated by upper-class men for money. Josephine Butler, in her 1879 address to the Social Purity Alliance, spoke on these issues, saying:

Worldly and impure men have thought, and still think, they can separate women, as I have said, into two classes; – the protected and refined ladies who are not only to be good, but who are, if possible, to know nothing except what is good; and those poor outcast daughters of the people whom they purchase with money, with whom they think they may consort in evil whenever it pleases them to do so, before returning to their own separated and protected home.[22]

---

21 William Acton, *Prostitution Considered*, p. 23.
22 Josephine Butler, *Social Purity* (London, 1879), pp. 9–10.

So where does that leave the thorny issue of prostitution? The sex trade being primarily seen by mid-century reformers as a connection between upper-class men and lower-class women, the rhetoric and criminal cases of the Victorian period focused on exposing the manipulation and dangers associated with it.[23] By focusing on working-class women they were able to discuss, debate and create identities for them on platforms that the women would not be able to access – newspapers, journals, medical symposiums – therefore denying them the opportunity to defend or correct a created cultural 'mask' now imposed upon them. This created an identity of active female sexuality as male-authored, and left the descriptions of pimps and procurers unchallenged. Arthur Munby recorded a gentleman approaching him in a photography shop in his diary as: "'Sir" replied the seedy one "I am a theatrical agent: I can supply you Sir with girls, for ballet or poses or artists models, at an hours notice"[24]; historians have used this as an example of how the women were being manipulated due to their position as objects of male

23 Walkowitz, Judith R., *Prostitution and Victorian Society: Women, Class, and the State* (Cambridge, 1982; Walkowitz, Judith R., 'Male vice and feminist virtue: feminism and the politics of prostitution in nine-teenth-century Britain', *History Workshop.* Editorial Collective, History Workshop, Ruskin College, (1982); Bullough, Vern L., and Bullough, Bonnie, *Women and Prostitution: A Social History* (Buffalo, 1987).

24 Smith, Alison, *The Victorian Nude: Sexuality, Morality, and Art* (Manchester, 1996), 57, believed to be from A.J. Munby's diary, 11 June 1870, quoted in Hiley, Michael, and Munby, Arthur Joseph, *Victorian Working Women: Portraits from Life* (London and Bedford, 1979), 116.

consumption. But we have not questioned whether or not the 'seedy one' was, in reality, a theatrical agent; if he could, indeed, procure the girls or if the women were actively seeking such work themselves and engaged the man to seek out clients for them.

The Victorian century is littered with examples of working-class women using their sexuality knowingly, as a form of income, and being acknowledged in the public press. Cora Pearl, the 'notorious demimondaine' of the French Republic – and a working-class English girl who had started her career in the brothels of London before moving to Paris, becoming the darling of the aristocracy and lover of Prince Napoleon – was hotly discussed by French and English newspapers alike.[25] Her 1886 tell-all memoir, published in middle age, was anxiously awaited; believed – or possibly hoped – to contain detailed descriptions of her sexual exploits among the social elites. On its arrival the disgust was palpable, although not for the reasons one might expect. One reviewer pronounced, 'her book, which is a species of blackmail levied upon those who fear the honour of a place in its pages, is a dull record of appalling extravagance.'[26] The reviewer does not draw the conclusion that the men of Cora's life had simply paid up. Sexual intrigue and illicit sex were so often believed to be carried out in the private spaces of the Victorian

---

25 'The Life of Cora Pearl', *Edinburgh Evening News*, 30 March 1886; Rounding, Virginia, *Grandes Horizontales: The Lives and Legends of Four Nineteenth-Century Courtesans* (London, 2004).
26 Ibid.

world – in rooms or alleyways, hidden from view – and yet the art of the period, and the press, drew constant attention to it. Female sexuality was a commodity to be consumed, and this is something the Victorians did by the truckload. In 1874, when the empty Pimlico studio and home of pornographic photographer Henry Hayler was raided, 130,248 photographs and 5,000 slides of erotica were discovered and packed on six different carts, which were then taken away and destroyed by the police.[27]

So the history of the sex trade is complicated. You cannot look at it and ignore the degradation and abuse of some of its members, but neither can you ignore the agency, passion and legitimate choice of others who have decided on it as their career. Since the Victorian era we have relegated those within sex work to the corners of our society, and allowed doctrines of abuse and dehumanisation to spring up and take control of sold sex. When a judge legitimises a rapist's access to any woman, and devalues her consent because she is a sex worker, how far are we from a system that legitimises a growing male viewpoint that sex is their right, and not a choice on the part of a loving partner? This is not what sex is for, this has never been what sex is about at any point in our historical culture, and it is our demonisation of sex workers that has brought us to where we are now.

27 *Western Mail,* 21 April 1874; Ashbee, H.S, *Index Librorum Prohibitum,* 1877, p. xixn.

13
Rape

'By its very nature, rape displays a "total contempt
for the personal integrity and autonomy" of
the victim ... the "ultimate violation of self."'
—Coker vs. Georgia, 1977

Sex, and its place in society, has given us a framework for laws, legal systems, politics, religion and pretty much every area of our lives. Although for many of us sex is about emotional and physical pleasure with those we love, our cultural understanding of sex has always had a far wider reach than simply our own bedrooms. Religion, race, class and gender have all played a part in restricting and governing our sexual lives. Power and sex have always been linked. For women, sex has been used as a form of social control – the immodest woman, the sexual woman, has become a centuries-old stereotype used to restrict and govern women's public voice. For men, sex has been presented as something to take, explicitly connected to ideas of virility, manliness, and domination of a passive subject. Today, we are beginning to understand how damaging these cultural stereotypes are to our societies. The idea of toxic masculinity and the desexualised woman is causing us serious problems. The most extreme example of this aspect of our sexual culture is rape, and examining how previous generations have dealt with this socio-sexual problem leaves us with one question: is rape something we will ever be able to stop?

Writing to Susan B. Anthony on 14 June 1860, Elizabeth Cady Stanton (1815–1902) identified one of the most important flaws in our Western culture and its systems of authority: 'Women's degradation is in man's idea of his sexual rights. Our religion, laws, customs, are all founded on the belief that women were made for men.'[1] Whether women were made for men – or from men, in the biblical belief of Adam and Eve – their autonomy had been defined in law as subservient to the men who surrounded them. Although our sexual culture is predominately built from our personal lived experience and the experience of those around us, we can't escape from the influence and power that systems of authority, such as the church and state, exert over the sex lives of their citizens. One of the most important tools women have had in the fight for their self-autonomy has been education, but this has taken centuries to obtain. 'Men have every advantage of us in telling their own story,' wrote Jane Austen. 'Education has

---

1 Sue Davis, *The Political Thought of Elizabeth Cady Stanton: Women's Rights and the American Political Traditions* (New York University Press, 2008), p. 69.

been theirs in so much higher a degree; the pen has been in their hands.'[2] This, perhaps, is the reason why our understanding of women's history, and the history of sex itself, has been so uninformed and confusing. We have lacked the voices of women, or have ignored those who have been recorded, in favour of male authority and a male-authored version of this history. The feminist history writing of the late twentieth century, on a determined mission to prove the horrors women suffered without their legal rights protected in law, focused, understandably, on the histories of those who had been degraded and victimised in our past. The importance of demonstrating the need for every citizen to be protected and supported in law was, and is, paramount. But one of the side effects of this approach is that it does not leave room for the lived reality and experiences of those who did not conform or successfully broke the system of control and power. The past is often presented as a time when women simply sat back and accepted, or did not question, their lack of rights, when that is simply untrue. We can hear, throughout this book, the voices of women who just did not care what society thought of them, and lived their lives as they wished – not as those in power dictated. The Anne Listers, Mary Hamiltons and Annie Besants of our sexual heritage. Beside them are the men who also refused or ignored the boundaries placed on them by moral or secular authorities. So if we are going to study or understand sex in our historical past we have to look beyond the laws of a period,

---

2 Jane Austen, *Persuasion*, 1818.

and look instead at its culture. And the culture that has had the most significant impact on our own today is that of the Victorians.

Although we often view the Victorian period as a period of great social regulation and control, it was actually a time of intense volatility. The nature of the mid-Victorian social order sought to establish recognisable social boundaries in the public urban space, where all classes mixed.[3] The idea of sexual respectability became an important social signifier, seen as the preserve of the middle classes, while the masses – both higher and lower – operated with a vulgar sexuality that ranged from illiteracy to bad language and lewd behaviour. Sex was being redesigned to be respectable. It had one purpose only – reproduction. In an attempt to solidify their own social status, the middle classes became focused on sexual respectability, guided by work on criminal cultures, mass observation and medical investigation.[4] We hear the echoes of the religious laws and state control of St Ambrose and Thomas Aquinas, but their influence had always been metered by a populace that embraced sexual expression and lust as a healthy part of an individual's life. But for a dominant group of law-makers and politicians in the latter half of the nineteenth century, the work of social investigators like William Acton, Henry Mayhew and John Stuart Mill – although demonstrating widespread and often liberal attitudes to sex in all classes

---

3 Peter Bailey, *Popular Culture and Performance in the Victorian City* (Cambridge University Press, 2003), p. 42.

4 Ibid., 235.

– became the referencing tools for converting female agency into victimhood, and sexual culture into social control.

Respectability was how one person communicated with another; it was defined by their 'sober' dress, their 'sober' mind.[5] And sexual respectability became the idea many of us have of the Victorians – buttoned-up, prudish, the Mary Gladstones of the world. But while the social elites were quick to see the working class as a singular entity, for 'those below' – who lacked the ability to act or comprehend respectability as an ideology – the truth was very different. Many people within the working classes lived 'sexually respectable' lives by their own standards: they worked hard, raised families, attended social occasions, whether it was in church or the music halls. Public discussions by church and state on sex in the nineteenth century became a constant balancing act between moral panic and moral reform – panic about uncontrolled sexual desires and reform to protect those who were not able to protect themselves. For the Victorians, part of this understanding came from controlled investigation. The Industrial Revolution had brought about large-scale population redistribution away from the rural communities of the previous centuries and into the towns and cities. People living in

---

5 Peter Bailey, '"Will the Real Bill Banks Please Stand up?" Towards a Role Analysis of Mid-Victorian Working-Class Respectability', *Journal of Social History* (1979), pp. 336–53; A. James Hammerton, 'The Targets of "Rough Music": Respectability and Domestic Violence in Victorian England', *Gender & History* 3.1 (1991), pp. 23–44; Mike Huggins, 'More sinful pleasures? Leisure, respectability and the male middle classes in Victorian England', *Journal of Social History* 33.3 (2000), 585–600.

very close and confined quarters provided the perfect conditions for mass observation – exploring the tastes, attitudes and lives of as many people as possible. The growth of divorce courts, and the slow shifts in marital law to provide women with a growing autonomy and protection within marriage, created enormous scrutiny over the sexual rights of men and women in the nineteenth century. Anne Humphreys has identified this as a period when 'the whole subject of marriage was under intense debate...in the press, the novel, and at dinner tables'.[6] The divorce courts existed as a form of social control, 'patrolling the boundaries of acceptable marital behaviour' and identifying what was and was not acceptable.[7] At the same time, sex outside of marriage, and the bawdy eroticism of sensual licentiousness that came from those for whom sex was *not* about marriage, but simply about pleasure, was increasingly seen as a social danger by those who wanted to control and regulate the sexual lives of the Victorians.

A culture of sexual danger was created by the tabloid press of the 1880s. It took hold in earnest with the feverish and fetishised coverage of the deaths of Mary Ann Nichols, Annie Chapman, Elizabeth Stride, Catherine Eddowes, and Mary Jane Kelly in the East End of London, at the hands of the press-created monster 'Jack the Ripper'. To

---

6 Anne Humphreys, 'Coming Apart: The British Newspaper Press and the Divorce Court' in (eds) Laurel Brake, B. Bell and D. Finkelstein, *Nineteenth Century Media and Construction of Identities* (London, 2016), p. 227.

7 Humphreys, 'Coming Apart', 227.

be a woman, in public and working, could now be portrayed as placing yourself, knowingly, in danger. Multiple accounts of female music hall artists dying by their partner's hand were reported: from Maggie Dudley, a singer, who was beaten to death by her husband, also on the stage as a comedian, in 1895,[8] to Cora Crippen (wife and victim of the infamous murderer Dr Crippen), better known as music hall singer 'Belle Elmore', in 1910.[9] Although the discovery of Elmore's murder was sensational at the time, it is her husband – and his status as the first criminal to be caught by wireless telegraphy – whose story has been remembered by history.[10]

Belle Elmore billed herself as a 'Serio Comedienne', and a review from 1900 of her performance at the Tivoli Theatre of Varieties, Manchester, claims she 'acquitted [herself] admirably.'[11] During her career, the *Sheffield Evening Telegraph* reported that she had 'appeared at various suburban halls, and she toured the provinces. She paid several extended visits to America and also to the Continent...a bright little artist, although not very powerful

8 'Music Hall Artists Death', *Nottingham Evening Post*, 4 January 1895.
9 'Music Hall Artiste Murdered!' *Fife Free Press*, 16 July 1910.
10 Foran, David R., Wills, Beth E., Kiley, Brianne, M., Jackson, Carrie B., and Trestrail, John H. 3rd., 'The Conviction of Dr. Crippen: New Forensic Findings in a Century-Old Murder', *Journal of Forensic Sciences*, 56.1 (2011), 233–40; Early, Julie English, 'Technology, Modernity, and "The Little Man": Crippen's Capture by Wireless', *Victorian Studies* (1996), pp. 309–37.
11 For billing: *Western Daily Press*, 25 January 1902, and for review: *Manchester Courier and Lancashire General Advertiser*, 23 October 1900.

in her acting.'[12] Although not achieving the same status
as Marie Lloyd or Vesta Tilley, two of the premier female
stars of their day, Elmore appears to have achieved enough
popularity that large crowds attended her funeral, which
included members of the Music Hall Ladies' Guild (of
which Marie Lloyd had been President), bearing a wreath
with the inscription 'To our dearly departed comrade'.[13]
Elmore had been the Guild's Honorary Treasurer since
its creation in 1906, designed to support young women
working in the halls, as well as to fight for safer working
environments and better pay for all female acts on the
music hall stage. It was Elmore's membership of the Guild
that led to the discovery of her remains and the flight of
her husband with his lover – Crippen had poisoned Elmore
and buried her body in the cellar of their home, before
fleeing on board a ship to Canada with his mistress, Ethel
le Neve. The Guild would meet weekly and Elmore's
sudden absence was decidedly out of character. They had
sent officials to her home to enquire after her health, but
when Dr Crippen answered the door, he informed the
Guild's enquirer that 'his wife had gone away to California
that morning'. This was so unusual that Elmore's friends
contacted the police.[14] This is the reality of women working
in the Victorian era, so often ignored and forgotten by the
stories of violent murder and sexual abuse. Cora Crippen
is not the victim of a notorious murderer, she is Belle

---

12 *Sheffield Evening Telegraph*, 16 July 1910.
13 *Dundee Courier*, 12 October 1910.
14 *Sheffield Evening Telegraph*, 16 July 1910.

Elmore, music hall actress and activist, whose murder was suspected, not by the police, but by a group of women who knew looking out for one another was incredibly important.

At Crippen's trial, a host of members of the Guild were called as witnesses: the current President, Madame Ginnett, 'now here training horses for a new act';[15] 'Miss Melida May, secretary of the Music Hall Ladies' Guild,[16] and the Welsh strongwoman, Miss Kate Robert, better known by her stage name of 'Vulcana'.[17] The unusual opportunity to see the women of the stage close up may explain the extensive press coverage of Belle Elmore's life. But it was also unusual; her married identity was of little interest to those by whom she was discussed. During the trial and in the press coverage, it is her performing name that is used. Under the heading 'Where is Belle Elmore?', Mr Muir, closing for the prosecution, said to the jury, 'Ask yourselves in this most important case: Where is Belle Elmore? Is your answer to be that she is dead? Whose remains were those in the cellar? Is your answer to be that they are those of Belle Elmore?'[18]

Interestingly, recent work by historians has begun to examine the role of mass media in creating a social reality that may have been perceived by its inhabitants, but did not *actually* exist. The relationship between newspapers,

15 Ibid.
16 *Sevenoaks Chronicle and Kentish Advertiser*, 19 August 1910.
17 *Hull Daily Mail*, 20 August 1908.
18 *Sheffield Daily Telegraph*, 22 October 1910.

social hysteria and the number of criminal prosecutions is one that emerges from any study of sexual morality in the late Victorian and Edwardian eras; while the mass media's role in constructing a reality of sexual crime and deviance is equally linked to the State's ability to generate new forms of social and legal control.[19] Newspapers and periodicals were often the voices of moral crusaders and were able to reach large numbers of literate, but not necessarily well educated, people for the first time. This created a space where the newspapers were able to direct social anxiety on a grand scale, which we see clearly in the hysteria created by the press around the murders of 'Jack the Ripper' in 1888.

Women, especially those in the East End, were depicted as one of the most vulnerable groups in Victorian society, with numerous reports of both common law and married wives being seriously injured or killed.[20] This narrative of sexual danger for women in Victorian London has been highlighted by the extensive scholarship of Judith Walkowitz; however, her scholarship carries with it – in relation to the music halls – an inherent misreading of the evidence. In her brief analysis of the construction of marriage on the music hall stage, Walkowitz claims, 'Female coster stars were even more critical of the daily performances of men as husbands and family men. Male costers responded by

---

19 J. Ferrell, 'Cultural Criminology', *Annual Review of Sociology*, vol. 25 (1999), 396–7.

20 D. Jones, *Crime, Protest, Community and Police* (London, 1982), p. 122.

depicting their own view of marriage as an unfortunate but comic calamity, with Charles Coburn making an enduring hit by celebrating the virtues of wife-beating in "'Two Lovely Black Eyes'".[21] Yet, Walkowitz's interpretation of 'Two Lovely Black Eyes' as a song extolling domestic violence between a man and a woman is utterly incorrect. In 'Two Lovely Black Eyes. An Interview With The Singer Of The Song', the *Pall Mall Gazette* related Charles Coburn's own story of the song's invention, and the message or codified meaning behind it:

'Two Lovely Black Eyes' is a parody of an American song of which the chorus is 'Nellie's Lovely Blue Eyes'. The air is the same, and had been sung in London by some lady vocalists, even at the Trocadero, long before I thought of it. I had an engagement at the Paragon in the Mile-end-road, and had to sing a new song one Saturday night... I was walking down Bethnal Green, thinking about it; the elections were on at the time, and I turned it over. So I got the first line:–

Strolling so happy down Bethnal-green,

Who, Why?

This gay youth you might have seen.

You see, 'seen', 'green'? The you would naturally meet someone. I met Tompkins. I wanted a word to rhyme with 'seen' and 'green' so I gave Tompkins a young lady:–

Tompkins and I with his girl in between.

---

21 Judith R. Walkowitz, *City of Dreadful Delight: Narratives of Sexual Danger in Late-Victorian London*, p. 45.

I had written 'Harry' at first, but it was too prosaic, so I changed it to Tompkins, which sounded funnier. Then I thought of the election, and the rest followed easily. What more natural than that we should fall out and that Tompkins should hand me 'two lovely black eyes'? That is how it grew.[22]

The lyrics of the song leave little room, even in the most metaphorical sense, for such a conclusion:

Strolling so happy down Bethnal Green
This gay youth you might have seen,
Tompkins and I, with his girl between,
Oh! what a surprise!
I prais'd the Conservatives frank and free,
Tompkins got angry so speedilee,
All in a moment he handed to me,
Two lovely black eyes!

Next time, I argued I thought it best,
To give the conservative side a rest.
The merits of Glad-stone I freely pressed, When
Oh! what a surprise!
The chap I had met was a Tory true,
Nothing the Liberals right could do,
This was my share of that argument too,
Two lovely black eyes!

---

22 'Two Lovely Black Eyes', *Pall Mall Gazette*, 8 February 1887.

The moral you've caught I can hardly doubt
Never on politics rave and shout,
Leave it to others to fight it out, if
You would be wise
Better, far better, it is to let,
Lib'rals and Tories alone, you bet,
Unless you're willing and anxious to get,
Two lovely black eyes!

CHORUS:
Two lovely black eyes!
Oh! what a surprise!
Only for telling a man he was wrong,
Two lovely black eyes!

But although 'Two Lovely Black Eyes' may not have been about domestic violence in itself, there does seem to have been a public connection of the song and gendered violence in the press. But it is here, and not in the music halls, that this cultural identity is born. In December 1889, the *Hartlepool Mail* carried a report of 'Two Lovely Black Eyes', stating that 'This morning, at Stockton, Bernard Burns, labourer, was charged with having committed an aggravated assault on Ellen Moran, his landlady, last night... It was alleged that he had knocked her about, and given her "two lovely black eyes". — He was remanded till Monday'.[23] And in the *Sunderland Daily Echo and Shipping Gazette*, 'Two Lovely Black Eyes' was·used as the headline to the report

---

23 *Hartlepool Mail*, 4 December 1889.

on Joseph Nesbitt after he was charged by his wife, 'the result being that she received two black eyes and other injuries'.[24] Not all reports using the title specifically identified male to female violence; in 1888, 'Two Lovely Black Eyes' headed the story of Mary Riseborough and Jane Miller, when 'Mrs Miller stated that the defendant blackened both her eyes, assaulted her husband, and overturned the furniture' during a dispute over money.[25] This press adoption of a popular song term to denote domestic violence occurs externally to the music halls, yet is clearly influenced by it. However, it would be wrong to interpret the halls themselves as responsible for these acts, as domestic violence was, as it still is, a widespread social and cultural issue that occurs in all classes. Walkowitz's desire to locate narratives of sexual danger specifically within the location of the halls is central to her desire to construct the history of women in the urban city. But this only works if we deal with the reality of those social spaces, and do not invent conflict where none is recorded.

In the nineteenth century, the identity of 'Womanhood' was projected as an ideal of sexual purity or innocence, while female sexual agency and autonomy were believed to be found only among the 'low and vulgar women': those who were identified as members of the working classes.[26] The social freedom afforded to working women was a double-edged sword; their independence came at a price.

---

24 *Sunderland Daily Echo and Shipping Gazette*, 23 October 1888.
25 Ibid., 30 May 1888.
26 Ibid.

It made them sexually accessible. The contemporary association between class identity and sexual agency has led much of our historiography; historians have an inherent perception that sex in the nineteenth century should be seen as part of a power system, where female victimhood is measured against male control.[27] It seems that sex has become historically accepted as an area of human experience where women have no agency; and middle-class women were given the mantle of sexual purity while working-class women, or anyone expressing female sexual agency and autonomy, had to be portrayed in history as either victims of male lust or a perceived danger to the moral fabric of society.

This view was created by those Victorian male authorities who sought to establish sex as an area of State control: 'Many men, and particularly young men, form their earliest ideas of women's feelings from what they notice early in life among loose or, at least, low and vulgar women,' wrote William Acton in 1857.[28] These 'low and vulgar' women were clearly not the domesticated mothers and matriarchs of middle-class households, but women with agency and independence, who populated the public arenas of the 'London streets, in casinos and other immoral haunts'.[29]

We cannot disconnect the act of sex from our narrative

---

27 Judith R. Walkowitz, *Prostitution and Victorian Society: Women, Class, and the State* (Cambridge, 1982).
28 Steven Marcus, *The Other Victorians: A Study of Sexuality and Pornography in Mid-Nineteenth-Century England* (Transaction, 2008), p. 31.
29 Ibid.

of womanhood in the nineteenth century. The fixation on the female body, both in a sexual and a reproductive sense, dominated both the literature of the period and the feminist history that has followed it. What happened to the female body, who used it and who consumed it, is undeniably part of the music hall stage; and yet it has only been previously examined through narratives of social control or class conflict. We need to understand sex against a new narrative of female agency in the music halls, not only through a narrative of victimhood.

The Victorians showed a vigorous interest in sex – both in its purely reproductive sense and also in its opportunities for pleasure.[30] From the intellectual to the medicinal and the cultural, sex was intrinsically linked to definitions of gender and gender roles, forming the basis for the 'separate spheres' debates and arguments for both men and women's emancipation.[31] The transmission of sexual

---

30 Fern Riddell, *The Victorian Guide to Sex: Desire and Deviance in the 19th Century* (Barnsley, 2014).

31 The ideology of 'separate spheres' was instrumental to the studies of British Women's History in the 1970s and 1980s (Leonore Davidoff, 'Gender and the "Great Divide": Public and Private in British Gender History,' *Journal of Women's History*, 15.1 (2003), 11–27) as the focus on middle-class women's lives came to the fore with Davidoff and Catherine Hall's *Family Fortunes: Men and Women of the English Middle Class, 1780–1850* (1994; reprint, London, 2002). However, this paradigm has come under considerable attack in recent scholarship, as it can only successfully apply to white Western middle-class women. Amanda Vickery's 'Golden Age to Separate Spheres? A Review of the Categories and Chronology of English Women's History,' *Historical Journal* 36, no. 2 (1993), 383–414, remains the foremost example of this critique.

knowledge – whether via books, pamphlets, erotic images, music halls, meetings or societies – was a focus for governmental discussion and legislation and much of this focus was led by the increase in female political activity and campaigns for women's rights. Annie Besant led a campaign to educate the working classes on birth control, appearing at lectures held in music halls, while Kitty Marion, the militant suffragette, used her experiences of sexual attitudes in the music halls to inform her militant activities and her campaigning for birth control. Sex, whether the physical act or allusions to it, in the form of direct reference, metaphor or innuendo, all featured on the music hall stage. For a century mired in sexual conflict, which has been used throughout the twentieth and twenty-first centuries as an ancestral ogre of sexually repressive attitudes, there has been no link made between the personal or individual interaction with sex in the Victorian period and the music halls. How the halls constructed sexual interactions – from courting to marriage and infidelity – between their audience members, and how these attitudes were alluded to or performed by their acts, are inescapably bound up in the identity of nineteenth- and early twentieth-century femininity.

Nineteenth-century studies on human sexuality and attitudes to human sexuality are many in number, by both contemporary and modern authors. This is, after all, the century that gave us the belief that women had 'little to no' sexual feelings; that homosexuality was an inversion, and gender difference identified from birth one's

suitability to certain social roles.[32] The later cultural backlash to these attitudes defined the historiography of sex
as revolutionary for tackling and exposing the Victorian
patriarchy. In the wake of third wave feminism, 'sex
history' has become primarily the property of radical
feminists, seen through strict boundaries of female victimhood and male oppression. This radicalisation of historical
research has widened in the last few decades to include
scholars of gay or 'queer' history, but has maintained an
approach that any form of sex history focuses on concepts
of otherness, displacement and victimhood. It is a
passionate and emotive arena in which to work. Although
the music halls have been examined as a space of otherness or of othering behaviour, they have been ignored by
scholars working in this tradition as a source for hege-
monic sexual behaviour.[33] Women who did not fit the
social or sexual stereotypes of this Victorian historiography have often been ignored by both nineteenth-century
contemporary (and later) feminists, as it ran against their

---

32 William Acton, *Functions and Disorders of the Reproductive Organs*
(London, 1865); Richard von Krafft-Ebing, *Psychopathia Sexualis: With
Especial Reference to the Antipathic Sexual Interest, A Medico-Forensic Study*,
translation and introduction by Franklin S. Klaf (New York, 1886);
Havelock Ellis, *Sexual Inversion*, vol. 2 (Philadelphia, 1915).

33 Tracy C. Davis is the only scholar to have dealt with the music halls
in this way, although her research focuses on the view of actress as
prostitute and the othering behaviour of women. See: Tracy C. Davis,
'Actresses and Prostitutes in Victorian London', *Theatre Research
International* 13.03 (1988), 221–234; 'The Actress in Victorian
Pornography', Theatre Journal (1989), 294–315; and, *Actresses as Working
Women: Their Social Identity in Victorian Culture* (London, 2002).

belief that female sexual agency could not be found in the working classes or the music halls.

For the Victorians, working-class women – the oft-adopted identity of music hall stars – caused a conundrum. Their agency, their perceived un-respectability and sexual freedom, were not part of the image with which campaigners for female enfranchisement wished to identify. The fight for female suffrage had to prove where female agency was lacking, not where it already existed, and so the identity of victimhood became ingrained into the early suffrage campaigners and has dominated our understanding of womanhood in the nineteenth century. Instead of being used as an example of female freedom, women's sexuality in the music halls became an area for social control. Perceived as inhabiting the dens of depravity and immorality, the music hall woman has become a two-dimensional construction, created to fulfil a specific social role. She must be a victim, firstly of male lusts and secondly of a society that judged her. But this is not the reality of the lives of the women who are to be found in the music halls. Our understanding of the enjoyment of pleasure is coloured by the influence of anti-sensualism doctrines drawn from legislation and intellectual writing, but these do not convey the will of the people. Popular culture, however, is capable of providing such evidence. Exploring this sexual culture demonstrates that sexual pleasure – shared intimacy between young lovers, married life and family – was not a taboo topic, but a nightly conversation.

There is one aspect of our sexual culture that

encompasses the most dangerous extremes that toxic masculinity and the sexual danger women face thanks to the creation of a newspaper culture that sensationalises and glorifies sexual violence. Looking back over history, how we have represented and reported rape through the centuries tells us a lot about the complex relationships between men and women and sex. The idea that a woman's sexuality, or her work, or involvement in the sex industry disqualifies her from being raped is not a new problem. Neither is the damage caused to women by the coverage of false accusations, even when they have been manipulated into them. On 26 March 1737, the *Newcastle Courant* reported a story occurring far from their county. 'The case of Maplesden, Coe and Shrove' in Canterbury, Kent, was the story of three teenage boys, all aged between 14 and 15 years, who had been accused of a gang rape 'on the Body of one, who 'tis said, is a notorious Common Whore'.[34] This unnamed woman had levelled the accusation in November 1736, and the boys had been sent to the Maidstone Jail. After months had passed, she had confessed that 'she had sworn falsely against them', having been pressured into the accusation by her Master. The real story was one of male pride and ego. Her Master had owed money, a significant sum, to Hayler Maplesden's father. Sending his son to collect the outstanding debt, Hayler had taken his two friends, Coe and Shrove, with him to collect it, only to leave empty-handed. The Master, 'out of Revenge against the Defendants, prevailed with

---

34 *Newcastle Courant*, Saturday, 26 March 1737.

her... to swear a Rape ... and had promis'd her Marriage for so doing'.[35] Having either refused to make good on his promise to her, or to ease her own conscience, the truth had finally been revealed and the Master himself was now in jail in the place of the boys, and 'There was great rejoicing upon the discharge of the young men'.[36]

Coverage of rape in the nineteenth century was surprisingly graphic, and shows us that, just as they did not shy away from the reality of sex, the abuse that could be executed in its name would not go unpunished. This tells us so much about the sexual attitudes of mid-century Victorians, who still received their cultural sexual knowledge from works like *The Art of Begetting Handsome Children*, for whom rape was the antithesis of what a sexual encounter should be. On 4 September 1857, the *Durham Chronicle* covered the 'Brutal Rape Case' of Ann Gibson. Aged only 16, Ann had been brutally beaten, robbed and raped by Thomas Osbourne and his companion, John Iveson, on the 14th of August, in a field near Elwick. Osbourne was 21 and a mason, from Stockton, and his attack had been so horrific that, the paper reported, 'some of the particulars of the case are too disgusting for publication, but the treatment to which the unfortunate young woman has been subject, as appears in evidence, will afford some idea of the crime of the brutes who have violently ill used her'. What is so important about this paper's coverage, and much of the

---

35 *Newcastle Courant*, Saturday, 26 March 1737.
36 Ibid.

coverage of cases like this, is that it would print the victims' testimonies verbatim. Rape was not an accepted part of Victorian sexual culture; it was aggressively punished – if not by law, then by the popular culture of the period. The press could operate almost as a form of mob justice for the victims, whose words would be read in the parlours, studies, libraries, offices, bedrooms and kitchens of the rest of England. The *Chronicle* printed Ann's testimony almost word for word:

I am a single woman, living in Middlesbro' with my uncle, Francis Kenward. On Friday, the 14th, I was at Sedgefield, at Margaret Gibson's, my aunt's. I left her house about 10 o'clock in the morning, to see my brother at Elwick. It is about seven miles from Sedgefield. When two miles from Sedgefield I met the prisoner on the footpath, in the fields. I am positive the prisoner is the man. I never saw him before that day. He was coming towards Sedgefield. He asked how far it was off. I said, about two miles. He went towards Sedgefield, and I to Elwick. I did not stop. When I got a mile further, I met another man. The last man spoke to me, and went in the same direction as the prisoner. I went on. On the road to Elwick, I called at Mr George Firby's house, and had dinner. It was between 1 and 2 o'clock when I got to Elwick and saw my brother. I had tea, and left between five and six o'clock the same evening to go to Sedgefield. When I was [a] mile off Embleton, as I was coming from Elwick to Sedgefield, I met the prisoner and another man. He was the same I met in the morning with the prisoner. I met the two coming in the field. The prisoner spoke and said, 'Now, Miss Gibson, you've got back from seeing your brother.' I did not answer, and walked on. It was a ploughed field. I went on the road towards the stile. Before coming to it I looked back, and saw they were running towards me. I ran on seeing them. The prisoner got hold of me first. I shouted 'murder.' The prisoner, as I was crossing the stile, took hold of my dress and pulled me back. The other man put one hand over my mouth, and held both my hands with his, and the prisoner took 3s from my pocket. He then threw me down, and the other man had hold of me. I could not shout, as the last named man had his hand still over my mouth. I fell upon my back. The other man knelt down as well as the prisoner. I struggled as much as I could to free myself. [The other particulars at this point are unfit for publication.] As soon as I shouted murder, the prisoner struck me a heavy blow over the mouth. He made it bleed.[37]

Ann's testimony continued in the most horrific way. After her attack, she returned to Sedgefield and confided in a family friend, who had taken her to the police, where she had reported her attack. A week later, standing in Middlesbrough Market Place, Ann felt a hand on her shoulder; it was Thomas Osbourne. During his attack he had forced her to tell him where she lived. Running from him, Ann attempted to seek refuge in a draper's

---

37 *Durham Chronicle*, Friday, 4 September 1857.

shop, but Osbourne continued to harass her. She managed to return to her uncle's home, and he fetched the police. Searching the nearby area, a local constable apprehended Osbourne, who gave a false name at his arrest. Refusing to believe it, PC Johnson marched him to the station. On the way, they were followed by a laughing, braying man, ridiculing Osbourne for his arrest. It was John Iveson, the man who had held Ann down as Osbourne raped her. He was quickly arrested and charged alongside Osbourne. Three months later, on Christmas Day, the *Chronicle* announced the outcome of the case, 'which, in the magnitude of the offence laid in the indictment, ranked next to murder'.[38] Osbourne was sentenced to twenty years, to the sound of cheering, as he protested his innocence and threatened the constable who had arrested him.

Ann Gibson's story is one with at least some form of justice at the end, but as we pick over the reporting of rape in the nineteenth-century presses, there is the consistent reappearance of the idea of 'respectability'. Women who suffered through horrific attacks were often tried on the stand, and their sexual past taken as evidence of their truthful nature, or even if they *could* be raped. On 7 April 1867, *Reynolds's Newspaper* reported on the charge of rape levelled against a surgeon who lived in Chigwell. Dr Charles Saunders appeared before the Epping Petty Sessions, accused of rape by Mrs Elizabeth Harrison, the wife of the railway stationmaster. She

---

38 *Durham Chronicle*, Friday, 4 September 1857.

alleged he had attacked her in her own home, on the 12th of March:

The prosecutrix, a very good-looking woman, about twenty-five years of age, said that on the 12th of March her husband told her that Dr. Saunders was below and had called to see her, she being in bed at the time. She said she could not come down then, but her husband said he wanted particularly to see her. She then got out of bed to dress herself, and her husband left the room, but in an instant, to her great surprise, she found Dr. Saunders in the room. He took a seat on a chair, but afterwards got up, took hold of both her hands, put his foot between her legs, and threw her on to the bed. (She then described what followed, all tending to prove that the capital offence had been committed.) She was unable to resist on account of the manner in which she had been thrown. She screamed as loudly as she could to Ann, her servant. The doctor had been attending her for diseased lungs. He did not leave her until he heard footsteps approaching. When the girl Ann came upstairs she could not open the door, and when she continued screaming out, the prisoner said, 'Hush, hush; no don't, Mrs. Harrison.'... The defendant then went and unfastened the catch, and the servant entered the room, Dr. Saunders having then his hand on the knob of the door. When the girl got into the room she told her to go and tell Mr. Harrison to come to her bedroom immediately. The girl went down stairs to tell her master, and while she was away she (prosecutrix) wanted to get out of the room, but Dr. Saunders prevented her from doing so. He wanted her to go with him to London, and to go to a theatre there with him. She refused to do so, and said she would tell Mr. Harrison what had occurred... The doctor entreated her not to say anything about it, and said he would tell Mr. Harrison that she was hysterical, and did not know what she was about.[39]

When Mr Harrison – Francis, who was, by all accounts, an utterly useless individual – returned, Elizabeth told him what had happened. She was clearly a woman who refused to be victimised. Putting on her things, and taking her servant with her, she went straight to the doctor's house and attempted to speak to his wife, determined to tell her what had just happened. At first unsuccessful, she managed to do so in the late afternoon, and what transpired represented the worst of Victorian middle-class pomposity and sexual repression:

...Mrs. Saunders came in. She [Elizabeth] complained to her of her husband's conduct in Dr. Saunders's presence. Mrs. Saunders said she could not believe it, but witness said she could positively swear that it was the truth. Mrs. Saunders said 'Can you swear before God and man that what you say is true?' and she said, turning to Dr. Saunders, 'You knew what I say is true.' Witness looked at him and said, 'You cannot swear before God and a bench of magistrates that what I say is not true,' and he made no reply. Witness said in the presence of Dr. and Mrs. Saunders that Mr. Harrison

---

39 *Reynolds's Newspaper*, Sunday, 7 April 1867.

wanted her to go to a doctor to be Examined. Dr. Saunders said he only called upon Mrs. Harrison out of friendship, and Mrs. Saunders said there ought to be no friendship between them. On the same evening Dr. Saunders called with the Rev. W. S. Meadows, and he said it was a very serious charge she was making against Dr. Saunders, and she replied that what she had stated was perfectly true, that she could swear before God and man that what she had stated was the truth and nothing but the truth. Dr. Saunders called God to witness that it was an untruth. Mr. Meadows said if she went on with the case it would be the worse for her. He referred to Mr. Harrison, and asked him if he believed it, and he said, 'Yes I believe my wife.' The servant was called, and asked if she did not hear Dr. Saunders say, 'Hush, hush; don't, don't,' and she said she did. Dr. Saunders said the girl would admit anything. She also told her female friends of what had taken place, and she bore marks on her person of his violence.[40]

From reading Elizabeth's account, the corroborating evidence of her servant, friends and family, as well as the revelations that Saunders had been obsessed with her for months – declaring his love for her, suggesting she go with him to Margate, even kissing her, even though she had soundly rejected his advances, and told her husband of them – this case feels open and shut. But what was about to face Elizabeth was the double standard of

---

40 *Reynolds's Newspaper*, Sunday, 7 April 1867.

Victorian moral prudery. For, in this court, nothing was
more important than the idea of a woman's sexual respectability, not even to her own solicitor, Mr Sleigh:

Mr. Ribton: I now wish to put a few other questions
to you, and I hope you will be careful how you answer
them. Do you know a Mrs. Debenham?

Mrs. Harrison: I do.

Mr. Ribton: Did you complain to her of having been
indecently assaulted in a railway carriage?

Mrs. Harrison: I did. But that has nothing to do with
this case.

Mr. Ribton: Do you know the person who assaulted
you?

Mrs. Harrison: I do.

Mr. Ribton: Did you tell Mrs. Debenham that a
certain person had assaulted you in a railway carriage?

Mrs. Harrison: Perhaps you will first tell me what you
mean by an assault.

Mr. Ribton: Did you not tell Mrs. Debenham that a
gentleman had put his hand under your clothes?

Mrs. Harrison: I told her that he said that I had got a
nice leg and foot, but I cannot say that I told her that
he put his hand under my clothes.

Mr. Ribton: Did he put his hand under your clothes?

Mrs. Harrison: He did not put his hand under my clothes.

Mr. Ribton: Did you tell her that he did?

Mrs. Harrison: I cannot swear that I did not tell her. He did not do so. He tried to put his hand under my clothes. I cannot swear whether I told Mrs. Debenham that he did or not.

Mr. Ribton: How long is that ago?

Mrs. Harrison: I cannot tell.

Mr. Ribton: Where were you married?

Mrs. Harrison: I decline answering that question.

Mr. Sleigh: Pray answer the question.

Mr. Ribton: Where did you first see your husband?

Mrs. Harrison: I first saw him at Peterborough.

Mr. Ribton: How long were you living at Peterborough before you were married?

Mrs. Harrison: I shall not answer that question. You can go amongst my friends, and find out what I am.

Mr. Sleigh: You are really bound to answer all the questions the learned gentleman puts to you. If he asks you any improper question, I as your counsel will interfere.

Mrs. Harrison: I was living in Peterborough, but I decline answering any questions as to how long I was there, or what I was doing there.

Mr. Sleigh: If I find such reticence on the part of the prosecutrix to answer such questions as may fairly be put to her by my learned friend, I shall feel it my duty to retire from the case.

Mr. Ribton: Were you a prostitute at Peterborough?

Mrs. Harrison: I decline answering any such questions.

Mr. Ribton: How did you get your living before you were married to Mr. Harrison?

Mrs. Harrison: I decline answering that question.

Mr. Ribton: Were you not a prostitute at Peterborough?

Mrs. Harrison: I was not.

Mr. Ribton: Then, were you on the town?

Mrs. Harrison: I decline answering any such questions.

Mr. Ribton: Let Mr. J. Thurlow come in.
(Mr. Thurlow entered the court.) Do you know that man?

Mrs. Harrison: I do.

Mr. Ribton: Now, having seen that man do you now say on your oath that you were not a common prostitute in the town of Peterborough?

Mrs. Harrison: I decline answering that question. (Murmurs.)

Mr. Sleigh: I am here to protect your interests, but if you hesitate to answer the questions which the learned gentleman has a right to put to you, from nothing but a sense of justice, which you will expect from my hands, I shall retire from this prosecution.

Mr. Ribton: You hear what your learned counsel has stated, and you see that man there. Now, were you not a common prostitute in the town of Peterborough?

Mrs. Harrison: I decline to answer that question.

Mr. Sleigh: You decline to answer the question, do you?

Mrs. Harrison: I do. A suggestion was here made by the chairman that the form of the question should be altered.

Mr. Ribton: Did you earn your living in the town of Peterborough by receiving the visits of gentlemen?

Mrs. Harrison: No.

Mr. Ribton: Then how did you gain your living?

Mrs. Harrison: I was a dressmaker.

Mr. Ribton: In the presence of the person whom I have called, do you say you were not known as a common prostitute in the town of Peterborough?

Mrs. Harrison: I am not aware that I was.

Mr. Ribton: Do you know a girl called 'Irish Oar'?

Mrs. Harrison: Yes.

Mr. Ribton: Did you live with her in Peterborough?

Mrs. Harrison: I decline answering that question.

Mr. Sleigh: I do not think that any counsel instructed in such a case would be entitled to any credit who would proceed with the case on the testimony of a witness who refuses to answer questions put to her seriously affecting her credit, and I shall therefore at once withdraw from the prosecution. I cannot do better in upholding my profession than by withdrawing from this prosecution. (Loud cheers in court.)

Mr. Ribton: The statement of my learned friend is only one that I expected from him, and he has done no more than a man of honour should do. At the same time I think it will not be merely necessary that my learned friend should withdraw from the prosecution, but the bench should give some expression of their feelings as to the merits of Mr. Saunders. There were within earshot a number of ladies who had been attended by him, and they would speak of him as a medical man whose conduct had been marked by the strictest morality and propriety in his demeanour towards them as his patients.

Mr. Sleigh: I have no hesitation in saying that you ought to discharge Mr Saunders after the way in which the prosecutrix has given her evidence and conducted herself this day. I need hardly say that Mr. Brown, the gentleman by whom I was instructed, was impressed with the truth of this woman's statement, or he would never have acted as her solicitor.

The Chairman: The course you have taken, Mr. Sleigh, is highly creditable to you. After the way in which the prosecutrix has conducted herself, no one can believe her testimony. Mr. Saunders, we entirely acquit you, and you leave the court with an unstained character.

Elizabeth was only 25 when she stood in court and watched the system that was supposed to protect her strip away her dignity and identity. She was a married woman, in the respectable position of stationmaster's wife, and her testimony of the attack, alongside its witnesses, made a compelling case that should have led to a conviction. But in the final statement made by the court it is clear that the truth of the assault did not matter. The only thing that mattered was whether or not Elizabeth was a respectable woman – the right sort of victim. We still deal with these concepts and stereotypes today. The judgements on women and their sexual history are so severe that modern-day rape victims are often advised not to seek therapy or professional support in the aftermath of an attack, as the records of their sessions will be made available to the defendant's legal team. On the stand, women still face questions on their morality and respectability, leading to cases that seem water-tight failing to secure a prosecution if the woman, or girl, had anything less than a pure, virginal sexual past. We seem so far from any evolution in understanding how to stop these attacks, or successfully prosecute their perpetrators.

14

The Future of Sex

'What's a fuck when what I want is love?'[1]
—Henry Miller, 1939

We are at a seminal moment in our sexual culture. Our modern sexual lives have become geared solely towards our own individual experience, and the emphasis on sex as shared pleasure – something that was so important to our ancestors – is being erased. We see the evidence for this in every aspect of our culture, from songs to films, to self-expression. But how has this happened? Why are we so keen to abandon the messages and beliefs of the past that advocated kindness, consent and sexual harmony in favour of selfish loneliness? Why has our quest for sexual pleasure become so utterly one-dimensional? Today, we demand perfection from our partners, we need them to fit an idealised image of what we think they should be, rather than celebrating and glorying in them, 'just as they

---

1 Henry Miller, *Tropic of Capricorn*, 1939, p. 224.

are'. Modern sexual culture is about instant gratification, it exists without care, and without a true understanding of what sexual pleasure can, or should, actually be. We require nothing more than for sex to meet our immediate needs, for another person's flesh and our own body; today the quest for our own orgasm is absolute and often at the expense of our partner.

We also operate in a climate of fear. #MeToo has brought sexual harassment out of the shadows, and now every person is aware of how broken the systems of power are, both at work and at home, and how little protection the laws our mothers and grandmothers fought for have actually protected us. For men, the ability to claim ignorance of the harsh reality many women have faced in our sexual culture has gone. They can no longer be naive – for all of us, our social innocence is gone. So where does society go from here? We have started to reassess our popular culture in light of the worst aspects of our sexual one. The backlash against sexually exploitative men like Michael Jackson, R Kelly, Harvey Weinstein and Woody Allen finds us asking whether we should continue to listen to, watch, read and consume the creative output of sexual predators. What happens if we apply that powerful cultural annihilation and erasure to our past? If we removed the work of Geoffrey Chaucer, what records do we have left to tell us about the lives, loves and culture of society at that time? Just as with the differing interpretations of the sex in 'The Reeve's Tale', Chaucer's own sexual life is unclear – if clarity is ever found, and it shows us he was actually guilty of rape, do we accept that and teach his work in context, or do we confine it to the bin?

Just as the language we use to talk and record sex is open to interpretation, in our culture sex itself is often seen as subjective. What we define as a 'sex act' has so many more different examples than our ancestors ever had to imagine. From couples who use sex toys that stimulate the touch of their partners, to the sex doll creators and deep fake pornographers, sex happens in a world defined by its absence of actual human touch. Across our society we are experiencing a disconnect from the sexual experience thanks to our cultural depictions of sex – no longer something that includes love and shared pleasure, now a fast fuck is all that matters. This is a significant and historic change. I believe we are experiencing a seismic cultural shift, as our global, shared sexual culture moves from the erotic to the pornographic. This move, from an erotic culture to a pornographic culture, is deeply damaging. We are losing the depth of emotion, joy, connection and extreme pleasure that our ancestors knew lay at the fundamental heart of the human sexual experience. The eroticism of the previous ages, which had so much to say about shared pleasure, is being lost to the technologic sanitisation of the commerce of sex. This is not the fault of the sex industry or sex workers – they are both as old as time itself, and have always been part of our sexual culture. But something has happened in the twenty-first century, something has emerged to dominate our sexual culture that erases everything that has gone before: the cult of self-satisfaction. This cult has turned sex, or the promise of sex, into a product. Programmes like ITV's *Love Island* or ABC's *The Bachelor* have promoted hyper-sexualised images of male and female bodies, and turned our natural desire for a sexual and emotional life partner into a monetised competition. If you do manage to find love and a lasting relationship, 'mommy bloggers' have economised the result. Pregnancy and parenthood are now commodities, social currency to be traded in for promotions and free advertising. In the same way we desire the latest phone, Kardashian make-up palette, or verified status, our sexual desires have become about what we can own, what we can use, or what we can claim to have experienced, rather than the experience itself. We care only about what we can get from sex, not what we give to it. So the answer to the question 'what is sex for?', in our modern sexual culture, is remarkably different to the one we find in the past. As this book has shown, historically our societies have always understood that sex is incredibly important, on both an individual and social level. And while we may be more aware and accepting of the myriad of sexual identities and sexual desires that are present in our societies, we are somehow losing the importance of sex itself. We believe we are the most sexually progressive and yet somehow we have also regressed back to one of our earliest sexual stages, the masturbatory, but now we just do it with other people next to us, or with robotic stimulation.

The widespread availability of free pornography websites must shoulder some of the blame for this, presenting as it does sex without context. But again, this does not mean sex workers, film-makers and the sex industry itself are to blame, rather the monetisation that came from the success of clip-sharing sites like YouPorn and Pornhub. The rest of the blame rests solely on us. We haven't fought hard enough for compulsory sex education and access to contraception, we have allowed people's basic human right to existence and acceptance to remain a debate. We have watched conservative commentators dominate and control our public arenas on sex work, rape laws and sex education. We have watched the idea of 'free thinking' and 'free thought' move from the hands of those who advocated for birth control in the 1870s, into the hands of those who believe 'free speech' means the right to advocate against every fair and equal law that protects our sexual culture, identities and gender. We need to claim sex back.

The sexual myths of our culture still rely on the belief that the Victorians were prudes and identity is a modern invention. But the Victorians were not prudes, and, while the language we use to talk about identity may be modern, what those words are expressing is actually as old as time itself. We find trans bodies in every century, just as we find those who are gay, lesbian, asexual and bi. In our modern world, the fixation of one branch of feminist identity, Trans Radical Exclusionary Feminists (TERFs) on the bodies of trans women (biologically born males who transition to female, often through a combination of hormonal therapy and surgery) has dominated our public discourse, as the lines between gender critical theorists (those who believe society has constructed specific gender identities for two specific sexes, male and female, inside rigorously policed social and cultural boundaries, to the detriment of men and women emotionally, spiritually and economically) and TERFs (those who believe trans women are not women, and pose a threat to female safe spaces) have been constantly blurred.

For those who are gender critical, the social markers of trans women: femininity, beauty, surgery to achieve a feminised body, self-expression via make-up and fashion, is to play into the prescribed female social stereotypes that they believe women are trying hard to escape. And yet, if a trans woman does not conform to the performative female stereotypes, does not have surgery, does not wear make-up or alter their physically male appearance, they are hounded and reviled by both those gender critical theorists, and the TERF faction of feminism, which tries so hard to proclaim they are the one bastion of the free woman, behind which we are all supposed to unite. Equally, for cisgender women – the modern term for those who identify with the sex assigned to them at birth – the 'trappings' of femininity are seen as just as detrimental.

There is a grotesque barbarism to the modern feminist sexual debate. We are horrific to one another and have created a world where 'how to be a woman' is an idea everybody has, and nobody can agree on. Consensus on the idea of womanhood is an impossible thing. If only this was something we could accept, rather than disagree on. Surely self-expression is a fundamental human right for all. But at the moment, on trans issues especially, feminism feels utterly stagnated. There is also a deep and unavoidable hypocrisy towards our trans brothers and sisters, fixated as it is on trans women while modern feminism is strangely silent on those women who become trans men. There seems to be an inability to comprehend the illogical arguments of their position, which would, logically, allow a trans man to sit in their 'female only' space, because at one point in their life they may have presented as female, yet deny access to a trans woman, who presents as female, simply because at one point in time they may have inhabited a male body. It doesn't make any sense, and requires an invasive and prying focus on the genitals of a person, rather than who they are, and what they believe.

In 2015, Germaine Greer, author of *The Female Eunuch* (1970), claimed, 'Just because you lop off your dick and then wear a dress doesn't make you a fucking woman'. She was forced to clarify her comments in 2018 on Channel 4's *Genderquake: The Debate*, initially denying that she said them, and then announcing, 'I'm very well aware there is a very lucrative industry that is lopping their dicks off...[but] being without a penis doesn't make you a woman any more than being without a womb makes you a man...it makes you a man without a cock!'[2] These crude judgements that much of mainstream, gender critical feminism employs never acknowledge that their biologically determined view of gender and womanhood erases and ignores women who are born without wombs, are infertile, or were born with high testosterone. In the world of Greer's feminism, trans men never cease to be women, and yet,

---

2 https://www.pinknews.co.uk/2018/05/09/germaine-greer-genderquake-debate-channel-4

if a trans man, who presented as male and/or had fully transitioned via surgery, attempted to access their female-only spaces, they would be instantly denied, due to the judgement that their physicality was not welcome. This fixation, on how a person looks, is the one thing gender critical feminists claim they are trying to break down, yet also seems to be the only thing they are determined to enforce. What is so grotesque about these judgements is that it is clear that none of those holding them have ever considered educating themselves on the reality of trans sex, especially for those who have transitioned from male to female via surgery. Interviewed by *Vogue* in 2016, singer and podcaster, Nomi Ruiz, wanted to raise awareness of what sex was like as a trans woman: 'There was this myth that you could never have another orgasm, that there's no sensitivity, and that you could never enjoy sex again. The conversation with my doctor beforehand was hilarious, because it's sort of customized. She asked me: "What are you looking to achieve? Like, are you a lesbian, are you interested in being penetrated? Is it more important to focus on the nerve endings in your clit, or do you want a lot of depth? Or do you want both?" I was like, "I want it all. Go for gold."'[3] Ruiz described the processes of dilation – an experience many cis women who suffer from pelvic floor dysfunction, fear of penetration and vaginismus are likely to be familiar with – which often take place over a period of six to seven months after surgical transition. 'They give you four dilators, with a ruler on

---

3 https://www.vogue.com/article/breathless-karley-sciortino-trans-sex

them. You're basically fucking yourself: You slowly increase the size, so that you keep the depth and width you've achieved. And then you have to dilate once a week for the rest of your life, unless you're having sex.'[4] After surgery, and once she had settled into her new body, Ruiz's sexual experiences will be utterly familiar to any woman who has experienced heterosexual sex. 'It took meeting the right guy, slowly fingering me, seeing how I reacted. You need someone to help you enjoy your body, not someone who just wants to fuck you,' she said. 'When I was turned on, I would get really wet, and I was shocked, because I'd never heard a [trans] girl say that her vagina got wet, I didn't realize that it would be this beautiful, natural part of me. I was like, "Holy shit, this is beyond what I thought my sex life could be."'[5] The beauty of sex in a body that is truly yours, with a partner who wants to share it with you, and cares deeply for your sexual pleasure as much as their own, is something that every single one of us deserves. And it is possible. A happy, healthy sex life does not have to exist solely in our historic past, as long as we rediscover the eroticism that has been lost, before it is too late. We need to acknowledge and accept that between consenting adults, everyone has a right to love who and how they want, and to be accepted for who they are. And that will only come true if we can get rid of our culture of sexual shame. This is born within ourselves, with our very first sexual explorations, it's the messages we received

4 https://www.vogue.com/article/breathless-karley-sciortino-trans-sex
5 Ibid.

from our family and friends, from our laws, ethics and systems of power. And if sexuality is a conscious individual design on the part of each person, a fiction that we create for ourselves of our likes and dislikes, our lusts and our disgusts, sex remains the universal human expression of that interior life.

We are the sum of our sexual experiences, just as we are the sum of any life experience. We need to understand sex for what it has always been – human, animal, intellectual, primal – sex expresses our most private desires and our deepest fears. We are at our most vulnerable in the moments we give our bodies to another human being. In a culture that celebrates overexposure of our lives and experiences, perhaps it is merely a logical consequence that sex becomes the one vulnerability we are withdrawing from, consuming it in the two-dimensional, digital world, out of fear of being seen for who we really are: messy, smelly, imperfect animal beings. Returning sex to the pursuit of a shared pleasure is a battle for our modern sexual culture. We have so much to learn from the sex of the past. Writing about the sexual attitudes of her female peers after the First World War, Dora Russell beautifully proclaimed:

> Sex, even without children and without marriage, is to them a thing of dignity, beauty, and delight. All puritans – and most males so long as they can remember – have tried to persuade women that their part in sex is pregnancy and childbirth, and not momentary delight... To enjoy and to admit we enjoy, without terror or regret, is an

achievement in honesty... The plain truth is that there are as many types of love among women of all classes as among men, and that nothing but honesty and freedom will make instinctive satisfaction possible for long. Grant each man and woman the right to seek his or her own solution without fear of public censure. Moral questions of this kind cannot be decided by some abstract rules... The wrong lies in rules that are barriers between human beings who would otherwise reach a fuller and more intense understanding of one another... There is no need to make these divisions into mind and body. There is no difference.[6]

This is the sexual culture we need to reclaim from the past. The celebration of sex has been part of our historic sexual society since people first decided to form communities. And if we learn any lesson from those who have gone before us it should be this: openness, understanding and acceptance. The people who have lived lives that laws and religions try to restrict even today have always been part of us. They are not new, they are not modern even if we make modern words to describe them. And we owe them their history. We are all owed a true retelling of our past, one that does not hide from either the best or the worst of us, but shows it side by side, so that we can learn and move on. History should not keep us in the past, but, like a child's night-light, should show us the dark before the dawn.

---

6 Dora Russell, *Hypatia*, pp.33–4.

Acknowledgments

It's a strange feeling, being an author during a pandemic. This book was originally slated to come out in 2020, and the subsequent delay and the difficulties of the last year made me fall a little out of love with it. Like many authors, my books feel like my children, and, at times, this one has been an unruly teenager, never quite saying what I wanted and not quite living up to how I expected it to be. When I sat down to write *Sex: Lessons from History* during 2018/19 I really felt I had a cause, a quest to write everything I could about the history of our sexual lives. But I realised very quickly this was an impossible task, and so it had to become something else: A series of lessons from the past, to teach us to be better today. As always, any errors will be mine, and mine alone.

But in this last year, for all its horrors, I managed to find some perspective: This book should not have all the answers. It is, in many ways, a collection of lives from our historic past so that we can understand we are not alone. My desire, as a writer and a historian, is to make sure the past showcases and remembers those who have gone before us, so that no one is left behind. Sex, and what it means to us, is a universal human experience. It shapes us, it creates our identities, and it informs many of the relationships and interactions we have across our whole lives. It has been used to abuse and suppress people's natural feelings in deeply damaging and dangerous ways, through the centuries. The battleground for today's sexual debates are as concerned with personal liberty as the arguments of a hundred years ago, and so it seems obvious to me that our belief in a free and equal society for all is still somewhat out of reach.

The only thing I hope this book will do is help people understand that human sexuality has always been a wildly different and exciting place, and that gender has never agreed to or accepted binary definitions. The past is not a place anyone can look at with rose tinted glasses, but it is a place to find out who you are, and that there have always been others like you.

This book would not have been possible without the help and support of those I love, and the men and women who have shaped my own sexuality. As a historian, the many archives and archivists who are fighting to recognise and preserve the lives of our LGBTQIA+ ancestors deserve nothing but respect and thanks, while the importance of the British Newspaper Archive remains paramount to capturing lives and wider attitudes in the past. Finally, I owe a huge debt of thanks to my brilliant agent, Kirsty McLachlan, my editor, Huw Armstrong, and the entire team at Hodder & Stoughton for holding on and supporting this book (and this author) during such a mad, weird, and historic time.

Index